Spirit Tree

Origins of Cosmology
in Shintô Ritual at Hakozaki

E. Leslie Williams

D1613314

UNIVERSITY PRESS OF AMERICA,® INC.
Lanham • Boulder • New York • Toronto • Oxford

Copyright © 2007 by
University Press of America,® Inc.
4501 Forbes Boulevard
Suite 200
Lanham, Maryland 20706
UPA Acquisitions Department (301) 459-3366

PO Box 317
Oxford
OX2 9RU, UK

Library of Congress Control Number: 2006902380
ISBN-13: 978-0-7618-3416-8 (paperback : alk. paper)
ISBN-10: 0-7618-3416-8 (paperback : alk. paper)

Contents

List of Photos and Figures

Preface

Shintô persists in Japan as a matrix of attitudes and ritual practices, but Japanese are increasingly unfamiliar with its cosmologies of origin. Shintô, as a discrete category of knowledge, is difficult for Japanese to discuss because this spiritual tradition is not approached in an explicit manner even though Shintô rituals occur on an annual, monthly, or even a daily basis. Exorcism of threatening influences is performed, gratitude is expressed, and future blessings are invoked from ancestral spirits (*kami*), but for the majority of practitioners, these rituals are "just what we do."

Some researchers have concluded that if practitioners cannot articulate a coherent set of principles, or if their statements reveal a multiplicity of understandings, then there must be a lack of comprehensively organizing thought structures. Other studies have emphasized that a fuzzy logic has allowed Shintô to be anything to anyone, and thus persist in perpetual metamorphosis across the centuries. Three decades ago Clifford Geertz issued an imperative (following Langer) that for scholars of religion "the concept of meaning . . . is the dominant philosophical concept of our time" [and] that "sign, symbol, denotation, signification, communication . . . are our [intellectual] stock in trade" (Geertz 1973: 89). The previous research, while earnest in its efforts to interpret meaning in Shintô ritual, has neglected some crucial sequences of cosmological thought that structure Shintô practice.

In my opinion, many Japanese are experiencing slippage from the previous bedrock of the Shintô worldview as a whole, that is, with three constituent cosmologies that synthesize a consistent Shintô worldview: Chinese Yin-Yang Five Phase cosmology (*ommyôdô*), the female medium tradition, and the Jungian archetype of the Feminine. These three cosmologies constitute cognitive vistas comprising the fundamental logic of this spiritual tradition, and significantly facilitate the interpretation of Shintô ritual practice. In particular, a major cognitive feature that structures Shintô ritual is Chinese Yin-Yang Five Phase cosmology, which is part of Japan's history, but the influence of this mode of thought has only perfunctorily been mentioned by researchers publishing in English. The female medium tradition that captivated Japan's early ethnologists, Yanagita Kunio and Origuchi Shinobu, which links Shintô practice to the larger realm of East Asia, has been addressed in only a couple of works (Blacker 1975, Rokkum 1998). And with the exception of Kawai Hayao (1988), there are no studies in English that have applied a Jungian conceptual framework to the study of Shintô. The Jungian archetype of the Feminine has an urgent applicability in the analysis of Shintô ritual.

Neither extensive aspects of history, nor psychology routinely comprise explicit knowledge for the majority of Shintô practitioners, but their unfamiliarity with these realms of knowledge does not negate the fact that such information can and indeed does structure the communal ritual life in which they participate. Such implicit knowledge, a familiarity produced by association with its products, is a routine aspect of life in human societies.

The issue of practitioners' implicit knowledge of cosmology structuring Shintô ritual practice is further complicated by the sweeping changes in modern-day Japan. New worldviews have been produced by industrialization, modernization, and the rise of scientific thought. The natural landscape, the environment in which a Shintô worldview is most significant, is now not a significant part of life for many Japanese. Many young people are leaving rural areas for better employment prospects in large cities. Only five percent of Japanese are involved in agriculture (Keizai Kôhô Center 1997). This was a venue in which Shintô worldview and ritual thrived, but fewer Japanese are tillers of the soil and, for those who are, mechanization has cognitively restructured this experience. The increasing disappearance of the traditional Japanese home, with its tutelary spirits, has further decimated another environment in which Shintô folklore and ritual thrived. Furthermore, a rise in the number of transient nuclear families (who regularly lack solid identification with a local shrine), a lower incidence of intergenerational living arrangements (and a regular flow of knowledge from grandparents to grandchildren), and an increasing unwillingness of adult children to care for their elderly parents, have all drastically reshaped social features that provided a congenial environment to the Shintô worldview. Shintô ways of knowing the world have been further eroded by a rising sense of individualism and a relentless emulation of Western lifeways that threaten to eclipse, on the level of individual and social cognition, previously more well-known aspects of history and psychology central to Shintô ritual practice.

While Shintô practice will certainly survive, for me there is a sense of urgency to explicitly articulate the Shintô worldview that structures the origin, logic, and purpose of ritual. This study is an attempt to interpret certain aspects of implicit knowledge embodied in Shintô ritual practice. It uses theoretical and methodological contributions from cultural anthropology and Jungian psychology. This research signals a new era in the study of Shintô in which an explicit acknowledgment of this spiritual tradition's conceptual continuity is presented.

The term Shintô, as used in this study, denotes: 1) all ritual practice focused on ancestral (kami) spirits, and 2) the cycle of beneficial ancestral spirits circulating between the seen and Unseen realms that bring abundant life energy to the human community. Japanese names are written as is customary in Japan, with family name followed by the given name.

I describe in these pages ritual practice that I observed in and around Fukuoka, on the island of Kyûshû, and then relate this practice to the Shintô worldview. Over a decade ago, I lived in Hakozaki as a Monbushô graduate research scholar studying Edo period history at Kyûshû University. During those two years, I became acquainted with priests at the Hakozaki Hachiman Shrine. As my schedule permitted, I attended the shrine's public rituals, including Tamaseseri and Hôjôya. Following three years of doctoral coursework in the United States, I returned to the shrine to conduct dissertation fieldwork. For one year (1995–1996) the priests at Hakozaki graciously allowed me to attend their annual cycle of rituals and interview them on numerous occasions. Interviews with shrine parishioners, with other inhabitants of northern Kyûshû, and attending rituals at a variety of shrines, provided important insights into what was unique to Hakozaki and what was not. I continue to regularly visit and do fieldwork at the Hakozaki Shrine.

Founded in 923 A.D. (Hirowata 1999: 7), the Hakozaki Shrine has a long and interesting history which we can only briefly consider here. The Hakozaki Shrine is mentioned in two important pieces of classical Japanese literature. In *The Tale of Genji*, dating to approximately 1015, Tô-no-Chûjo's hidden daughter, Tamakazura, while living in Kyûshû is said to have made pilgrimages to Hakozaki Shrine to pray that she be reestablished to her rightful place in the Capital (Waley 1993: xxii, 517; Seidensticker 1993: 394). And in *The Tale of the Heike*, its present canonical form dating to 1371, as members of the harried Taira clan made a retreat from Dazaifu, they offered petitions at the Hakozaki Shrine that the child emperor Antoku (and the Taira themselves) would be restored to the reigns of government in Kyôto (McCullough 1994: 252, 364).

In 1587, the great unifier of Japan, the Regent Toyotomi Hideyoshi, after subduing the Shimazu clan in Satsuma, lodged for more than a month at

Hakozaki (Hirowata 1999: 158; Papinot 1988: 695). While residing in Hakozaki's Main Hall, Hideyoshi surveyed the city of Hakata, ordered its rebuilding and restructuring, made donations to the Hakozaki Shrine, and redistributed the fiefs of Kyûshû among the feudal lords (Hirowata 1999: 159, 161). During this month, the grand master of tea, Sen no Rikyû waited on Hideyoshi and coordinated tea gatherings (*chakai*) for the Regent and the wealthy merchants of Hakata (Hirowata 1999: 158–163). Hakozaki's treasury is home to seven fancy poem tablets (*tanzaku*) that record waka poems written by Hideyoshi and his guests at Hakozaki's pine grove tea gatherings in 1587 (Hakozaki 1993: 24). Sen no Rikyû is said to have donated the Kamakura period stone lantern that stands next to Hakozaki's Main Hall (an Important Cultural Treasure), and since 1968 the successors of Rikyû's tea tradition, the head masters of both the Urasenke and Omote-senke schools annually prepare tea as an offering before the Main Hall (Hakozaki 1993: 42–43).

My gratitude knows no bounds to the Chief Priest at Hakozaki, Tamura Yasukuni, and his kind brother, High Priest Tamura Toyohiko. Their support and patience in the process of my learning are magnanimous and remarkable. Okada Takeshi and his family have indebted me as gracious hosts and introduced me to the Great Shrine at Izumo. High Priest Senge Yoshihiko, at Izumo, provided me with profound insights in my study and inspired me to persevere in the explication of the Shintô worldview. Priest Miyajima Michihisa at the Grand Shrine of Ise provided me with wonderful insights concerning Shintô worldview; I am grateful for his sincerity and exceptional hospitality. Chief Priest Ueda Sakan at the Grand Shrine of Kashii taught me a great deal. There are countless other individuals whose kindnesses have furthered this work; their combined assistance has made this research an exciting reality. I am grateful to the following readers of this manuscript: Pam Draper, Jeff Love, Sandy King, Constancio Nakuma, Arne Rokkum, and Joyce Williams. My dear wife, Michelle, has been a source of wonderful support to me during the revision process. My family has been most loving and understanding throughout the long research process; they are most precious to me.

E. Leslie Williams
Clemson, South Carolina
February 2005

Chapter One

A Paradigm Shift: Roots and Shoots

The gnarled, knotted trunk of an ancient zelkova tree, having flourished for 500 years at a mountain spirit (*yamanokami*) shrine in Nagano prefecture, now stands in Kyôto University of Art and Design (see Photo 1.1). The tree was felled after a hollow space developed in its trunk, making it wither. Thereafter, it was brought and put on display in the university's main lobby. During its lifetime, it was known as the Spirit Tree; as such, it was the focus of local mountain spirit ritual. Now, at the university, its limbs and branches have been removed, together with its bark and roots. Only a bulging trunk remains, perched on a large cube of granite. Alive, the Spirit Tree was rooted in the local earth where it breathed, took in nourishment, and thrived with the seasons. Now it stands a piece of modern art, a shadow of its former grandeur.

Striking parallels exist between Japan's spiritual tradition called Shintô and the remains of the Spirit Tree. The denuded trunk standing in a sterile lobby environment approximates the plight of twenty-first century Shintô. Boasting a long history, this spiritual tradition faces an uncertain future following its appropriation and reorganization by Meiji era politicians, the shock to its system accompanying the end of World War II, and the ongoing erosion of the Japanese family system.

What we see today are the remains of a thriving Spirit Tree that once stood firmly rooted in the cognitive landscape of Japan (see Figure 1.1). This tree grew in the fertile soil of the Feminine archetype; its roots were a set of locality-based traditions presided over by female mediums and its trunk an inheritance of all-encompassing Yin-Yang Five Phase (*ommyôdô*) cosmological concepts supported by male priests. Its limbs extended as ritual appeals to ancestral spirits, and its branches and foliage flourished as petitions for both abundant harvests and numerous offspring.

1

Photo 1.1.　The Zelkova in Kyôto University of Art and Design

Figure 1.1. The Spirit Tree

For participants in Shintô ritual in Japan, the Feminine archetype, the female medium tradition, and Yin-Yang Five Phase cosmology still persist, but these aspects of cognition are shadowy realities for many. The Feminine archetype consists of implicit realities which seem largely out-of-awareness knowledge for practitioners. Aspects of the female medium and male-led Yin-Yang Five Phase traditions survive, but appear far removed from most practitioners' experiences. The majority of present-day Shintô ritual is focused on petitions to ancestral spirits for abundant life. Without explicit awareness of their antecedents, these rituals constitute a collection of mute surface facts. Notwithstanding sweeping changes in this spiritual tradition, there exists a great strain of continuity. Though in a precarious position, the Spirit Tree (*shimboku*) still lives.

FOCUSING ON CONCEPTUAL ORIGINS

The particular Shintô examined in this study signifies a cycle of spirits (or, way of the kami) and embraces all ritual activities focused on *kami*, or ancestral spirits, and notions concerning their operation in the seen and Unseen realms. Shintô presents unique challenges for all who seek answers concerning why certain socially-scripted perceptions and practices have persisted for centuries.

Previous scholarly literature on this topic falls into one of three categories: 1) descriptive treatments of the subject in which a long-needed organization of facts is conducted (Herbert 1967, Ono 1962, Picken 1980, Plutschow 1996, Takatori 1993, Ueda 1996); 2) historical summaries of particular shrines or forms of belief (Hardacre 1986, Hardacre 1989, Grapard 1992, Nelson 1996, Picken 1994, Smyers 1999, Teeuwen 1996); and 3) popular theoretical topics for academics including invention of tradition (Nelson 1993), political, social, or economic dynamics as they figure in ritual practice (Ashkenazi 1993, Guthrie 1998, Nelson 2000, Reader 1991), and gender issues (Bargen 1997, Miyata 1987).

This scholarship represents vital contributions to the study of Shintô. Most of this work is descriptive and does not address the conceptual origins of this tradition. A prime objective of this study is to introduce a new means of interpreting Shintô by presenting the cognitive origins and underpinnings of this tradition. The organizing foci of Shintô are found in aspects of history and social thought about which many Japanese seem explicitly unaware, and therefore incapable of articulating effectively.

Jungian analyst Kawai Hayao claims in *The Japanese Psyche* that the psychic orientation portrayed in Japanese folklore and mythology is feminine in character (1997: 26). Kawai does not provide a coherent framework for Japan's Feminine orientation, but the issue of female-centeredness in Japanese social cognition is thought-provoking. And yet, a study has long been needed that addresses the social-psychological heart of this issue, one that exposes the cognitive underpinnings of this tradition of Female orientation.

Research is easily frustrated because Shintô ritual, in shrine and non-shrine contexts, is obscured by kami-focused practices performed to obtain abundant harvests and offspring. In present-day Japan both rice harvests and the birth rate are curtailed, so neither petition appears to make much sense amid the twenty-first century realities of life. And yet Shintô shrines, and other venues where kami ritual is performed, tenaciously continue to offer these same petitions, oblivious that such ritual concerns might be out of touch with people's lives. It is little wonder that when Japanese feel drawn to religious practice, they most often are not attracted to kami shrines or Buddhist temples, but instead find their needs fulfilled in new combinations of familiar rituals and ideas in the form of new religions (see Arai 1996, Ishii 1996).

For more than a decade, my academic curiosity and research efforts have been focused on ethnographic research at Japan's third most prominent Hachiman shrine: the Hakozaki Hachiman-gû in Fukuoka. Priests and parishioners regularly participate in ritual there to ensure rich harvests and numerous offspring. Nonetheless, description of ritual behavior is an insufficient means to address the conceptual foundations underlying what is perennially performed at Hakozaki.

Conducting research for extended periods at Hakozaki provided me with opportunities to grasp essential aspects of Shintô. During this time, taboos focused on earth and females attracted my attention. These taboos, together with practitioner interviews, led me to insights that began to provide information that led deeper, beyond the routine ritual level of cognition.

In my view, the crux of my research is the Feminine archetype, a conceptual linking of woman and earth, a fundamental conceptual foundation of Shintô ritual.[1] This archetype consists of the collective womb from which all life emerges; it is associated with the endless natural cycles that shape temporal life in the shrine locality. The Feminine archetype is the earth that devours the corpse (or seed), only to cast forth new life as the life-giving womb. Implied here is the mystery of interpenetrating life and death. Practitioners tend to identify this set of understandings under the rubric of "nature" (*shizen*). The important cognitive role of females and their intimate relation to kami beings resulted from an awareness of the Feminine archetype and is confirmed by previous scholarly research (Blacker 1975, Miyata 1987, Yanagita 1970, Yanagita 1971). This ancient female priest tradition was brought into vivid focus by Arne Rokkum's monograph on Ryûkyûan female priests (1998). Articulation of the Feminine archetype itself is intellectually indebted to the work of the Jungian psychologist Erich Neumann (1963). Neumann's contributions will be more fully covered in Chapter Two. Rather than subscribing to the notion of the "psychic unity of mankind" (Neumann 1963), this research situates the generation and use of archetypes within the realm of social cognition; or in other words, the socially constructed, accessed, and regulating features of shared knowledge which functions as conceptual currency within any given society.

Pursuing the cognitive origins of contemporary Shintô ritual at Hakozaki makes imperative a revisiting of history. This study includes a brief survey of Yayoi period history, situated within the larger context of East Asia, to reclaim precious and vital aspects of social cognition that structure the worldview of contemporary Shintô ritual practice. To explicate ritual practice at Hakozaki, northern Kyûshû must be considered as a constituent element within the more comprehensive ritual sphere of East Asia. In isolation, Hakozaki's ritual life has very little information to divulge regarding the conceptual structure of Shintô cosmology. Ritual practice at Hakozaki is based on a worldview that on one level is grounded in the Feminine archetype dating to at least Japan's Yayoi period, and on another level is structured by the principles of Yin-Yang Five Phase cosmology that arrived in Japan during the sixth century.

CYCLING ANCESTRAL SPIRITS

If knowledge concerning the Feminine archetype and Yin-Yang Five Phase thought is implicit cognitive content for practitioners, on what then is their ritual explicitly focused? Spirits, known collectively as kami, the souls of deceased human beings (see Yanagita 1970) are the focus of Shintô ritual. One priest at Hakozaki elaborates: "Kami and Buddhas are both ancestors. Nearby ancestors are called Buddhas (*hotoke*) and are given ritual according to Buddhist rites; far-away ancestors, after 33 years, are known as spirits (kami) and are venerated in the Shintô manner." Kami spirits are perceived by practitioners to be the agents of growth and decay. Kindly spirits (kami) are the agents which grant blessings of growth and development; menacing spirits (*onryô*, or *mamono*), unhappy with their fate in life, are identified by some practitioners as being agents responsible for disease and degeneration. All kami ritual behavior consists of managing individual and collective relationships with nature and ancestral spirits.

The Feminine archetype of understandings, grounded in nature and natural cycles, unite both the seen and the Unseen realms. In life, individuals operate in the realm of the seen. At death, persons are transformed into spirits, and become part of the Unseen Realm. "High spirits" (kindly ancestors, or kami; following Rokkum's term 1998: 62) reside in nature (particularly in the sky) before returning to the seen realm as the life-force behind new life in *any* of its forms, particularly as offspring or as rice. At death, high spirits return to nature before being reborn as agents of growth in the realm of the seen. Hence in Shintô ritual, petitions and gratitude for both abundant harvests and offspring are a means of harnessing the goodwill and power of the Unseen Realm for the benefit of the seen (see Blacker 1975). However, maladjusted, low spirits of the dead (onryô, or *oni*) do not return to the seen realm as the life-force for new life forms. Instead, their invisible forms remain in limbo on the earth, maliciously intent on robbing the living of their vitality and dragging them to an early demise. Low spirits are the focus of perennial exorcism and purification, to block their pull upon the living. High spirits are a social manifestation of the life-giving Feminine archetype, the Good Mother. Low spirits are a social expression of the life-taking, Terrible Mother. This is the unique vision provided by this particular spiritual tradition. These conclusions have been substantiated by Umehara Takeshi's work (1995: 53–54). These spirits objectify the positive and negative characteristics of the Feminine archetype.

Contact between the seen and Unseen realms occurs at boundaries. As junctures between the known and unknown, boundaries are thresholds at which spirits from beyond can enter the dimension of the seen. But spirits from the seen realm can just as easily slip into the Unseen at these same interstices. For practitioners of this spiritual tradition, kami (beneficent and otherwise) preside over boundary phenomena. To negotiate boundaries is to come into their realm of power, and therefore, kami ritual is performed at these junctures for safe passage. For practitioners, boundary crossing represents an existential danger and to neglect the appropriate ritual would be foolish. Informants explain that careful participation in ritual at each juncture in life prevents harm and provides an extension of life, or rebirth (*saisei*). In addition to being intervals redolent with kami power, temporal and spatial boundaries are junctures at which cognitive contact with the Great Mother is made, in both her devouring and generating aspects. Practitioners, repositories of cultural knowledge, identify the dual aspect of the Feminine archetype at boundaries in terms of both sinister and benign kami.

Culture in this study denotes a non-essentialized phenomenon consisting of out-of-awareness understandings held by collectivities of individuals which represent a not completely shared overlapping of viewpoints. This culture concept is influenced by Marshall Sahlins' superorganic view of culture (Marcus and Fischer 1986: 142–43). Culture in this sense of the term indicates cognitively-shared semiotic codes that are implicitly followed and that impart patterned responses to shared, or cultural expressions and responses (Marcus and Fischer 1986: 144). These shared sets of information that individuals hold more or less in common "mediate all human perceptions" (Marcus and Fischer 1986: 142). For Sahlins, the objective of anthropology is to "produce accounts of cultures which reveal their distinctive structures of meaning," or in other words, to discern the superorganic mediation of perception embodied in the overlapping viewpoints belonging to informants. This concept of culture resonates with Clifford Geertz's definition of culture: "an historically transmitted pattern of meanings embodied in symbols, a system of inherited conceptions expressed in symbolic forms by means of which men communicate, perpetuate, and develop their knowledge about and attitudes toward life" (1973: 89). This study will consider a range of "inherited conceptions" about kami to produce a reconstructive model of the worldview that organizes ritual practice in northern Kyûshû.

PROBLEMS OF INTERPRETATION

Notions surrounding kami beings, shrine structures, and local festivals in Japan, at first glance appear to be uniquely Japanese cultural phenomena. This view is substantiated by the opinions of many Japanese themselves. For example, "Shintô is the exclusive belief [system] of Japan," or "Shintô is the religion of the ancient Japanese," or even, "Shintô consists of the accumulation of Japanese lifeways." The tendency to parochialize this set of cultural attitudes and practices is a stumbling block that has stymied the efforts of scholars and others to penetrate this tradition. Approached from this perspective, and considered in isolation from other East Asian spiritual traditions, research into Shintô topics has been handicapped.

A further problem of interpretation has been perpetuated by the conceptual limitations of the intellectual and linguistic concepts employed in examinations of the subject. The modern conceptual framework has been challenged to explicate Shintô ritual; this seems an outcome of interpretive presuppositions inherent to the West. One example of semantic and conceptual difficulty should suffice at this juncture.

Who or what is the Japanese emperor? For some Allies during the Second World War, the emperor was God to the Japanese. This understanding might conjure up images of the Japanese reverencing the emperor as God incarnate on earth, perhaps similar to the figure of Jesus Christ. Was this the wartime understanding in Japan of the emperor? From another Western perspective the emperor might have been a god, in a Greco-Roman sense; something like Zeus or Hermes who periodically walked among humans to test them and grant favors to deserving mortals. Then some Allies might have seen the Japanese as a group of pagans, who fanatically believed their emperor to be divine, and with this idea the Japanese rallied themselves to take over the world in a righteous cause, like a Holy Crusade. There are endless roles in Japanese society that could have been ascribed by the Allies to the person of the emperor. But the likelihood is very remote that an Allied soldier would have immediately reached the conclusion that the emperor holds a position of *the* imperial ancestor embodied in mortal guise, reincarnated in each generation and renewed again each year by means of Shintô ritual, and for these particular reasons is held in great reverence as a living link to the past.

Such a conclusion would have been difficult for the Allied forces because they were mortgaged to their own cultural inheritance and therefore prejudged toward what they saw in Japan. According to orthodox Judeo-Christian doctrine, when a grandparent becomes deceased, they go to inherit their eternal reward and are removed from among the living. Historically, no hard and fast distinction separated the living and the dead in Japan. Hence, ancestors have been a living, known reality in everyday Japanese life, while in the United States they are not perceived similarly.

Shintô ritual practice in Japan is no less problematic to comprehend for inheritors of orthodox Judeo-Christian conceptual traditions than the social role of the emperor might have been for the Allies half a century ago. The kami-focused spiritual tradition could be labeled an amalgamation of magical practices, religion, and superstition. And yet, these convenient and more or less familiar terms do no justice to the subject of inquiry. Magic, religion, and superstition are three rather slippery lens through which to view the Spirit Tree of Shintô, but simply employing these labels does not present us with a truly accurate image of the subject. These arbitrary terms provide their own distortions and may, in actuality, speak volumes more about the history of thought in the West than they reveal anything about an accurate map of spiritual orientation in Japan. In order to accurately interpret the conceptual significance of the Shintô tradition, three essential aspects of cognition must be addressed.

SHINTÔ'S THREE PILLARS

All kami ritual revolves around three pillars of cognition: kami beings, rice, and the emperor. Kami are spirits that live in all aspects of the locality and are the main focus of this ritual tradition. Kami has been routinely translated into English as "god" or "deity;" but in reality, they are spirits of the deceased: ancestors (see Yanagita 1970). Japan's first modern ethnologist, "Yanagita Kunio . . . firmly believed that all kami had their origin in the dead ancestral spirit, and were merely superior and proliferated forms of an original deified ancestor" (Blacker 1975: 45). I agree with this conclusion. Kami bear more than a passing resemblance to the very source of "the mysterious spiritual power" of the Polynesian islands, *mana*, itself the power of the "spirits of the dead" (Leach 1984: 670). Kami lodge within and animate each feature of the landscape, either natural or man-made and there are both kindly and injurious varieties. Any kami can bestow blessings on the living if given proper ritual attention, but just as easily, a spirit can be offended and can punish mortals. All kami-focused ritual consists of exorcising the threatening variety and propitiating the kindly spirits. On a whole, beneficent high spirits are known, named, and receive regular ritual attention; menacing low spirits often have no name and receive irregular or no ritual from the living community (Williams, forthcoming manuscript). Ancestor spirits native to the local area continue on in the locality as either tutelary beings or as a bane to the living. Similar ideas have obtained in many traditional societies in the form of ancestor veneration; Chinese and Korean ancestor ritual is particularly well-developed (Itô 2000: 256–57; Noguchi 1994: 353–54; Swanson 1960: 103–8).

High spirits attach themselves to everything, animate and inanimate, and are reincarnated into the seen realm as the life-force that quickens all life forms. In Japan, the food most prevalently associated with kami beings, truly indispensable in kami ritual, is polished white rice. Rice and offspring (human and other forms) are most immediately emblematic of the life-giving kami, the high spirits. Therefore, raw rice, rice cake (*mochi*), and rice wine are perennially employed in kami ritual as a means of invoking high spirits, and also in a sacramental usage by participants as a means of obtaining the abundant life energy of these beneficent spirits for themselves. Rice of the local area, being the essence of the local kami, has always been highly valued by the local population. This represents a tacit understanding that *local rice* is the actual embodiment, or reincarnation of the *local ancestors* and their potent life-energy. In June 2003, the host father of a Clemson University Study Abroad student in Kyôto told her that she should eat all of her rice because, he explained, "each grain of rice in your bowl is a kami" (Werkhoven, Jennifer 2003, personal communication).

Prior to the Meiji Restoration, kami ritual throughout Japan was localized and performed by unaffiliated shrines, clans, and families with slightly divergent practices. Variations in which the kami, the local ancestors, were venerated varied from place to place, but one spiritual linchpin remained: the emperor. In the earliest kami myths recorded in the *Kojiki* (712) and the *Nihon Shoki* (720), the emperor is identified as the lineal descendent of the "Heavenly Resplendent" female sun spirit, Amaterasu-ômikami who commanded her grandson Ninigi-no-mikoto to descend to the Japanese islands and to rule them. In the Daijôsai ritual, each emperor is incubated in a ritual womb so that the spirit of Ninigi is revived in his person; and at each winter solstice, this same ancestral spirit is renewed within the emperor at the Niinamesai ritual (Tanikawa 1983: 400–403). Hence from ancient times the emperor has been called the "manifest ancestor" (*akitsukami*) (*Manyoshu* 1959: 189; *Nihon kokugo dai-jiten* 2000: 184) or the "ancestor appearing in human form" (*arahitogami*) (*Manyoshu* 1959: 176; *Nihon kokugo dai-jiten* 2000: 631). Thus, a special reverence surrounded the person of the emperor and successive military rulers of Japan sought imperial sanction to rule the nation. In effect, the emperor functioned as an unofficial, yet widely recognized high priest of the kami tradition, himself being the living Ancestor eternally manifest in human guise.

This set of elements has a particularly unique Japanese configuration, but there is much that serves to unite Shintô with other spiritual traditions in East

Asia. Knowledge that kami are ancestral spirits is one common denominator that unites Japan with its neighbors Korea and China. Exploits of the Yamato clan (progenitors of Japan's imperial family) and other powerful allied and rival clan ancestors, identified as kami, are recorded in the *Kojiki* and *Nihon Shoki*. Guy Swanson found a positive correlation between societies in which there are "sovereign kinship groups," clans for example, and commonly held notions that ancestor spirits "are active in human affairs" (1960: 108). My assertion is that ancestral spirits (kami), displaying varying degrees of remembered human identity, animate the features of the seen and Unseen realms and manifest themselves most prominently in the seen realm as rice, and in the sacred figure of the emperor. Active ancestral (in the case of Japan, kami) spirits in the realm of the living appear to be a product of societies in which powerful clan organizations are an integral feature, such as is found in a chiefdom; such a level of social organization was definitely in evidence by the Kofun period, and certainly in the Yayoi period, if considering the Kyûshû site of Yoshinogari.

Female mediums have played an important role in the formation of Shintô ritual; in my own work, this impetus persists mainly at the level of popular, ritual practice not coordinated by male priests. Mediumistic systems of practice appear to be more characteristic of band and tribal levels of social organization, as is evidenced in Japan's Jômon period (see Umehara 1995). Shintô's mediumistic characteristics are prominent and serve to further connect kami ritual practice and understandings with spiritual traditions far-removed from Japan geographically and temporally. Rather than using the often used term shaman, which in the Ryûkyû islands exclusively denotes a medium that performs rituals focused on deceased spirits and aspects of decay (Lebra 1966: 75; Rokkum 1998: 76, 110), I prefer to use the term medium. Medium is an "intermediary . . . an individual held to be a channel of communication between the earthly world and a world of spirits" (*Webster's Ninth New Collegiate Dictionary* 1983: 738). This is precisely the role played by sacral women in the Shintô tradition, and medium applies equally to females who perform rites focused on either generation or decay. Since cognition in the Shintô ritual world is organized in terms of these two poles, use of the neutral term medium is significant. In this study, mediums performing decay-focused ritual are shamans; ones that specialize in generation ritual are priestesses (this follows Rokkum 1998: 76, 110).

There are three salient aspects of the medium tradition as I define it: an emphasis on the Unseen Realm and its spirits, a predominance of medium figures, and an abiding interest in boundary phenomena. In mediumistic systems of thought, in addition to the seen realm, there exists another dimension of existence hidden within or behind the features of everyday experience. This

Unseen Realm is inhabited by invisible gods, demons, ancestors, and other spirits that largely exist beyond the control of mortals, and yet exercise considerable power over the seen realm (Blacker 1975: 20–21). For most humanity, these beings are unknowable; and yet, the Unseen Realm intersects in countless ways with the seen.[2]

Mediums are conversant with the Unseen Realm and its beings. Many mediums, including shaman figures, have experienced a sudden shock, illness, or near death experience that provided egress beyond the barrier, and access to extraordinary knowledge and powers. Mediums are conversant in ritual means of influencing the spirits from beyond; this knowledge and power can benefit those around him or her who do not similarly see or know.

The cosmos envisioned from the mediumistic worldview is perceived in terms of boundary phenomena. In band-level societies where mediumistic figures and practices are widely found (see Service 1962; Swanson 1960), there are less rigid divisions between socially-constructed systems of categorization as there are for state-level societies. For example, in Japanese folklore, our categories of animal and human being are challenged by the anomalous cases of the fox, badger-dog (*tanuki*), cat, and snake. Such animals are traditionally considered to be able to assume human form; these interstitial beings distort our categories of animal and human being. It is not unusual for shaman figures the world over to employ a familiar (in Japan, *o-tsukai*) in their shadowy work, or even for a shaman to take the form of the animal in their travels to the Unseen Realm. Mediums generally are conversant with the cosmos of boundary phenomena; these anomalies linking conceptual categories are the sources of power that confer upon the knowing individual socially-recognized abilities to travel to the Other World and influence spirits.

Ancestor spirits (kami) are interstitial beings linking our categories of known and unknown phenomena, of the seen and the Unseen realms. Rice is an interstitial food, in premodern Japan, conflating our categories of food and ancestor. The emperor, an interstitial figure combining the cognitive categories of mortal being and ancestor, functions as a medium himself given his ritual duties to renew his ancestress, the Sun. Nevertheless, very few kami priests, including the emperor, are presently practicing mediums who travel to the Unseen Realm, heal the sick, and foretell future events. Their place in a contemporary state-level society largely obviates the need for them to perform such functions. Rather, they officiate in ritual affairs which have become increasingly secularized, politicized, and merchandised. They stand at the pinnacle of the great Spirit Tree, conducting kami ritual for abundant harvests and offspring; in other words, generation, or "fruition" (following Rokkum's term 1998: 105, 204, 238).

RESEARCH OVERVIEW

The primary aim of this study is to analyze contemporary Shintô rituals conducted by priests and parishioners at the Hakozaki Hachiman Shrine in Fukuoka. Data from Hakozaki will be augmented by Shintô ritual performed in non-shrine contexts in northern Kyûshû. As this ritual behavior is an outgrowth of premodern antecedents, it is imperative to examine its origins in Yin-Yang Five Phase cosmology, female medium ritual, and particularly the Feminine archetype. Strands of social cognition from the Yayoi and later periods will be pursued to reveal the unique conceptual framework that serves to constitute the fundamental, dual-structure cosmology for kami tradition ritual practice.

This cosmology is a combination of two distinguishable traditions, one strain dating from Japan's Yayoi period and the other being of a later date, more continental, and Chinese in persuasion. The Yayoi period cosmology dates from a period when northern Kyûshû was linked by trade to both the Ryûkyûs and Korea and will be reconstructed by employing ethnographic comparison of ritual behavior in present-day mainland Japan, Korea, and the Ryûkyûs. This Yayoi period worldview is female-affirming in its emphasis. The second cosmology came into mainland Japan during the sixth century in the form of Yin-Yang Five Phase thought, known in early Japan as Ommyôdô. This second cosmology of Chinese origin is female-denying. This second worldview informs the majority of contemporary Shintô ritual in mainland Japan largely without its being identified as Chinese in origin; in fact, many Japanese implicitly perceive all that takes place in shrine contexts as natively "Japanese."

Examination of this dual structure worldview is facilitated by employing a comparative approach. Both cosmologies, Yayoi and Yin-Yang, are based on the cognitive foundation of the Feminine archetype, but the former values the ritual and cosmological role of females more so than does the latter. This study represents a dramatic shift in conceptual paradigm used to analyze kami ritual practice to overcome the limitations of prior conceptual challenges by situating this ritual within the larger context of its own cognitive history.

Chapter Two, "Living Landscape," presents the assertion that the ancient, Yayoi period kami worldview is attuned to the bodily experience of the female. Situating this worldview within a general historical context, a broad overview will be presented to highlight the unique ways in which the Yayoi period human community related with the local landscape. Introduction to the general mechanics of the Feminine archetype and the supporting theoretical constructs for this study will be highlighted. This chapter relates to the cognitive soil in which the Spirit Tree stands firmly rooted.

Chapter Three, "Great Mother as Woman and Topocosm," pursues the Yayoi period worldview, in which women functioned as the prime priestly figures, by comparing folklore and ritual practices focused on specific landscape features found in mainland Japan, in the Ryûkyûs, and in Korea. These ritual practices identify some topocosm features with the life-granting auspices of high spirits, while others are identified as the haunt of threatening low spirits. All of these features are treated as interstices into the body of the Great Mother, and by examining attendant ritual practices closely, her dual character is exposed. Furthermore, these ritual practices are preserved within the contemporary female priestess tradition; women are presently perceived as the Great Mother personified. This section presents the root strata of the Tree, a complex of Yayoi period understandings presided over by females.

Chapter Four, "Yin-Yang Five Phase Cycles of Time," introduces salient aspects of the nature-based, female-centered Yin-Yang Five Phase cosmology of cycles, chiefly managed by male priests in the Japanese mainland. This cosmological, proto-science based on *The Book of Changes* became the official means to conduct divination and ritual *vis-à-vis* the spirits of Japan. While the Yayoi period worldview examined in Chapter Three is female-affirming in outlook (despite the ambivalent nature of the Great Mother), this second system of cognition is female-denying by taboos it conceptually focuses on foci of female power, menstruation and ovulation. Corresponding to the trunk of the Tree, this chapter provides for the first time in English concrete details of Later Heaven Sequence cosmology as it relates to Shintô ritual in mainland Japan.

Chapter Five, "Spirits High and Low," examines the ambiguity of spirits (kami) as an outgrowth of the imprecise definition of spirits (*kijin*) from early times in China. These commonalities will be explored as an attempt to further demystify the concept of kami by situating it more broadly within the context of East Asia generally and, more specifically within the cognitive framework of the Feminine archetype. This section is an attempt to more fully expose the limbs of the Great Tree.

Chapter Six, "Hakozaki's Spirit Tree," applies the tools developed in the preceding chapters to explicate the pattern and significance of ritual life at the Hakozaki Hachiman Shrine in Fukuoka. Grounded in the connectedness of this particular region of Japan to the continent, and in the soil of the Feminine archetype, a dual structure to ritual life at Hakozaki is exposed. One set of ritual is of a later date, presided over by male priests in the central shrine compound, and focused on the veneration of Emperor Ôjin and his mother, Empress Jingû. Another set appears to be earlier, is observed largely by women in peripheral areas of the shrine, and appears to be equated with a female sea spirit, Tamayorihime. These two sets of practice relate to the Yin-Yang cosmology and the Yayoi period complex of understandings, respectively. This chapter relates to the branches and foliage of the Tree.

Chapter Seven, "Fruit of the Spirits," reiterates the main conclusions of this work and recommends directions for future research. In particular, it presents relatedness of pattern in Hakozaki's ritual life with ritual practice in East Asia, particularly the Ryûkyû Islands and Korea. It also shows how this mediumistic, female-oriented tradition has been marginalized at Hakozaki in favor of Yin-Yang influenced forms of practice, presided over by male priests who control the central and legitimate ritual forms.

This study signals a new era in the study of Shintô, one in which the subject matter can be approached as an organic whole, grounded in a new acknowledgment of the tradition's conceptual continuity. Kami-focused ritual practice has been neglected by interpretive borders imposed upon the subject to define it as a unique entity rather than as a segment in a continuous pattern of East Asian ritual expression. Rather than performing a dissection of the subject in terms of nineteenth century disciplinary thought, kami ritual practice needs to be appreciated as a living organism within its own unique environment. As the effects of Western-influenced capitalist, materialist, and scientific modes of thought continue to reduce the level of resonance that routine Japanese experience with the kami-focused worldview, its elucidation takes on greater urgency, even while an ominous hollow grows within the trunk of the Spirit Tree.

NOTES

1. Capitalization of Feminine archetype, and terms associated with it including Good Mother, Terrible Mother, and Great Mother, in this study are a means of acknowledging the central organizing function of the Feminine principle in mediumistic systems of thought. This convention follows the convention found in Erich Neumann's *The Great Mother: An Analysis of the Archetype* (1963).
2. Unseen Realm is capitalized in this study as a means of making it a proper noun and therefore an explicit and legitimate subject of inquiry (as pioneered by Blacker 1975). Scholarly dismissal of this subject or an implicit acknowledgement will impede a more comprehensive understanding of Shintô ritual practice.

Chapter Two

Living Landscape

Ritual practices focused on kami beings in contemporary Japan present an undeniable, albeit fragmented view of a living landscape. Japan's Central Bureau of Shrines (*jinja honchô*) has capitalized on the notion of this ancient worldview, claiming that Shintô inculcates a "reverence and appreciation for nature" that is unique and presupposes modern environmentalism in the West. A recent pamphlet published by this organization explains:

> . . . the Japanese spirituality inherited from our ancient ancestors has been gradually lost or hidden somewhere deep in unconsciousness. It might not be too exaggerated if we said that not only environmental conservation but also all problems of modern society have been caused by a lack of awe, reverence, and appreciation for nature that ancient people used to have and taught us about (Jinja Honchô 1998: 13).

This position is correct in identifying a preexistent worldview that was focused on the natural world and also deeply meaningful to the ancient Japanese. Furthermore, this early cosmology has with the passage of time and changes in social relations, technology, and political structures, become more fragmented and divorced from the realities of life for many urban dwelling Japanese in the twenty-first century. As claimed by the Central Bureau of Shrines, there are ancient ways of experiencing the world that still persist in the kami tradition, but the relationship the ancient inhabitants of Japan possessed with the natural world was undeniably different from our own.[1]

YAYOI PERIOD MAINLAND JAPAN

It is my opinion that Japan's Yayoi period (200 B.C.–250 A.D.) was a pivotal juncture at which a unique kami-focused cosmology initially obtained. During the Yayoi period, rice cultivation and its attendant technology arrived in Japan from the continent (Kodansha 1983: 321). My claim is that communities in this period were led by religious leaders that directed coordinated efforts to produce rice. The introduction of agriculture, including new technologies that supported this development, provided the Yayoi period Japanese with components that spawned a new worldview. In particular, the planting of seeds in the earth resulted in a new perception of human conception. The overarching planting of seeds metaphor led to a conceptual linking of earth and female that was instrumental in the formulation of the Feminine archetype. This archetype is a central cognitive feature in Shintô, and similar spiritual traditions led by female medium figures, which we will examine in this chapter and in Chapter Three.

The Yayoi period comprises part of Japan's prehistory; during this era the Japanese possessed no written language. This fact alone presents unique challenges, and our knowledge concerning Yayoi lifeways comes from two sources: archaeological excavations and the written records of Japan's literate neighbors.

The preeminent Yayoi archaeological site found to date, Yoshinogari, is located in southeastern Saga prefecture, in northern Kyûshû (Hudson & Barnes 1991: 214–15). Remains of a moated village surrounded by a palisade, watchtowers, pit dwellings, and high floored rice storehouses, several of which have been reconstructed, have made this site the most publicized and visited of all Yayoi sites (Hudson & Barnes 1991: 214–19), with some 900,000 persons visiting the site annually ("Japan Times Online" 2002: 1).

To date, 2,500 burial jars and the skeletal remains of 300 individuals have been recovered (Hudson & Barnes 1991: 213, 224). The deceased at this site were buried in very large ceramic urns (*kamekan*). In the Early Yayoi, two urns were placed mouth to mouth to enclose the corpse; in later periods, one urn was used with a wooden or stone lid being used to seal the burial vessel (Hudson & Barnes 1991: 224). At least two high status burials contained red ochre, sprinkled inside the urns (Hudson & Barnes 1991: 221).

The site itself was occupied throughout the Yayoi period, its occupation being divided into three periods: early, middle, and late (Hudson & Barnes 1991: 214). An abundance of stone reaping knives in the early period were re-

placed by iron ones later on, and grain storage facilities indicate that rice culture was a major feature in Yoshinogari's subsistence (Hudson & Barnes
1991: 227). In addition to silk fabric remains, swatches of finely woven linen
made of hemp fibers, with a very high fiber count per square centimeter of
30/30 (modern linen is 35/35), have been recovered from burials and represent the most advanced Yayoi period linen weaving found to date (Hudson &
Barnes 1991: 226). Many inhabitants were also buried with bracelets made
from tropical shells native to regions south of Amami Ôshima in the Ryûkyû
Islands, more than 400 kilometers to the southwest (Hudson & Barnes 1991:
225). These gohora and imogai shells were associated with males and females
respectively, and are theorized to have marked elites, pointing to the fact that
Yoshinogari was one point in a trade route of rare shell that connected the
Ryûkyû Islands, Kyûshû, and Korea (Hudson & Barnes 1991: 225–26).[2] Hudson and Barnes estimate that the population of Yoshinogari during the third
century to have been approximately 1,000 persons (1991: 233).

The most notable written document dealing with the Yayoi is *The Chronicles
of Wei* (Mandarin: *Wei chih*; Japanese: *Gishi*), dated 297 A.D. (Brown 1993:
97). It describes Yamatai, a chiefdom level society ruled by a sequestered female medium named Himiko, who ruled from a fortified palace, served by one-
thousand female servants and a lone man, her younger brother ("Gishi." 2002:
2). The record indicates that Himiko practiced "sorcery" (*kidô*). Her subjects
grew rice, hemp, mulberry, and raised silkworms. Unlike the Chinese, the subjects of Himiko ate raw vegetables, went barefoot, and smeared their bodies
with red ochre ("Gishi" 2002: 2). They also were very fond of rice alcohol
("Gishi" 2002: 2). This chiefdom was divided into social classes and had storehouses in which taxes, in the form of rice and cloth, were stored ("Gishi" 2002:
2). Furthermore, men and boys tattooed their bodies ("Gishi" 2002: 1). The
record claims that when Himiko died, a huge tumulus was constructed and 100
servants were immolated to accompany her ("Gishi" 2002: 3).

While the location of Yamatai is still a matter of no small debate, *The
Chronicles of Wei* does provide a rare glimpse of Yayoi period Japan long before the Yamato court adopted Chinese writing and recorded the earliest surviving written document in Japanese, the *Kojiki* in 712. But, before Japanese
scribes could effectively produce a document like the *Kojiki* in Chinese characters, a great deal of study and imitation of continental manners first took
place.

Manifold changes occurred between the late Yayoi period chiefdom over
which Himiko ruled (ca. 230) and the Chinese model state that flourished during the Nara period (710–794). In 552, Buddhism was officially introduced
into the island nation from the Korean state of Paekche (Aston 1990: 65–66;
Papinot 1988: 278, 815; Tamaru 1996: 44); this new system of belief not only

changed the spiritual landscape of Japan, it also served as an important medium by which the process of rapid and far reaching Sinicization took place (Tamaru 1996: 45–46). Carmen Blacker identifies the Taika Reform of 645, a conscious restructuring of the Japanese clan political system in favor of the T'ang dynasty civil administration, as the *coup de grâce* which ended the influence of female mediums that functioned so prominently at court. She claims that their influence persisted in the Japanese mainland thereafter at the level of folk practices (1975: 30).

RECONSTRUCTING A YAYOI PERIOD WORLDVIEW

In order to go back in time and revisit Yayoi period lifeways, including the female medium tradition and worldview that has significantly influenced Shintô ritual practice, the mediumistic ritual practices of three rural societies surrounding the island of Kyûshû will be examined: Dunang (Yonaguni) Island located in the Ryûkyû island chain, Enduring Pine Village in Korea, and three areas in mainland Japan. This comparative method is informed by the tendency for peripheral, in this case rural, populations to be more conservative in their habits than urban centers. Common features strongly uniting these three sets of behaviors will provide insights concerning the ways in which a Yayoi period worldview was constructed. These commonalities will also present issues that will, in turn, force us to confront even broader theoretical questions.

Yayoi Lifeways in the Ryûkyû Islands

Located on the periphery of mainland Japan's cultural sphere, the Ryûkyû Islands offer unique glimpses into Yayoi period lifeways that have eroded and been eclipsed with the passage of time in mainland Japan. Both Yanagita Kunio and Origuchi Shinobu found social practices in the Ryûkyû Islands which they considered typical of society in the Japanese mainland prior to its process of embracing Chinese models of civilization (Blacker 1975: 112; Lebra 1966: viii). I feel that Yanagita and Origuchi were accurate in this regard. Several factors seem to indicate that the Ryûkyûs have preserved lifeways, beliefs, and practices that still do exist in the mainland islands, but that with time have become secularized, less immediate, and more fragmented with the increasing adaptation of continental and later Western modes of thought. Contemporary ritual practice in the Ryûkyûs resonates quite strongly with Yayoi period lifeways preserved at Yoshinogari and in the third century record, *The Chronicles of Wei*.

First, the Ryûkyû Islands still preserve a strong tradition of female priest-esses and shamans (Blacker 1975: 113; Hagiwara 1993: 103; Lebra 1966: 24, 70, 74–75; Rokkum 1998: 72–74; 76–78), not unlike the medium Himiko. Blacker, summarizing the work of Nakahara Zenchû, elaborates:

> . . . we have the nuru or noro [the Ryûkyûan priestess figure], a majestic sacral woman who exercises spiritual power over a village or group of villages. . . She possesses a personal kami who is in fact the apotheosis of her own ancestors, and who provides her with a direct link with the spirit world. Her residence is a shrine where these ancestors have their tablets . . . All of these signs are imme-diately reminiscent of the ancient miko [medium] . . . in the nuru we glimpse a parochial Himiko . . . (1975: 113).

Much like Himiko, the chief priestess of the Ryûkyûan kingdom (*chifijing*) prior to 1650 wielded considerable social, religious, and even political power (Lebra 1966: 102). In addition, this priestess was served exclusively by female servants, her shrine was taboo to males, and she spent her time secluded from others, focusing on developing her spiritual prowess (Lebra 1966: 111). In a similar fashion, in 749 A.D., at the dedication of the Great Buddha image at Nara's Tôdai-ji, the female medium (*ôga-no-morime*) from the Hachiman Shrine at Usa in Kyûshû attended the ceremony borne in a purple litter, as was Emperor Shômu himself (Nakano 2002: 58). Even one century following the Taika Reform, this venerable priestess was afforded the enviable honor of re-ceiving from the emperor the lower Fifth Rank at court, complete with its rights to receive an audience with the emperor, claim a government stipend, and the right to wear attire suited to her rank ("Hinode-cho" 2002: 2; Morris 1994: 63–65). The tradition of powerful female mediums persisted beyond the Yayoi period in Kyûshû, and longer in the Ryûkyû Islands. Female medium figures officiate in prominent roles even at the present-day in the Ryûkyûs.

Second, rice culture figures prominently in the ritual life and subsistence patterns in the Ryûkyûs (Hagiwara 1993: 103; Lebra 1966: 51, 60, 189; Os-hima 1992: 320–22; Rokkum 1998: 34, 42, 180), much as it did in Yayoi pe-riod Kyûshû. Even the raised floor rice storehouses were an important feature in rice culture in the Ryûkyûs as they had been in the Yayoi, as evidenced at the Yoshinogari site.

Third, until 1899 when it was outlawed by the mainland Japanese, tattoo-ing was practiced among Ryûkyûan women who had reached adult status and even formed part of a woman's coming of age ritual (Lebra 1966: 194; Os-hima 1992: 332). This also mirrors the account of *The Chronicles of Wei* that indicates men and boys in Himiko's kingdom were tattooed.

Fourth, a close affinity exists between Ryûkyûan and mainland dialects. Hanihara's (1987) computer simulation estimates that 1.5 million persons migrated into mainland Japan between the Early Yayoi (300 BC) and the close of the Tomb period (700 AD) (Ômoto & Saitô 1997: 441). It appears that during this influx of outsiders and continental influences into Western Japan, the split between mainland Japanese and Ryûkyû speech patterns took place. Hattori's linguistic analysis of the Kyôto dialect of mainland Japanese and the Shuri dialect of the Ryûkyû Islands identifies the separation of these two languages at approximately the year 500 A.D (1959: 83; see Philippi 1968: 20), approximately 200 years after the end of the Late Yayoi period. It is my hypothesis that migrations took place in which some inhabitants of Kyûshû retreated to the Ryûkyû Islands. Or, if this was not the case, then at least by the advent of the sixth century the old trade routes that had routinely connected the Ryûkyûs to Kyûshû and Korea were interrupted, severing the contact that had once been common.

Arne Rokkum (1998) provides a wealth of ethnographic data in his monograph devoted to contemporary ritual life in Dunang, the southernmost island in the Ryûkyû island chain (see Figure 2.1). His work defines the ways in which an elaborate, institutionalized priesthood of females served the religious needs of the Ryûkyûan kingdom during its heyday in the fifteenth century (1998: 43–48). This female priesthood was later fragmented into several, locally operating religious specialists as warriors from the Satsuma domain in mainland Japan conquered the polity in the sixteenth century (1998: 43–48). In the course of this study, data from Rokkum's ethnography of contemporary Dunang will be utilized primarily as a means of accessing the particulars of ritual practice coordinated by the island's female mediums.

The Korean Connection

Vast numbers of Korean immigrants bearing continental influences also made their way into Japan during the Yayoi period. These large numbers of Koreans entering mainland Japan are implicated by Hanihara's computer simulation mentioned earlier.

Korea played a major role in the cultural and technological development of mainland Japan as a transmitter of Chinese civilization. Korean language bears strong affinities to mainland Japanese, and genetic research has indicated that the mainland Japanese and Koreans are of the same stock (Horai et al. 1996: 581, 584, 588). Although Korea and Japan presently have separate national boundaries, during the Yayoi period, these contemporary boundaries were much less meaningful. For centuries, Korean ritual life has been oriented around a prominent mediumistic spiritual tradition (Chang 1988: 30–31). Like the Ryûkyûs, female mediums have wielded considerable power in Korean folk religion. The medium tradition in Korea also revolves around

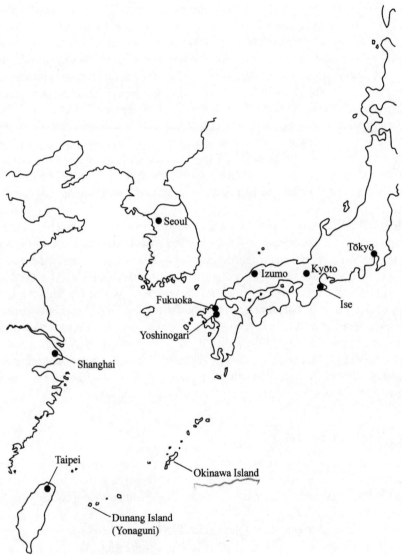

Figure 2.1. Significant Locations

an emphasis on the Unseen Realm, female mediums, and boundary phenomena. Laurel Kendall's (1985) thick description is an ethnography that details ritual practices coordinated by Korean, female mediums in a community she calls Enduring Pine Village (a pseudonym), located north of Seoul. A lively sub-culture exists in which housewives function as household god priestesses who are directed in their practice by female mediums (1985: 25–30). This female practice operates beyond the pale of, yet complements, male-controlled Confucian ancestor rites and male-structured society (1985: 25–30). Korean folk belief, in addition to Ryûkyûan ritual practice, will provide us with another means by which to recover the kami-focused belief and rituals practiced in Yayoi period Japan.

Ritual Practice in Mainland Japan

Ritual practice in the Japanese mainland will also be examined as a further means of recovering salient aspects of Yayoi period worldview. Carmen Blacker's (1975) classic ethnography of Japanese female mediums is devoted to the practice of women in the Kinki, Kantô, and Tôhoku regions of Japan. Her research aims at explicating the significance and role of integral symbols that are employed in kami tradition ritual practice. Clifford Geertz has defined all religion as "a system of symbols" (1973: 90). By analyzing key symbols, Blacker's work represents a primer in kami tradition symbology that divulges several essential elements upon which the ritual and belief of this spiritual tradition is predicated. Blacker's study is also extremely sensitive to the explanations of practitioners regarding the Unseen Realm, a fundamental topic around which kami tradition myth, symbol, and ritual revolve. Perhaps most significantly, the vision of Blacker's work is comprehensive enough that it provides generalizable insights not bound to place or time.

By considering belief and ritual practice in the Ryûkyûs, Korea, and mainland Japan, we will come to see a triangulated worldview that flourished in the Yayoi period, Japanese mainland. This reconstructed cosmology of the Yayoi is our key to grasping more fully the specifics of Shintô ritual practice. By considering the contemporary ritual of the Ryûkyûs and Korea, or mainland Japan's Yayoi period kin groups, our view of Shintô ritual in contemporary mainland Japan will become more heightened and focused.

LIVING LANDSCAPE

The ancient Shintô worldview was structured in terms of the bodily experience of the female. For the residents of Yayoi period mainland Japan, such as the inhabitants of the Yoshinogari site in Kyûshû, this ancient worldview was a lens through which they viewed their environment. The following five concepts are essential in understanding this ancient cosmology, which underlies and informs the worldview of contemporary kami tradition ritual practice in Japan.

The Topocosm

The combined features of the local landscape were considered an all-encompassing living, containing entity (vessel) composed of topological features such as vegetation, earth, rivers, rocks, trees, mountains, and valleys. Native mammals, birds, insects, reptiles, and human beings were no less a part of this local organism. None of these single parts is divorced from the whole; all of these elements blend into one great being that is known and experienced as a united entity. Moreover, cognitive experience of this local landscape was perceived in terms of an archetypically female entity (this concept will be examined further later).

Theodore Gaster has dubbed this "total corporate unit of all elements, animate and inanimate alike," the "topocosm" (1961: 24).[3] Collectively this great organism is alive, bristling with energy, and numinous. Erich Neumann defines numinous as ". . . the action of beings and forces that the consciousness of primitive man experienced as fascinating, terrible, overpowering, and that it therefore attributed to an indefinite transpersonal and divine source" (1963: 5).

There are potentially an endless number of topocosms but for any given community, the local topocosm is the most immediate, for it is the source of all local life. In the topocosm, community has its origin, and to it they are connected in terms of subsistence, shelter, and spirit.

The Landscape as Corridor to the Unseen Realm

Features of the topocosm were not seamless; at certain places and times, egress (interstices) from this world opened into an Unseen Realm inhabited by supernatural beings. Important aspects of the living earth, such as a sacred mountain or mighty river, were named and known, revered and remembered. Not only did such places serve as cognitive points of reference (Rokkum 1998: 36, 160, 212), but salient features of the landscape were noteworthy since they could serve as portals into another realm beyond, the Unseen Realm of spirits. Important locations in the home compound also provided access to this other dimension.

For inhabitants of Dunang Island, various features of the local landscape are still considered by inhabitants to be portals of access to the other world where the spirits of animals, deceased humans, and other more impersonal entities can be encountered (Rokkum 1998: 185–87). In particular, mountains and springs are significant features in the spiritual landscape, while lithic monuments and shrines around the home figure as important ritual sites at which the power of mountains can be accessed (Rokkum 1998: 68, 99, 193–94).

In Korea, too, mountains are believed by women to be sacred places of power which should be ascended, with extreme care, in order to seek blessings for their families; in fact, the mountain god is considered to preside over ancestors buried in the hills, and certain areas in the home are also linked with the veneration of mountains and ancestors (Kendall 1985: 6, 128, 130).

In the traditional Japanese home, certain features, in addition to the kami and Buddhist altars, are areas at which spiritual beings are recognized, including the entry, the hearth, the well, the garden, the veranda, and the toilet (Williams 1997: 97–101, 108). Similarly, female mediums in Japan recognize many aspects of the landscape at which the otherness of spiritual beings can be encountered. Among these features are: huge evergreen trees of great age, rocks that exhibit phallic features, pools, lakes, caves, riverbeds, and mountains (Blacker 1975: 40, 75, 83; Nomoto 1990: 233–36). Female mediums explained to Blacker that mountains in particular are the location from which they invite the kami spirits and kindly ancestors into the realm of the living; it is in mountain areas, too, that shamans perform ascetic training to augment their spiritual powers (1975: 79). Oba Iwao asserts in his research on mountain belief in prehistoric Japan that mountains themselves were extremely sacred areas into which members of the human community were not allowed to enter, since these heights were considered to be the precincts of kami beings (Blacker 1975: 81). Mountains were also consistently considered to be inhabited by beneficent ancestral spirits, as determined by Hori Ichirô's analysis of eighth century elegy poetry recorded in the Manyôshû (Blacker 1975: 81). The earliest date for poems in the Manyôshû has been identified, by Gary Ebersole, to be the mid-seventh century (1989: 10), so by that time at least, both kami and ancestors seem to have been thought to inhabit mountains.

Cycles of Growth and Decline

The local landscape was not perceived as a static reality, but rather as a dynamic organism that experienced regular cycles of growth and decline. This waxing and waning of life energy for the Yayoi period inhabitants of Japan was no trivial matter. The waning of life energy, as in the dormant state of various life forms in the winter, was a matter of trepidation regarding the survival of the topocosm. At important junctures, such as the winter solstice, rituals would have been performed to revive the life energy of the local earth entity: the topocosm.

Gaster indicates that time for ancient man was reckoned in terms of successions of cyclical time, cycles that followed one after another, rather than a linear progression of time stretching from birth to death. Yet these renewed cycles of time and, subsequently, a renewal of topocosmic life energy did not come about automatically and effortlessly. Rather, this renewal was "fought for and won by the concerted [ritual] effort of men;" this ritual battle for the resurgence of renewed life, he claims, was the origin of seasonal ritual observances in human communities (Gaster 1961: 23; 37–38).

Two Classes of Spirits

While aspects of the local landscape were perceived as benign, many elements of the topocosm were held to be menacing and threatening to the human community; these inherent dangers and apprehensions concerning the locality would have served as a major, if not predominant feature of their ritual practices. For many Westerners, a day of hiking, camping, or rafting out in wilderness areas is an exhilarating recreational experience. But for the Yayoi period inhabitants of Kyûshû, among the sentient aspects of the land, and in many of the interstices of those features, there lurked spirits and forces filled with ill-will or spite, who desired to attach themselves in a parasitic fashion to members of the human community. And, if possible, these dark forces would steal the life force from hapless persons. Ritual precautions were always necessary, and the services of ritual specialists including mediums would have been in high demand when the uncertainties of life presented themselves. Much of Yayoi ritual was directed by fear of supernatural danger, or apprehension that such danger might impinge upon their lives. As a result, the inhabitants of Yayoi period Kyûshû would have had a much greater dependence upon ritual and a more spiritually complex existence than either ourselves or even their contemporary descendants.

Two general classes of spirits appear to have been recognized by the Yayoi period inhabitants of Kyûshû as being contained within the various features of the topocosm: beneficent spirits and ancestors, and menacing, life-sapping ghosts and spirits in the landscape.

In Dunang, spirit visitors from beyond the horizon visit at regular intervals bringing with them blessings for the community (Rokkum 1998: 62–63), but other beings, such as "tree hosts" can curse human beings and even drain a person's vitality if their influence is not thwarted (Rokkum 1998: 172). In addition, islanders perceive certain sacred features so spiritually dangerous and powerful that they are loath to approach, even when accompanied by an island priestess (Rokkum 1998: 164).

In areas around Enduring Pine Village, not only is the home compound full of gods and spirits, but the entire area beyond the gate of the home is identified by women as being the haunt of ghosts and other less humanized, yet pernicious influences (Kendall 1985:). While ancestors and gods do visit the living to bestow blessings at rituals (Kendall 1985: 20–22), the local landscape is more often associated with disease-causing earth spirits, wood spirits, jealous ghosts, and restless ancestors (1985: 99).

In Japan, both kami and kind ancestors bring life and fertility to the topocosm; unhappy ghosts and the wandering spirits of those who died without family (*muenbotoke*) are identified as the source of illnesses and other forms of misfortune (Blacker 1975: 20–21, 41, 43–44, 47–49).

Women as Intermediaries

On Dunang, women including priestesses and shamans, are universally recognized as having a special closeness and access to the island spirits (Rokkum 1998: 40, 76, 195). In particular, these women are identified by islanders as possessing spoken words of power that in prayer they use to invoke the living landscape (Rokkum 1998: 198). In Korea, as well, women are identified as having an automatic closeness to the gods, ancestors, and spirits; housewives function as priestesses in their own homes, and female mediums officiate in rituals at which housewives converse with spirits and make pilgrimages to mountains (1985: 128; 131). In Japan, women have from early times been perceived as the "natural intermediaries" between the community and the Other World (Blacker 1975: 28). Yanagita Kunio was very impressed that women doggedly fulfilled the role of medium, particularly in the Ryûkyûs, and Blacker identifies the female medium (miko) of the "late prehistoric period" that appear in the *Kojiki* and *Nihon Shoki* as oracles that served both the nobility at court and the farmers in local villages (Blacker 1975: 104; 113). Without exception, females are recognized as being the inherent mouthpieces and mediums for spirits given their closeness to and intrinsic affinity to these beings.

I. M. Lewis has called this the "sexual bias of the spirits" in that spirits have a pattern of manifesting themselves in the persons of women (Lewis 1971: 309). Lewis' conclusion as to why women are the preferred vehicle is that spirit possession is a socially recognized way for women to voice their displeasure with their place in a male-controlled world (1971: 89). Kendall, takes issue with this conclusion; instead, she asserts that Korean "women and shamans perform essential ritual tasks that complement men's ritual tasks" (1985: 25).

While both of these previous positions have merit, I will argue that it is the bodily experience of the female that 1) structures the perception of the local landscape as both container and portal, 2) informs the positive and negative character of spirits equated with the landscape, and 3) ultimately predisposes women to be the a priori officiants in the world so ordered.

THE ARCHETYPE OF THE FEMININE

Clinical social worker and Jungian analyst Gareth Hill identifies archetypes as "patterns or forms for expectable, typical human experience" (1992: xiv). Archetypes are "universal patterns or motifs" that in the individual manifest themselves in "dreams, visions, and fantasies," while in the realm of society these models of and for experience are evinced in the realms "of religions, mythologies, legends, and fairytales" (Platania 1997: 58). For Carl Gustav Jung, archetypes came into existence from the collective, rather than individual, experience of society (Platania 1997: 59). Archetypes are expressed by particular aggregates of symbols (Neumann 1963: 6) and function on the individual and collective level to impart meaning to human experience (Platania 1997: 59).

For nearly all persons, the central experience in infancy is the presence of mother. Human perceptions of self, society, and the world are all largely based upon "the child's bodily tie to the mother" (Dinnerstein 1976: 34). Cognitive psychologist Dorothy Dinnerstein claims that "the mother is in a literal sense, not just a figurative one, "the intermediary. . . in charge of the most intimate commerce between child and the environment: the flow of substances between the flesh and the world" (1976: 131). Out of this experience with mother, develop the individual's perceptions and primal "prototypes" and "archetypes" which will cognitively structure subsequent experiences of safety, fear, happiness, and disaster (Dinnerstein 1976: 131).

Analytical psychologist Erich Neumann, concurs with Dinnerstein, asserting that the "positive, primordial experiences" with mother are ones in which she is known as a "vessel that gives nourishment," as a provider of "abundance" for the child (1963: 123). Ultimately, the experiences with mother in infancy and early childhood have far-reaching ramifications with regard to how an individual, and even society, comes to view the world and their place in that cognitive realm (Dinnerstein 1976: 41–53; 124–30).

Out of this early relationship with mother, emerges the archetype of the Feminine. Neumann explains that in the archetype of the Feminine, woman is analogous to body and vessel (1963: 43). For the Yayoi period inhabitants of Kyûshû, the woman as body/ vessel appears analogous to the perception of the earth, or the topocosm.

Like a human mother, the vessel of the topocosm provided life. An understanding of how the topocosm occupied a central, omnipotent and omnipresent location in the lives of the resident human community, not unlike the role of a human mother in relation to her infant child, casts Dinnerstein's cognitively structuring "child's bodily tie to the mother" (1976: 34) in a brand new light. Early experiences of the human mother archetypically continued to function as the "intermediary . . . between the child and the environment" (Dinnerstein 1976: 131) and mediated Yayoi period perceptions of the topocosm itself as a Feminine entity. Every aspect of the topocosm—rivers, hills, forests, and mountains—was simply part of the Great Mother upon whom her children were dependent (Neumann 1963: 12).

The topocosm was not only perceived to be a vast container that surrounded and sustained all life, various features in the living landscape were held to be portals into the Unseen Realm of spirits. Margaret Miles identifies the female bodily processes of "menstruation, sexual intercourse, pregnancy," and birth as means by which "women's bodies loose their individual configuration and boundaries" (1989: 153). Citing Bakhtin, she asserts that the female body is "a body in the act of becoming. It is never finished, never completed; it is continually built, created, and builds and creates another body . . . in short, [the female body] outgrows its own self, transgressing its own body" (1989: 153). In short, she argues that the female body is "permeable" when compared to the "closed, self contained, controlled male body" (1989: 153).

The penetrable, constantly evolving characteristics of the female body were, for the Yayoi period inhabitants of Kyûshû, metaphorically linked and applied to the local landscape. Victor Turner calls metaphor "a means of proceeding from the known to the unknown" (1974: 25); in metaphor, two items are fused in such a way so that the "subsidiary subject" is used to illuminate the "principal subject" (1974: 30). Knowledge of the changing female body, then, was applied to elucidate the more removed, and unknown nature of the topocosm, and visa versa. This shared form of cognitive reality (metaphor) is based on "implicit generalizations from social experience," (Turner 1974: 13) that shape and give meaning to existential reality. Systems of ideation are based on a root metaphor which Turner claims are products of the "rational, discursive understanding [or, mind]" (1974: 46, 48). Turner employed the term "root metaphor," which philosopher Stephen Pepper preferred to call a "conceptual archetype;" both terms denote a major cognitive model by means of which social groups apprehend a given reality (Pepper 1972: 91–98; Turner 1974: 25–26). In the present study, following the terminology of Jungian psychology, I will simply use the term archetype. For Jung, experience of a supernatural being originated in a projection, a reflection of aspects "of the unconscious," or psychological realities from within (Neumann 1963: 20). Having been trained in the field of cultural anthropology, rather than speaking of "the unconscious," I prefer to speak of cognitive realities, or aspects of cognition resulting in the perception of spirit entities that are projections of socially-conditioned aspects of shared cognition. Jung elaborates on the function of metaphor in the human experience:

> An archetypal content expresses itself, first and foremost, in metaphors. If such
> a content should speak of the sun and identify it with the lion, the king, the hoard
> of gold guarded by the dragon, or the power that makes for the life and health
> of man, it is neither the one thing nor the other, but the unknown third thing that
> finds more or less adequate expression in all these similes, yet,—to the perpet-
> ual vexation of the intellect—remains unknown and not to be fitted into a for-
> mula (Neumann 1963: 17).

In metaphoric manner, the female body has three aspects that serve to structure a meaningful Yayoi period view of the landscape: process, creativity, and permeability. First, the changes inherent in the fertile female body's monthly cycle parallel the seasonal changes in any given topocosm over the course of a year. The cycles of fertile woman and landscape are ongoing and embody dynamic change focused on endless birth of new life. Second, woman and earth embody a creativity that goes beyond their own physical limits. In the processes of birth and vegetative growth, the boundaries of woman and the earth are surpassed as the emergence of new life takes place. Woman and earth experience transcendence as new life forms incubate within, and emerge from, their physical being. Finally, woman and earth exhibit a permeability of body. In the woman, blood and offspring emerge from her body; the seed that finds a home within her sets in motion changes that create a new life. For the earth, humus (the organic portion of the soil originating in decayed animal and plant matter) and vegetative life come forth; it too receives seeds and also absorbs the lifeless remains of flora and fauna. This metaphoric linking of woman and earth created, for the Yayoi period inhabitants of Kyûshû, a topocosm that was viewed as being as permeable as the female body.

The metaphoric linking of earth and woman precipitated the creation of a cognitive complex we will call the archetype of the Feminine which, in Yayoi period Kyûshû and in contemporary Japan, implies the figure of an Earth Mother, or Great Mother. While in other societies and time periods, the Earth Mother is named, graphically portrayed, and addressed, in Japan at the present, her existence is only implicitly acknowledged, despite the fact that all aspects of ritual practice indicate this Feminine archetype to be the focus of attention. This implicit acknowledgment of the Great Mother in Japan, I claim, is a result of Ommyôdô thought via China (examined in Chapter Four) that deemphasized females on the basis of their cosmological association with cognitive margins which challenged the predominant male-ordered society. Prior to the arrival of Chinese cosmologies in Japan, a more explicit focus on the Earth Mother structured ritual life, the evidence of which still remains in Ryûkyûan, Korean, and mainland Japanese ritual practice.

Neumann identifies the archetype of the Feminine as possessing both positive and negative aspects, "the Feminine not only shelters the unborn in the vessel of the body, and not only the born in the vessel of the world [topocosm], but also takes back the dead into the vessel of death, the cave or coffin, the tomb or urn" (1963: 45). He elaborates concerning the destructive aspect of the Feminine: "beside the fecundated womb and the protecting cave of earth . . . gapes the abyss of hell, the dark hole of the depths, the devouring womb of the grave and of death, of darkness" (1963: 149). The seed in both woman and earth result in the emergence of new life: in offspring and in vegetative life. The earth receives the spent bodies of flora and fauna which rot and create new earth, thus maintaining the fertility of the soil. In an analogous fashion, menstrual blood in the woman is also a means of maintaining her own fertility; but symbolically is representative of the failure to produce offspring. Among the Maori, menstrual blood was seen as a twice anomalous case of a corpse that had never lived (Douglas 1966: 96). In one case, the Feminine is life-giving; in the other, it is life-taking. Previously, I have called this constellation of understandings the Earth-Womb root metaphor (1997: 19). The Feminine archetype possesses both a generating aspect and a devouring aspect; each aspect is implicitly acknowledged and addressed in the ritual practices we will examine.

NOTES

1. Even though the Central Bureau of Shrines prefers to emphasize that Shintô is a wholly unique product of a privileged and separate culture and nation, I maintain there is much that connects Shintô ritual practice to East Asia in terms of basic cognitive processes.

2. This seems to have been a continuation of trade patterns that Mori (1989) and Warashina (1990) indicate existed in the Jômon period in which high grade obsidian from Mt. Koshi at Imari Bay was traded via a route that extended from the Ryûkyûs in the south to Hyôgo prefecture to the east; this obsidian has also been found at three sites in Korea (Hudson & Barnes 1991: 230).

3. The term topocosm come from the Greek words *topos*, or "place" and *cosmos*, denoting a "world order" (Gaster 1961: 24).

Chapter Three

Great Mother as Woman and Topocosm

GAPING INTERSTICES IN THE LANDSCAPE

Mediumistic ritual practices in the Ryûkyûs, Korea, and Japan indicate certain landscape features are identified with life-giving aspects of the Feminine archetype, while others are indicative of its life-threatening manifestation. These perceived attributes have important cosmological implications *vis-à-vis* the Yayoi period inhabitants of Kyûshû. Five topocosm features are recognized interstices from which high spirit influences emerge: mountains, monoliths, springs, ceramic vessels, and soil.

Interstitial locations in the landscape are metaphors for the generative life forces of the Feminine archetype, ultimately the womb of the Great Mother. Examination of ritual practices will illustrate this assertion and identify similarities between practices in the Ryûkyûs, Korea, and Japan.

Mountains

In the Ryûkyûs, Korea, and Japan, mountains are major spatial interstices equated with the life-giving Feminine archetype. Mountains are: (1) the realm of spirits who are the source of life, growth, and fertility; (2) the Other World home to the spirits of the dead; (3) taboo areas; and (4) an interstice from which spirits descend to visit the human community.

Mountains as the Realm of High Spirits

Mountains form salient loci along Dunang's Spirit Trails (*kan-nu-miti*), pathways that form "closed circuits" in the island along which "high spirits" navigate, affecting the fortunes of the human community (Rokkum 1998: 167). In fact, the term for a priestess' shrine is "High Peak" (*utaki*), indicating that the spiritual "highness" of mountains is there accessible to the human community (Rokkum 1998: 115, 168). The high Peak Spirits of Dunang Island are petitioned by priestesses (either *k'a* or *bunai*) for "fruition" (*dû* or *jû*), explained succinctly by Rokkum as "births and crops" (1998: 105) and "the moment of female life-invigoration" (Rokkum 1998: 110).[1] These generative forces are known locally as "of today," or "of this world" (*sunka*) (Rokkum 1998: 76, 110) and are manifestations of the life-giving aspect of the primal Earth Mother.

In Korean ritual practice, mountains are "pure, powerful, elevated, and sacred space" (Kendall 1985: 130). Branch families make pilgrimages to the mountain associated with the lineage founder precisely for the reason that *this* particular mountain is recognized as the "source" of their familial "blessings" (Kendall 1985: 131). Women make mountain pilgrimages to petition a Taoist spirit, the Seven Stars (*chilsông*) of the Big Dipper, considered to preside over: "conception," "birth" in general, the birth of sons, "fertility," the welfare of a woman's children, including their career development and long life (Kendall 1985: 127–30). All of these blessings correspond to the life-giving aspect of the Feminine archetype. Women take with them rice or, if they are petitioning the mountain for conception, rice, kelp (seaweed), and fruit (Kendall 1985: 127, 129). Rice metaphorically represents the seed that makes the Great Mother (and reflexively the female supplicant) fertile, while kelp and fruit are tangible produce of the Feminine. Each item is indicative of the Feminine's life-giving aspect. Some women petition both the Seven Stars and the mountain spirit in the same visit to the mountain (Kendall 1985: 128).

Certain mountains are identified in mainland Japan as the "sacred dwelling place" of kami, functioning as an "object of worship" (*goshintai*). The association of kami with mountains (as well as other interstice locations) will be explored throughout this study.

Mountains as a Home to Spirits of the Dead

Beneficent high spirits and others associated with the local landscape have a direct relationship to, if not origin in, ancestor spirits. In Korea, the mountain spirit presides over the ancestors, and Kendall shows revealing evidence that Korean high spirits, or "gods," also have an origin in ancestral shades. This merging of high spirits and ancestors is a logical corollary to the cognitive function they serve as projections of the Feminine archetype's generative aspect.

On Dunang Island, "death forces" are presided over by female shamans and address the realm "of yesterday," or of the "other world" (*nunka*), or mortuary ritual (Rokkum 1998: 76, 110). Ancestor spirits become part of the Peak Spirit host equated with mountains, circumambulating the island along the numinous Spirit Trails. Sister priestesses (*bunai*) preside over rituals performed for their ancestors enshrined at stone altars in their family house site; island priestesses conduct rituals in their High Peak shrines for island high spirits. These Peak Spirits preside over the life-giving forces inherent in the living landscape (Rokkum 1998: 76–77; 185). Rokkum explains that with time, ancestor spirits in the house site become island spirits; "enshrined human souls [eventually] fuse with the Peak [Spirits]" and are addressed in island ritual, rather than by sister priestesses (1998: 185). Here becomes visible the transition of familial ancestral spirits into more impersonal high spirits of the greater island.

In Korean ritual life, the dead are clearly identified as going "to the mountain and away from the world of men and women" (Kendall 1985: 107). At the close of seasonal ancestor rituals presided over by men in the Confucian manner (*chesa*), spirits are sent back to the mountain (Kendall 1985: 146). Branch families perform their most solemn, Confucian ancestral rites at the mountain equated with their lineage founder (Kendall 1985: 131). The mountain spirit (*sansin*), popularly recognized as controller of deceased spirits, keeps the dead safely in place in hillside graves and prevents them from wandering among the living (Kendall 1985: 6, 130). Women also venerate the mountain spirit when they make pilgrimages to a mountain (Kendall 1985: 128). Kendall claims that in her female mediums' ritual practice, "gods (*sillyông*) are above ancestors (*chosang*)," but in certain instances, it is apparent that "some gods are also known ancestors. They are grandfathers and grandmothers writ large" (1985: 55). This pattern also indicates a process whereby ancestors become more exalted spirits, "gods" if you will, with the passage of time.

Based on analysis of one hundred twenty-two, seventh century *Manyôshû* elegy poems, Hori Ichirô claims that mountains were very clearly the domain of kami and kindly spirits of the dead (Blacker 1975: 81). Forty-seven poems, or fifty percent, mention spirits of the dead identified with mountain locations, which is twice the number of any other single location represented (Abe 1995: 160–61). In Yayoi period Kyûshû, mountains were considered to be the Unseen Realm where the beneficent dead resided. Work by Ôba (1970) and Hori (1963) indicates that mountains in prehistoric Japan and into the seventh century were the other-worldly domain of kami and ancestor spirits. The reputation of particular mountain areas including Kumano, Tateyama, and Osorezan have persisted for centuries (and into the present) as especially noteworthy portals into the realm of the dead (Blacker 1975: 82–83).

Mountains as Taboo Areas

Mountains receive much collective attention as spiritually significant features of the Dunang landscape (Rokkum 1998: 68, 37). In Rokkum's experience, island inhabitants endeavor to avoid these places; when approaching mountains, no one is "lighthearted" about the prospect since to "linger in the sacred nuclei" is to risk having life-souls (*mabui*) separated from one's body (1998: 37, 164). Vegetation-clad mountains and other dense concentrations of growth, such as overgrown house compounds, are indicative of the mountain, and assume an aura of other-worldly power that is best left alone by the non-priestess (Rokkum 1998: 172–73, 184).

Lebra mentions that on the island of Okinawa (in the Ryūkyūs), priestesses were to refrain from performing their ritual duties during times of their menstrual period (1966: 50–52). Women were also perennially taboo on fishing boats because of their menses; their presence aboard was said to impair the fisherman's relationship to the sea spirit. This female taboo, one informant explained, existed "because the sea kami is a jealous female" (1966: 52).

While Rokkum does not mention ritual taboo surrounding menstruation for female priests and shamans on Dunang Island, he does mention that priestesses and shamans very carefully separate ritual matters focused on the generative forces "of today" and the death ritual directed toward the forces of "yesterday" (1998: 110). In addition, before important ritual occasions (*kanbunaga*) that access the life-giving forces of Peak Spirits, island priestesses scrupulously avoid meat, animal products, and sexual relations (1998: 101). Rokkum (2003: personal communication) indicates that for inhabitants of Dunang, menstruation rather than being a source of taboo, is rather an evidence of female generative, and hence, ritual power.

Based on his own fieldwork, Lebra indicates that Chinese ritual influence was most pronounced on Okinawa, but that in other areas including remote Dunang, such ideas were less evident or non-existent (1966: 99). Dunang appears to be an exception to the Chinese-influenced menstrual taboos found on Okinawa, and cognitively closer to the Yayoi period worldview we are seeking.

Pilgrimages into the mountains of Korea are fraught with ritual danger and taboo (Kendall 1985: 129). The Feminine archetype is equated with the mountain and taboo serves to shield female pilgrims from the Great Mother's dangers. Women do not explicitly identify the mountain as a point where contact with the Great Mother is made, but their behavior implicitly acknowledges that such a meeting does take place. While petitioning the life-giving aspect of the Feminine, its life-taking aspect must be strictly avoided. Taboos observed include: no fish or meat three days prior to the ascent, no contact with those in mourning, no menstruation, and scrupulous attention to cleanliness (Kendall 1985: 129). In addition, social contact is taboo going to or coming from the mountain, lest one compromise taboos. Taboos on meat, death, and menstrual blood (analogous to fruition failure) sever ties with the life-taking aspect of the combined woman/ earth Feminine archetype. Lapses of taboo observance have deleterious effects for those involved (Kendall 1985: 129–30).

In prehistoric Japan, and into the Nara period, mountains were major cognitive interstices in the topocosm equated with kami and ancestor beings. Based on archaeological excavation of offering caches at mountain bases, Ôba Iwao asserts that in prehistoric mainland Japan, mountains were considered taboo areas inhabited by kami spirits (Blacker 1975: 79–81). Before the end of the Edo period (1867), several mountains were completely off limits to women including Mount Fuji, Dewa's Yudonosan (opened to females in 1993), and Ôminesan, which is still off limits to women. In 1969, women were allowed to advance twelve miles closer to Ôminesan, but it is still off limits because it is "too holy and pure to risk contamination by women" (Blacker 1975: 215–16). Female contamination in the context of kami ritual is explained by my Japanese informants to be "red impurity" (*akafujô*), menstruation, which based on the Feminine archetype is analogous to fruition failure, and even death pollution. Such thought appears to be continental in origin and will be examined further.

In mainland Japan, the mountain spirit (*yamanokami*) was a female spirit around whom taboos were commonly focused. Nomoto Kan'ichi identifies a female mountain spirit near the rural village of Momoie in Akita prefecture (1990: 93). When hunters and villagers entered the mountain, special "mountain language" (*yamakotoba*) had to be used, and if "village language" (*satokotoba*) was used by mistake, water purification had to be performed (1990: 93–95). Game taken on the mountain was offered before her shrine and thanks given, and only after so doing could hunters use everyday language again (1990: 95). Folklore in northern Honshû, the central Japanese Alp area, and in the mountainous areas of Kyûshû, identifies the mountain spirit as a female entity (Nomoto 1990: 98). In these areas, male hunters who took a large trophy or who lost a tool on the mountain exposed their genitals and called in prayer on the mountain spirit to thank her or to implore her aid; exposure was said to please the female spirit (Nomoto 1990: 98).

In legend, women had to carefully avoid the female mountain spirit's wrath (Nomoto 1990: 97–98). At entrances to at least three mountains, Ishigamiyama (Tôno-shi, Iwate prefecture), Iwakiyama (Tsugaru-shi, Aomori prefecture), and Hakusan (Tsuruki-chô, Ishikawa prefecture), "old woman rocks" (*ubaishi*) stand where legend claims women tried to climb the sacred mountain and were punished by being changed into a large rock (Nomoto 1990: 96–97).

Mountains as Interstices from which Spirits Descend

On Dunang Island, during the festival of the First Fruits, the Peak Spirits "descend from mountain tops" and are conveyed to waiting priestesses in their

High Peak shrine by means of swaying palm fans held by island women (Rokkum 1998: 194). The Peak Spirits' gift to the human community is topocosm invigoration: these mountain spirits "induce growth in living matter" and quicken the "regenerative process in humans, domestic animals, and plants" (Rokkum 1998: 194, 204).

In Korea, ancestral spirits repair to the mountain realm at their demise, descending together with the mountain spirit as summoned in female medium rites (*kut*) or in male-oriented Confucian rituals (*chesa*) and, following these rites, return to the mountain heights (Kendall 1985: 6, 107, 146).

In Japan, mountains have been identified for centuries as vehicles of descent for beneficent kami spirits into the realm of the everyday (Blacker 1975: 39); both ancestors and kami are said to descend from these heights to the human community below at certain festival times (*Basic Terms of Shintô* 1985: 58). At Higanezan (*jikkoku tôge*) in Shizuoka prefecture, at the equinoxes, ancestor spirits are venerated in the mountain heights; with successive rituals and purification of the deceased, these spirits are said to move to higher points on the mountain and to become tutelary beings (*uji gami*) for their descendants (*"Ohigan wa naze nihon dake no gyoji?"* 1999).

In mainland Japanese folklore, the generative forces of life are also equated with the mountain and the mountain spirit, which is a projection of the Great Mother. The mountain/ field spirit, most often identified as a young female (Kishi 2002: 54, Ôshima 1983: 181), is said to descend to the village in spring to fructify the crops as the field spirit (*tanokami*); after the harvest, this spirit returns to lodge in the mountains as an old hag during the winter months (Ôshima 1983: 181, 184). At planting time, the descending field spirit (known as *sanokami*) was traditionally served in the fields by young, marriageable "field-spirit maidens" (*saotome*) who transplanted rice seedlings into the paddies (Nomura 1998: 517; Shintani 1999: 91). The term *sa* signifies field-spirit (Nomura 1998: 517; Shintani 1999: 91), so descending to the fields, the female field-spirit seems a fertile young woman, the Good Mother, whose likeness is reflected in the persons of the field-spirit maidens.

The hag-like manifestation of the mountain spirit, invoked in the proverbial image of fingers placed like horns on either side of the head by a Japanese man referring to his wife, is touchy and fierce when angered. Her most representative image is a mountain hag of ravenous appetite (*yamamba*). The fearsome aspect of the mountain hag most closely represents the Terrible Mother, and appears to be equated with the harvest and her return to the mountain. The mountain spirit, often identified as an ugly or fierce woman who aids the process of human birth (Hafuri 1969: 366) is the source of life, "without whose aid human birth may not be safely accomplished;" in remote mountain recesses she can be found suffering the pains of childbirth (Blacker

1975: 84). Yanagita Kunio identifies the mountain spirit/ field spirit as the "mutual ancestor" of the human community below the mountain who "forever protects the holdings of the family" (1970: 149). In the image of the mountain spirit/field spirit, as in the case of the Peak Spirits of Dunang, the image of the Feminine archetype originating in the mountains is extremely clear. These spirits preside over the collective, generative aspect of both woman and earth: offspring and vegetative life.

These ritual practices identify mountains as major interstices in the landscape, sources of life-giving powers, as they certainly were in the Yayoi period. Mountains are sanctuaries, interstices at which emerge kindly ancestor spirits that bestow fertility and growth, in the form of birth and crops in the topocosm. Births and crops (in addition to other vegetation) represent the collective product of the "seed" in both woman and earth. Emphasis on woman and earth indicates the Feminine archetype that obtains in the metaphoric linking of these two "females," and which presupposes a Great Mother figure. Rituals focused on a female mountain spirit in the mountainous areas of mainland Japan bear out her gender with the greatest clarity.

Mountains are approached with the ritual purpose of claiming the blessings of "female life-invigoration" (Rokkum 1998: 110), but these same mountains are the interstice through which the dead come and go. These two aspects are reconciled in the two aspects of the Feminine archetype: both life-giving and life (or corpse)-receiving. This dual character equated with the mountain interstice of the Great Mother is substantiated in taboos on death (meat, mourning, and menstruation) which must be observed if the mountain is to bestow its bounty of life. The Great Mother is a touchy and jealous being, yet powerful and willing to bless with abundant life so as long as she is not offended, confronted with, or excited by death and other life-taking influences, including menstruation. In the Yayoi period worldview, mountains were important interstices of great power in the topocosm through which, periodically, the blessings of life and fertility could be invited to reinvigorate all the features of the local landscape.

Monoliths and Storage Platforms

Upright stone altars, or "monoliths," are also significant interstices in the living landscape equated with the life-giving forces of the Feminine. On Dunang Island, monoliths function as metaphoric links to the mountains, and are the objects to which ancestor spirits immediately "attach themselves" (Rokkum 1998: 68, 185). Most house compounds on Dunang contain one or two such altars; in "Origin Houses," the "house site" of a lineage founder, the number of monoliths increases (Rokkum 1998: 193). These stones, called "ensouled objects" by Rokkum, are the focus of sister priestess-led ancestor rituals (1998: 68, 185). In ritual practice, "Mountains are reproduced and accessed in prayer through the vehicle of the upright stone [the monolith]" (Rokkum 1998: 193). Inhabitants of Dunang endeavor to keep decaying vegetation away from stone altars and, during times when life-giving force ritual is performed, shamans (who shed animal blood in some of their ritual activities) must not approach a monolith (Rokkum 1998: 184). These practices parallel the taboo of death *vis-à-vis* mountains, and bespeak the ritual care in approaching the Great Mother. With time, ancestral spirits equated with the household monolith become one with the high, Peak Spirits (Rokkum 1998: 185)

Rather than stone altars, Korean households access the powers of mountains through another metaphoric link: the storage platform (*jangdokte*). Kendall explains that among her informants, the storage platform, located out in the household yard, holds large jars of fermented sauces; it is "high off the ground" and is commonly held to be "the cleanest place within the walls" that surround the dwelling compound (1985: 130). Korean women explain that the platform is "the proper analogue to a mountain" and that ashes are ritually placed next to the platform, signifying the return of ancestors to the mountain (Kendall 1985: 146). This place is the site for ritual focused on the house site spirit (*toju*), or the serpent spirit (*opu*) who directs the family fortunes (Chang 1988: 36; Ito 2000: 417). These two tutelary spirits are represented by a ceramic vessel filled with grain (Chang 1988: 36; Ito 2000: 415, 417); the images of serpent and grain indicate that these spirits are ancestral. Women also set out offerings for the mountain spirit on this platform; it is a space set apart, an interstice analogous to either a mountain or a temple (Kendall 1985: 150, 195).

While upright, stone altars do appear in mainland Japanese ritual life, they do not consistently do so within the contemporary household compound. Might ritual practice in the Ryûkyûs preserve ideas that have been lost in mainland Japan? Origuchi Shinobu indicates that in ancient Japan, rocks were indeed considered to be "ensouled objects" just as they are considered in Dunang. The concept of "sealed vessel" (*utsubo*) appears in early folklore and mythology: a sacred, spiritual power inside the "womb-like" vessel "gestates, grows, and emerges," often in the person of a hero (Blacker 1975: 98). Rocks in this early period were alive with a spirit force within, and far from being inanimate; they were thought to grow larger with the passage of time (Blacker 1975: 98).

Ethnologist Honda Sôichirô identifies "stone vessel altars" (*iwakura*) as "the focus of prehistoric and ancient kami ritual; a location to which the spirits descended or which they inhabited" (Honda 1991: 93). These large rocks or groups of rocks, located in or at the foot of mountains were considered the focus of worship and are the "oldest form of shrine" (Honda 1991: 93–94).

Ôba Iwao identifies mountain base ritual sites as stone vessel altars, places where the power of mountains was accessed without entering the heights themselves (Blacker 1975: 80–81).[2] Stone vessel altars and "rock boundary" sites (*iwasaka*), gravel areas surrounded by large stones (*Basic Terms of Shintô* 1985: 20), both early sites for kami ritual in mainland Japan, appear in the *Kojiki* and *Nihon Shoki*, and seem analogous to the "inner enclosure" (*ibi*) of landscape shrines in the Ryûkyûs (Rokkum 1998: 68, 77, 187; Tatematsu 1993: 172). In the Yayoi period worldview, monoliths were cognitive contact points to mountains and the Unseen Realm. Through stone altars the generative forces of ancestral spirits were accessed by the living community. The auspices of the Good Mother are evinced in these sacred objects.

Springs and Wells

Island priestesses on Dunang make pilgrimages twice annually to "New Water places," springs in the landscape, to reestablish their relationship to living water (Rokkum 1998: 94, 99). Priestesses on Miyako Island in the Ryûkyûs explain that the "continual" welling up of water from island springs is the "breath of the island; if this breath of the island were to stop, it would mean that the island itself would die" (Tatematsu 1993: 171). In the Ryûkyûs, little difference is seen between natural springs and made-made wells; both are "places at which the island takes its breath" (Tatematsu 1993: 172). "Spirits ascend from crevices in the ground," explains Rokkum (1998: 195–96). Dunang priestesses are initiated into "sisterhoods" that venerate these "ensouled freshwater springs." Relationship with the "water host" of these water sources confers upon women guidance and "protection" which they, in turn, extend to the men of the island (Rokkum 1998: 94, 99). Priestesses take small amounts of this spring water which they "domesticate" in their sacred vases within their personal shrines (Rokkum 1998: 94, 99–100). Spirits of living water are enshrined in sacred vessels in the priestess shrine, providing a continual means of accessing their protective power. Spring spirits bear a striking resemblance to the mountain/ field spirit of mainland Japan, the collective Ancestor who continually cares for local descendants.

Korean women also utilize springs as centers of ritual attention, and invoke mountain springs for conception, taking with them rice and produce from land and sea. One of Kendall's informants describes the way in which she petitioned the Seven Stars spirit:

> I couldn't get pregnant. Everyone said I should go to the mountain. I went with a *mansin* [female medium] and a friend. I took rice grain, kelp [for soup], and fruit and prayed beside a mountain spring (1985: 127).

In mainland Japan, the term for well (*ido*) originally designated a gushing or bubbling water source (Ôshima 1992: 72; Shinmura 1969: 137). This term is currently applied to wells only, while "spring" has its own term [literally, "emerging water"] (*izumi*) (Shinmura 1969: 112). It appears that the present ambiguity between springs and wells in the Ryûkyûs was a feature for earlier mainland Japanese, too. In Chapter Six, we will examine the ritual use of wells in contemporary Kyûshû, but for the present, one piece of mainland folklore will suffice. Formerly, in the mainland there existed a ritual called "soul restoring" (*tama-gaeshi*) (Ôshima 1992: 72). When a loved one was near death, family members would run to the well and yell the person's name down the shaft as a means of calling their spirit back, and saving their life (Ôshima 1992: 72). In Sashima, a town in Ibaraki Prefecture, this ritual was practiced up until the 1930s, and is said to have been effective because practitioners recognized that the Other World was at the bottom of the well ("Sashima-chôshi" 2002: 1). This belief seems validated by the fact that the expression "below the spring" (*izumi no shita*) denotes "the land of the dead" (Shinmura 1969: 112).

In summary, springs offer an interstice into the Other World at which access to protective, life-giving spirits is evident, and also at which the spirits of the deceased are pulled into that other dimension beyond. The life-proffering and life-swallowing aspects of the Feminine archetype both obtain at this interstice. With the spirits of the dead sinking below and the spring spirits rising up to bless and protect, these deep water sources are home to kindly ancestors spirits who emerge to watch over their living family members. This conclusion is given credence by the name given to the well spirit in Dunang: "[going] Up-Down" (*nundan-uridjan*) (Rokkum 1998: 161). In this instance, congress with ancestors takes place at the metaphoric interstice that leads into the Great Mother's permeable body: the spring. Just as monoliths are means of accessing the power of mountains, sacred vases in the priestess shrine appear to fulfill a similar function with regard to springs.

Ceramic Vessels

Island priestesses on Dunang keep in their shrines "sacred vases" (*kandin*) which they use to venerate the "birth-spirit" [as opposed to the devouring spirit], and which they invoke as a medium of personal tutelary protection. In addition, at least one of Rokkum's priestess informants claims that she receives "insights" from her sacred vases (Rokkum 1998: 94, 261).

Ceramic jars for storage figure prominently in the domestic rituals of Korean women; these jars may be located on the storage platform, or in other places about the traditional home. Jars are a means of indicating the presence of a spirit being (Kendall 1985: 113, 193). Filled with grain, these jars mark the presence of "particularly powerful gods" that are female, such as Birth Grandmother, the Talking Female Official, or the Seven Stars who preside over female concerns including conception, birth, and the growth and health of children (Kendall 1985: 113–14, 127–28). The mountain spirit, another focus of mountain pilgrimage ritual, also receives offerings in ceramic jars on the storage platform (Kendall 1985: 130). Kendall explains, ". . . the Seven Stars and the mountain spirit oversee birth and death, entrance and exit from life in the villages and towns below the mountain;" (1985: 130) these two spirits also neatly delineate the dual aspect of the Feminine archetype. George Jones (1902) offers the insight that grain pots and other "spirit placings were far more numerous and elaborate at the turn of the century," and Akiba Takashi (1957) observes that there were great numbers of "spirit pots" in homes in all parts of Korea (Kendall 1985: 193).

In contemporary, mainland Japan, ceramic vases hold evergreen (*sakaki*) branches on the household kami altar (*kamidana*). Familiarity with ritual practices in Dunang and Korea adds new significance to these extremely common vases used in ritual contexts. Evergreen branches suggest vigorous, unabating life energy, which resonates with the veneration of the birth-spirit in the sacred vases used by island priestesses in Dunang. Markets throughout mainland Japan offer fresh evergreen branches for sale year-round, and while I am not aware of any Japanese who receives revelation from these vases, these ceramic vessels do appear to be one ritual means by which practitioners petition high spirits for the blessings of life, health, and protection.

In Yayoi period Kyûshû, ritual use of ceramic vessels was also a means of accessing the life-giving forces of the Feminine archetype. Over 2,500 burial jars (kamekan) found in burial contexts at the Yayoi period Yoshinogari site (Hudson & Barnes 1991: 213, 224) initially seem to indicate this to be so. In light of contemporary ritual practice, use of large ceramic vessels to inter the dead at Yoshinogari would appear to be a means of ensuring the deceased's rebirth by placing them in a metaphoric womb of the Great Mother. In the three ritual cases considered, ceramic vessels are used to: 1) venerate the birth-spirit, 2) effect tutelary protection, 3) signify the presence of powerful female spirits, and 4) invoke generative powers associated with the mountain. Urn burials at Yoshinogari seem to suggest that a similar process of logic obtained in the Yayoi period: the life-bestowing aspect of the Feminine archetype was evoked by placing the dead in a womb-like environment.

Soil

Soil is also an interstice in Yayoi period cosmology. Earth itself is the fundament of the topocosm, another feature at which the permeable body of the

Great Mother is manifest. The Great Earth Mother is, after all, the local earth itself (Neumann 1963: 303). The Feminine archetype, in this case the topocosm, is a reality that prefers homeostasis; in other words, a relative state of equilibrium among the various parts of the whole (Hill 1992: 5, 8–9, 22).

The Feminine archetype denotes a ceaseless cycling (Hill 1992: 7) between the dual aspects of growing and shrinking, of life-giving and life-taking. Both woman and earth alternate between periods of fertility, conditions that favor the reception of the seed/growth, and periods of sterility, conditions of disso- lution and reabsorption, where the old is sloughed off in preparation for the next period of fertility. There are no other alternatives than these two poles; if other options should arise, the Feminine automatically opts for decay as an automatic resumption of the endless cycle (Hill 1992: 5). In a word, "con- stancy and balance" are paramount, "change [beyond the regular cycle] is ab- horred" (Hill 1992: 5). These are the rhythms of nature itself, one reason that natural cycles, vegetation and particularly trees (with their dependent limbs, branches, twigs, and leaves), are so prevalently utilized metaphoric devices to convey insights regarding the Feminine archetype (Neumann 1963: 48).

The Great Mother is both generative and destructive and, above all, she is very possessive and jealous of all the life forms found within her pervasively encompassing womb (Neumann 1963: 25): the topocosm. Compliance with the eternal cycle of local patterns of growth and decline results in continuing support from the Mother; variance from this pattern invokes her ire and is dangerous.

Rokkum explains that on Dunang, inhabitants address "prayers to samples of Dunang soil" (1998: 34). They do so because, according to inhabitants, the soil, or the soil spirit (*dinaranuci*), of the island exerts a pull on persons liv- ing on the island (Rokkum 1998: 116). Special affinities accrue between in- dividuals and the soil of the island in general, and also to the particular soil of their home site (Rokkum 1998: 116). But no individual's relationship to the soil is personal; persons on Dunang experience a "collectivity of fates" *vis-à- vis* the island soil (Rokkum 1998: 117, 151–53). Maintaining an amicable re- lationship to the soil becomes a social responsibility, and in the event that this relationship sours, it becomes even more so (Rokkum 1998: 117, 151).

In terms of "soil belonging" on Dunang, some matters are easy and others are more complicated but, routinely, the services of either a priestess or a fe- male shaman are required to keep the relationship good (Rokkum 1998: 116, 159). A relatively easy matter is moving the location of a small island shrine from one location to another: the transferal of shrine stones and a pinch of soil from the original site accomplishes the act (1998: 186). Life on the island ne- cessitates moving through the landscape, but callously disregarding such pas- sage is dangerous. In particular, deserted (overgrown) house compounds (with monoliths), thick groves, and boundary locations are places at which one of a person's seven "life-souls" (*mabui*) might be snatched from the body (1998: 163–64, 169, 197). One island priestess identified a boundary area between villages, a place that many persons found creepy, to be a location where a woman "lost her life" (1998: 163–64). Which came first in that particular case, the feeling of apprehension associated with the site, or the untimely loss of life, we may never know, but certain boundaries between worlds carry a sense of unease all the same. Rokkum summarizes: "South Ryûkyûans find in the trails set upon their island territories . . . the impressions of growth affected by decay, of inertia affected by transit" (1998: 63).

Crossing boundaries between worlds or, in other words, negotiating interstices (crevices between topocosm areas) in the landscape can cause a person to experience shock in varying degrees. Islanders know that a "sudden shock" can result in the dislodgment of a life-soul; experiencing a shudder is one indication that such a separation has taken place (Rokkum 1998: 160). A stray life-soul is an event in Dunang that "prefigures" death (Rokkum 1998: 160). Eating rice balls is considered an immediate means of restoring the errant life-soul. This action was also formerly a means of preventing apprehension prior to taking a sea journey (Rokkum 1998: 180) and, in this latter case, appears to have been a preventative measure observed to protect one's life-souls when leaving the confines of the island. Another means of recovering the soul is to return to the place where the shock was experienced and to toss soil from that location on one's head (Rokkum 1998: 151). In lieu of soil ritual, dousing the head with seven portions of sea water followed by the sacrifice of a chicken to the ocean spirit Nira, the being considered to "exert a deadly pull" on the living, will suffice to save the afflicted person (Rokkum 1998: 151, 183). Nira, spirit of ocean depths, is the Great Mother herself. Rokkum elaborates:

> The nira spirit . . . figures in people's imagination all over the archipelago [of the Ryûkyûs]. . . The spirit's character is somewhat ambiguous. The nira is a promoter of ample harvests. As a sea spirit, it makes way for the arrival of seed . . . a life-sustaining agency. Yet in a somewhat double-edged, fuzzy logic, it comes out also as an adversary. It bequeaths growth, but at the same time it can exert a deadly pull from its subterranean and sub aquatic regions. It delivers and it pulls. Shamans exchange souls for commodities, foods, and money to extricate their patients from this drag. . . The nira signifies a movement which delivers upon the islanders the blessings of fruition just as it signifies a movement which pulls the living into an abyss of death matter (1998: 182–83).

No image could present so perfect a portrayal of the dual aspect of the Feminine. This female spirit, in addition to the sea, holds sway over the island land itself (Rokkum 1998: 181). In the logic of the priestesses and shamans of Dunang, it appears that careless negotiation of interstices in the landscape, in addition to other forms of shock, are means by which injury (loss of one or more life-souls) occurs. This injury, if unaddressed, eventually leads to an untimely death unless, in ritual, a food ransom is offered in place of the afflicted person and, concomitantly, the substance of the Great Mother's being, sea water or soil, is poured over the discomfited person's head. In this, there surfaces a tacit understanding that the stray life-soul has been snatched by Nira, and that its restoration will only come in *quid pro quo* exchange. Another acceptable ransom food offering in rites of soul restoration are rice balls; the image of a round rice ball conforms to the roundness of a "life-soul," the latter being signified by the former (Rokkum 1998: 180). Transgression of local interstices causes spiritual impairment which precipitates predation by Nira, eventually resulting in a pull of the person (and others) toward death if the infraction is not resolved. The devouring Feminine archetype, like a hungry shark, drags the unfortunate, offending person in a dizzying spiral down toward death and decay if not halted by ritual intervention.

While life-soul mishaps can occur by negotiating the island landscape, much greater problems can accrue when persons leave the island or return from elsewhere. Leaving the island, and subsequent fear of losing life-souls in the process, prompted the former practice in Dunang of eating rice balls before an ocean voyage. Lebra notes that on Okinawa Island, men leaving for long sea voyages took a small amount of soil from the local shrine and, when safely returning home, this soil was replaced with thanksgiving (1966: 56). Leaving or returning to Dunang from abroad is considered to be an event that can precipitate "sickness or misfortune" (Rokkum 1998: 157). When an inhabitant of the island plans to leave and does not plan to return, a shaman is employed to perform a ritual of "soil release" in which the soil spirit, fire spirit, and well spirit of the home site are addressed and a bit of soil is retrieved for the traveler (Rokkum 1998: 157). Under no circumstances is it explained to the spirits that the person is leaving; instead, the individual is sent on a "journey," regardless of whether the journey will end or not (1998: 157–59). Even in conversation on the island, only the euphemism of "journey" is employed (1998: 159). Indeed, a person's tie to the island cannot be severed, nor spoke of as such. If such were to be done, it is likely that the spirits, and ultimately Nira, faced with the prospect of being abandoned indefinitely, who for lesser infractions on the island snatches a life-soul or two, would react by quickly taking the person's life as a means of reincorporating them into the topocosm. The cognitive understanding is that the Mother affects decay to prevent a person from leaving the land, thus resetting the regular topocosmic cycle. Here emerges the image of an overly possessive and jealous Great Mother. In keeping with the Feminine archetype, inhabitants of the Great Mother's womb must not leave the confines of the topocosm. To do so is an attempt to disregard, escape, or transgress their preordained roles in her endless cycle of growth and reabsorption. Taboos surrounding boundary transgression in the previous instances obtain or are mitigated by the lack of, or observance of local soil ritual, the Great Mother's body.

Understandably, island and sister priestesses, who must be on intimate terms with the island spirits (and the Great Mother), and must act as effective intermediaries between them and the community, epitomize the ideal relationship with the Great Mother. They observe proper ritual at topocosm interstices, they are restrained to maintain permanent residency on the island (Rokkum 1998: 115), and at ritual functions, they wear yellow robes of office, dyed with an extract of the island soil (1998: 81). They enjoy an intimate relationship with the Great Mother; in fact, they become a means of maintaining the continuing life-giving support of the soil and the Feminine archetype, and function as cognitive projections of the goddess (Rokkum 1998: 175), the Great Mother herself.

In Taoist-influenced Korean ritual practice, attention focused on the soil takes the form of recognizing earth spirits (*chisin tongbap*) that carouse together with tree spirits (*moksin tongbap*) (Kendall 1985: 98). These spirits are "malevolent imps [that] instigate or perpetuate illness" and are conjured by disregard of cardinal direction taboos that are linked to certain days of the Chinese lunar calendar (1985: 97–98). Rousted spirits infest the offender's house, attach themselves to weak or offending persons, and must be exorcised by a female medium who will afterwards attach "charms" to "[re]secure the house boundaries" (1985: 98–99). When the displeasure of more powerful spirits is serious enough, a shaman will rub the afflicted person with a live chicken, vicariously sacrifice it, and have it buried on the hillside "like a human corpse" to release the individual from their life-draining grasp (1985: 19, 90).

In mainland Japan, similar ideas existed. The enduring distinctions of Western Japan and Eastern Japan, literally "west of the barrier" (*kansai*) and "east of the barrier" (*kantô*) are reckoned from the ancient barrier station of "Meeting Slope" (*ôsaka*) in the modern-day city of Ôtsu. By at least the Heian period (794–1185), Meeting Slope was an important barrier linking the familiar and cultured regions of the capital with the untamed eastern provinces beyond. Travelers leaving the capital stopped at this pass and presented offerings (*tamuke*) and prayer to the spirits of this place for safe passage. Folklore identified this slope as the trysting place of a male and female spirit who were locked in an embrace. Travelers who crossed the pass disturbed this divine couple; if offerings were made with prayer, the intrusion was forgiven, and protection in travel and a safe return were granted. Failure to do so was to incur the wrath of the local pair of spirits and would have dire consequences (Matisoff 1978: 9–10). To offer ritual at this regional interstice was to seek and receive the Great Mother's blessing to "journey" beyond and return safely; a lack of a soil release would have been to risk a loss of life-souls or worse.

Additionally, an ethnographic example from contemporary Japan. A 79–year-old lady at the Hakozaki Hachiman Shrine in Fukuoka, after receiving sacred beach sand from the shrine beach said:

> I have humbly received some sacred beach sand. This sand, every morning when the children leave for school and the grown-ups go to the company, you sprinkle a little on [your body] for that day [in the entryway] so that there will be no calamity (*sainan*): no traffic accidents nor injuries. And we even put it in a little envelope and carry it with us on trips and such. *Like a protective-talisman (o-mamori)?* Yes, yes. That's right. My granddaughter is a student in New Zealand, and she has an envelope of it with her now!

LIFE SOULS IN JAPAN

Heian period Japanese recognized a plurality of spirits attached to the individual, much like the inhabitants of Dunang in their concept of life-soul. In *The Tale of Genji* (written ca. 1005 -1014), through a medium employed during exorcism rites conducted for the beleaguered Lady Aoi, spirits ("some of them belonging to living people") attached to the lady were made known:

> They were a heterogeneous, insignificant lot—some of them apparently deceased nurses, others the wraiths of men with hereditary grudges against the family, taking advantage of her weakness. Aoi sobbed and wept incessantly. . . [but] there was one [spirit, belonging to Lady Rokujô] that clung with great obstinancy, frustrating every effort to transfer it to a medium. It did not inflict horrendous pain, but it never left for an instant. There seemed small likelihood that the spirit of an ordinary person would be so persistent. . . (McCullogh 1994: 7, 8, 138).

Apparently, in addition to whatever life-souls were thought to belong to the individual, there was the possibility that the souls of living persons could attach themselves to other living individuals.[3] The spirit of Lady Rokujô, Lady Aoi's living and estranged rival for the nobleman Genji's attentions, was the prime source of Aoi's torment. Ivan Morris asserts that female jealousy at this period was seen as having such "maleficent power" as to drive the

disgruntled woman's spirit from her body to commit heinous acts unbe-
knownst to the perpetrator (1994: 250). Jealousy was "regarded with . . . dis-
taste" in the mainland because it "forced" the afflicted person to wreak spiritual "revenge," during life and even after death (Morris 1994: 132). Lebra
notes that on Okinawa, the wandering spirit of a living person was called a
"living life-soul" (*ichimabui*) while a "dead life-soul" (*shinimabui*) was one
belonging to a deceased individual (1966: 25).

Life-souls, attached to the individual, are a socially-defined, cognitive
means of objectifying and intertwining the individual, community, and local
landscape into a single spiritual whole that is articulated with the Feminine
archetype complex of understandings. In Heian period Japan, malevolent possession by the spirit of a living, human rival (in the case of Lady Rokujô)
could cause illness and death. The case of Lady Rokujô appears to be the
gruesomely jealous, curse-wreaking aspect of the Feminine played out at the
individual, female level. In the case of Lady Rokujô, the nobleman Genji's
failure to obtain soil-release (tacit permission) to direct his affections elsewhere became the means by which the devouring Feminine consumed the
jilted lady, driving her to possess her rivals.

Nevertheless, the concept of life-soul, attached to the individual or wandering through jealousy to attack others, is a unifying theme that firmly links
this mainland phenomena to the Ryûkyûs. Furthermore, the concept of curse
or retribution (*ichiining*, *tatari*) performed by spirits upon the living is also a
unifying concept in the Ryûkyûs (Lebra 1966: 40; Rokkum 1998: 64) and on
the mainland that brings Lady Rokujô's behavior into the realm of soil ritual
and the Feminine archetype.

THREATENING SPIRITS IN THE LANDSCAPE

In contrast to life-giving spirits, which are cognitively equated with the ordered universe of society, life-threatening spirits are perceived to represent
the pale beyond social order. They are also associated with features of the
topocosm. On Dunang, in addition to the Nira spirit lurking in watery depths,
menacing spirits are perceived in terms of "nature spirits" that inhabit soil,
 trees, or stone, as the hungry dead, or ghost entities (Rokkum 1998: 159).
These forbidding beings are of the "other world," "of yesterday" and are part
of the "death forces" presided over (outside of the home) by female shamans
and are addressed by "mortuary ritual" (Rokkum 1998: 76, 110). For inhabitants of Dunang, it is imperative that the life-sapping forces of "yesterday"
are kept "safely apart" from the life-giving powers of "today" (1998: 110).
Female shamans also preside in rituals that address the death forces of the

"other world" (*nunka*), including "prayer and sacrifices" to protect the living from the forces of that other, threatening dimension (Rokkum 1998: 76).

Although spirits are said by islanders to move about the topocosm, none of them are perceived independent of a physical location in the landscape (1998: 159). These "hosts" (*nuci*) residing in the landscape are demanding, and are constantly looking for offerings (1998: 154). Human beings must beware that they "do not fall prey to the cravings of the dead or of a nature spirit" (1998: 159). Trees and wood are said to be significant abodes of suspect beings.

Tree spirits inhabit trees and wood and are said to "drain vitality from human bodies" (Rokkum 1998: 172). Dunang legend identifies the origin of tree spirits with a covetous man whose hands were nailed to a tree, left to die by the angered widow of the man he had previously killed to have her (Rokkum 1998: 172). Thwarted in his desire, and jilted by the woman he would have as his wife, his spirit filled with ill will (in mainland Japan: *urami*) and he became hostile to humanity, a potent source of torment to others (Dunang: *ta'tai*, mainland Japanese: *tatari*) (1998: 172).

Ghosts also manifest themselves in animal form. Rokkum returned several times to Dunang for fieldwork. A shaman informant confided in him that his on-going, reoccurring relationship with the island was the reason that he had several "uncanny metamorphic sentients" (*kidimunu*), or ghosts visiting his lodgings in the form of "a pigeon, a snake, a pig, a cat," and also swarming bees (1998: 151–52).

Rocks (other than the monolith shrines), gravel, and earth are also the abode of spirits even around the house; Rokkum identifies these with the "soul fragments of dead prior inhabitants of the compound" (1998: 154, 161). These life-souls attached to rocks and gravel in the home appear to be analogous to "house ghosts" that are harmful to the living (Rokkum 1998: 86). House ghosts are indicative of decay, the opposite of fruition (Rokkum 1998: 86). A man's sister on Dunang Island is his personal priestess and goddess who brings him access to fruition (birth and harvest) while his wife fulfills the role of exorcist and keeps the ghosts of the home (the realm of death and decay) under control (Rokkum 1998: 86). Rokkum asserts that ancestor ritual in the home celebrates the continuity of deceased male lineage members and functions as a "symbol of house integrity," and on these occasions, men take the leading roles (1998: 110).

In Korean mediumistic ritual practice, ghosts, "restless ancestors," "red disaster," and offended water spirits (Kendall 1985: 99, 102) are some of the threatening forces which must be confronted by the living.

Ghosts (*yongsan* or *chapkwi*) wander in the realm outside the gate of the home, along roadways; everyone, with time, accumulates a following of life-sapping ghosts about their person (Kendall 1985: 99, 100–101). The home, unlike the realm outside the gate, is usually a refuge from ghosts since it is periodically the site of ritual exorcism (Kendall 1985: 103). As with spirits, when ghosts are exorcised from the home, the shaman pays particular attention to "vulnerable spots" in the compound and is sure to "secure the house boundaries" (Kendall 1985: 91). Ghosts are hungry beings belonging to two groups: previous family members and anonymous, unknown spirits (Kendall 1985: 99). Ghosts "died unmarried, without issue, often violently or suddenly when far away from home;" without descendants to offer them proper rituals and food; they are "unsatisfied, [and] they wander angry and frustrated, venting their anguish on the living" (Kendall 1985: 99). They are particularly attracted to new clothing, to feasts and to guests at family observances for weddings, longevity, and mortuary rites, with the spiritually weak being particularly susceptible to their life-sapping influences (Kendall 1985: 98, 100).

Restless ancestors (*chosang malmyong*), originating from the broader category of ancestors (*chosang*) in general, are a source of affliction for the living (Kendall 1985: 99). The general profile of well-adjusted ancestor spirits includes the following factors: during their lifetime they were married, had offspring (particularly sons), died at home, and were well advanced in years (Kendall 1985: 99). Such an ancestor is considered in Korean villages to bring blessings to their descendants and to remain close to the family home (Kendall 1985: 55, 100). Ancestors become unhappy and cause problems when the home's spiritual defenses have been compromised, when high spirits in the family home have been neglected, or when the ancestors themselves possess unfulfilled longings, or nurse a grudge (Korean: *han*; Japanese: *urami*) (Kendall 1985: 99–100). While there are several formal ritual occasions during which offerings are presented to the placid family ancestors through male-directed, Confucian mortuary rites (Kendall 1985: 29–30, 144–47), it is in the person of the female medium that disgruntled ancestors voice their pent-up longings so that they might be properly addressed (Kendall 1985: 99–100). Restless ancestors roam among the living, joining forces with ghosts and other wandering spirits, drawing attention to their plight by touching family members, which touch brings disease (Kendall 1985: 99–100, 102). Fulfillment of persistent longings transforms wandering ancestors back into their proper niche as sources of blessing for the family.

"Red disaster" (*hongaek*), a less personalized source of affliction, lingers on roads, bridges, at sites of previous accidents, and at places associated with sickness and death (Kendall 1985: 102). Individuals coming into regular contact with this store of negative energy accrue its deleterious effects which cause misfortune for the bearer if not exorcised (1985: 102–103). Red disaster can be exorcised from persons and places with a sprinkling of millet (1985: 102–103).

When a Korean funeral procession must cross the site of a known underground water course, the services of a female medium are enlisted to perform a rite to placate the spirit of water. Otherwise, having the corpse carried above its lair, the water spirit will be angered and lash out in retaliation at the family for the offense. To avoid this threat, lengthy ritual complete with elaborate offerings are made and permission is sought to prevent misfortune (Vindenes, Haakon 1992, personal communication).

In mainland Japan, two classes of threatening spirits are simultaneously recognized: a vague, Ryûkyûan-type strain (Lebra 1966: 21) equated with particular features of the topocosm, and a second variety, more in keeping with Korean ideas, which is more personalized and more articulated with social realities.

The nature of spirits in the natural landscape, which comprise the first class of threatening spirits, is more abstract; the names applied to these entities are also quite ancient. The terms for landscape spirits include: *chi, mi, hi/bi,* and *mono.*

The oldest of these terms is *chi* (Kamata 1993: 125). It is preserved in the names of nature spirits in the *Kojiki* and the *Nihon Shoki* including: field spirit (*nozuchi*), tree spirit (*kukunochi*), fire spirit (*kagutsuchi*), water spirit (*mizuchi*), and thunder spirit (*ikazuchi*) (Kamata 1993: 124; Philippi 1968: 55–56, 63). Chi denotes "spirit" or "elder" (Philippi 1968: 459, 622) and seems to have been applied to "great, powers in nature" that were reverenced (Kamata 1993: 124). By itself the term "expresses powers in nature that flow and move" including the landscape features of wind and roads, as well as blood, milk, and spirit (Kamata 1993: 124).

Kamata Tôji identifies the term *mi* as more recent in origin than chi (1993: 4); it also appears in spirit names in the *Kojiki* such as sea spirit (*watatsumi*) and mountain spirit (*yamatsumi*) (Philippi 1968: 56, 70). The designation mi indicates "spirit," "ruler," or "lord" and appears to have been applied to spirit beings that "preside over a wide area" (Kamata 1993: 125–26; Philippi 1969: 499, 552).

The most recent and abstract term for spirit entities is *hi / bi* (Kamata 1993: 125). It also is recorded in *Kojiki* names including: generative force (*musuhi, musubi*), healing spirit (*naohi, naobi*), and misfortune-working spirit (*magatsuhi, magatsubi*) (Kamata 1993: 4; Philippi 1968: 47, 69, 596). While chi and mi are connected to concrete locations in the landscape, hi identifies spirits of "abstract functions" such as generation, healing, and misfortune-working (Kamata 1993: 4).

Finally, *mono* is indicative of earthly spirits (*kunitsukami*) as opposed to the spirits of heaven (*amatsukami*) (Kamata 1993: 125). Mono also appears in the *Kojiki* in the name Great Lord of Earthly Spirits (*Ômononushi*); the term mono signifies "[earthly] spirit," "[physical] object," or "rascal" (Kamata 1993: 125). Use of the term "mono" has also been applied to "low ranking, malicious, curse-bearing (*tatari*) spirits" (*mononoke*) (Kamata 1993: 125). Ueda Kenji calls mono spirits "demons" (1996: 35). Kamata identifies chi spirits (as in the *Manyôshû* phrase *chihayaburu*), as "possessing terrible powers by which they act" (Kamata 1993: 125–26) in the landscape; to which category I would add both mi and mono, as well. These local, earthly spirits (chi, mi, and mono) are "strange, deformed, low-ranking spirits," and non-anthropomorphic beings, while high spirits (*kami, tama*; this second term denotes spirits of the kindly dead) are more "high-ranking and more inclusive terms" for beneficent spirits in general, and are perceived as being anthropomorphic (Blacker 1975: 43; Kamata 1993: 125–26; Ueda 1996: 35). Earthly spirits are identified by contemporary mainland Japanese as "bad spirits" (*warui kamisama*), while high spirits are called "good spirits" (*ii kamisama*).[4] Good spirits are enshrined and are recipients of regular veneration; bad spirits jealously inhabit features of the local landscape—plants, animals, mountains, and rivers—and receive irregular or no ritual attention (Williams 2002: 16–18; Ueda 1996: 35). In contemporary mainland Japan, earthly spirits are the focus of soil pacification rites (*jichinsai*) so as to not harm construction efforts nor plague inhabitants of the future dwelling (Ueda 1996: 35).

The second class of threatening spirits consists of disgruntled ancestors and relationless spirits of the dead. They bear more than a passing resemblance to their counterparts in Korea. In the Japanese mainland, like in Korea, contented ancestors (*tama, gosenzosama*) married a spouse, raised children, and passed away at home surrounded by family (Blacker 1975: 43). These kind beings continue to have an interest in their progeny, are given serious ritual attention, and "will continue to act as mentors and monitors to their descendants" until their ritual term is completed (usually 33 years) and they merge with the corporate Ancestor of the family (Blacker 1975: 44). If ancestor spirits are not given proper ritual attention, most often at the family Buddhist altar (*butsudan*), they become offended, distant, and retaliate by cursing the family (Blacker 1975: 47). Yanagita Kunio relates that in the regions of Yamato, Kawachi, Mikawa, and Kyûshû at the completion of 33 years the ancestral spirit is said to be "cleansed," and to become a kami spirit (in Shikoku this process only took three to six years) (1970: 118, 120). Lack of proper veneration before the requisite 33 years, when their spirits become purified and free, transforms ancestral spirits into beings "less than human, malevolent, spiteful, in need of succor and restitution" (Blacker 1975: 48). Once proper rituals are resumed, however, they become the kindly sources of blessing they once were (Blacker 1975: 48). Obviously, the incentive to perform assiduous ancestral ritual is great; in many Japanese homes, these observances are also largely the provenience of Buddhist ritual forms. On significant ritual occasions in the realm of Buddhist ancestor ritual (at Obon and on important memorial dates), members of the male, Buddhist priesthood officiate in the home.

Ghosts, or relationless spirits of the dead, are a heterogeneous, pitiable, and lonely class of beings which can be divided into two categories: common ghosts, and angry ghosts. Ghosts in general are the social inverse of kindly ancestors. Much like ghosts in Korea, common ghosts died without spouse or children, or in a far away place separated from family and relatives; as such, they are known collectively as "relationless spirits" (*muenbotoke*) or "hungry ghosts" (*gaki*) (Blacker 1975: 48; Smith 1974: 41). Because they suffered an unusual death, they are doomed to roam in the landscape forever on an "endless search for food and comfort" (Smith 1974: 41, 48, 65). Receiving irregular or no ritual attention, they linger at their grave, or the site of their death, filled with "bitterness and spite," leading unsuspecting and susceptible persons to an untimely demise (Blacker 1975: 48; Smith 1974: 44, 45, 50). These beings in limbo include the deceased spirits of: aborted fetuses, children, childless persons, women who died in childbirth, victims of drowning, casualties of war, and suicides (Kawara 1995: 56; Smith 1974: 43, 44, 49, 65). Ritual intervention by the living can deliver such ghosts; in contemporary Shintô ritual, one means to pacify such spirits is by designating them a low-ranking kami that receives more regular ritual attention (Blacker 1975: 49). Buddhist rites to pacify common ghosts (*segakie*), held "under the eaves" or at a temple, revolve around food offerings and sutra readings to fill and comfort these wandering spirits and keep them from harming the living (Smith 1974: 42–43).

Collectively, unredeemed ghosts are identified by shrine priests and practitioners at Hakozaki as being "bad spirits" (kami). As such, they are recognized in particular spatial boundaries: crossroads, corners, shorelines, entrances, and other spatial boundary areas (Williams 1997: 17). Common ghosts are also perceived by contemporary mainland Japanese persons at suicide sites (suicides), former battlefields (casualties), at rivers (victims of drowning), hospitals (victims of sickness and death in childbirth), graves (unhappy or childless persons), and special areas (particularly associated in folklore with spirits of aborted fetuses and young children) called the "Riverbed of Boundary" (*sainokawara*) (Williams 2002: 6).[5] Robert Smith reports that persons who, for unexplained reasons, continue to suffer "misfortune" suspect the interference of a ghost and seek out a female medium to intervene, ascertain the problem, and offer ritual solutions (1975: 44). Sakurai Tokutarô indicates that according to female mediums, ghosts and ancestral dead must not be summoned during months when high spirits are "active," especially when the field spirit (*tanokami*) descends to the village, as this might provoke a "quarrel" between her and the dead (Blacker 1975: 154–55).

"Angry ghosts" (*onryô*) are those who died an especially "violent" or cruel death, consumed with feelings of "rage and resentment" (Blacker 1975: 48–49; Smith 1974: 41, 44). The influence of these virulent entities is said to affect the entire topocosm, and may extend beyond it. The wrath of these angry beings is historically credited with causing various diseases, epidemics, floods, droughts, and raging thunderstorms; notable examples include Sugawara no Michizane (845–903) (Blacker 1975: 49), Taira no Masakado (circa 940), and Emperor Sutoku (1124–1141) (Papinot 1972: 604, 611, 618). These raging spirits require extraordinary ritual attention to abate their fury and, as in the case of Michizane, will only be appeased when raised to the level of very high spirit (for Michizane, the title *Tenjin*, or Heavenly Spirit) (Blacker 1975: 49).

In summary, threatening spirits in the landscape are needy, threatening forces in the Yayoi period worldview because they: 1) fall beyond the pattern of social bounds, and 2) are cognitive features representing the life-taking aspect of the Feminine archetype.

Ghosts, whatever their status, do not belong to the mainstream of society as is represented in the person of contented ancestors. They are unusual in their circumstances and represent anomalies in the expected social norms and patterns. Their negative perception is due in part to their embodiment of "liminality" (Turner 1969: 95–96). Liminality represents a mode of being that is "disordered," "unlimited," "indefinable," and outside of social structure and, as such, challenges and threatens the ordinary "pattern" and "order" that is defined and maintained by society (Douglas 1966: 94–95). Their liminal status is further reinforced by their being identified with boundary sites: roads, gates, crossroads, corners, and shorelines. These places, as the meeting of two dimensions, are metaphoric signs analogous to the marginality of these anomalous spirits.

Ritual identifies these liminal spirits as projections that threaten the living with destruction. Threatening spirits do not embody the intact bond of marriage or the production of offspring, and collectively are analogous to defiling menstrual blood that denotes decay and the failure of fecundation. From an Ommyôdô perspective, which will be dealt with in Chapter Four, female blood that is not channeled into offspring is "matter out of place," just as are the spirits of those who died beyond the bonds of the conjugal family. This dual failure to procreate and subsequent death represent a life-threatening reality to the continuation of society as a whole. This social reality is couched in metaphysical terms. In Ommyôdô cosmology, menstrual blood, likewise, presents a threatening social reality; it represents a failure to produce offspring, a menacing prospect to genetic and social survival.

Lebra notes that female shamans (*yuta*) on Okinawa, who mainly perform ritual for ghosts and other malcontent spirits, uniformly lead dysfunctional lives and are socially marginal (1966: 82), just as the spirits they endeavor to address in ritual. These women routinely have had serious disagreements with spouses and family members, display "personality disorders, suffer from incurable illnesses, report persistent hallucinatory experience," and are not firmly linked in lines of ritual and familial kinship as are priestesses. Lebra reports that, whereas shamanic services were formerly socially restricted on Okinawa, overall incidence of shaman ritual has increased as the level of community organization to support priestess ritual practice has waned (1966: 84).

As inheritors of the Yayoi period spiritual tradition based on the Feminine archetype, female mediums are intimately aware of the features in the topocosm and the spirits associated with these features. Mediums are capable of invoking these spiritual beings because they know their names, and can adjust their own behavior and direct others given their knowledge. An influential figure in the upbringing of mainland Japan's well-known animator of supernatural beings, Mizuki Shigeru, was the medium who as a child he called Nonnonbâ. This woman, a native of Mihoseki-chô in Shimane prefecture, awakened in young Mizuki an awareness of "supernatural beings" (*yôkai*; *obake*) that inhabited the features of the home and landscape (Komatsu 1994: 64–67). Komatsu Kazuhiko asserts that Nonnonbâ lived within the landscape in a means unlike the way we presently do; she possessed a different "worldview" and was forever relating her experiences to an invisible dimension of spirits (1994: 66). He summarizes: "Even though she saw the same landscape and features within it, she had a vastly different understanding of it than we [presently] do" (1994: 66). Naturally, her divergent point of perception gave rise to a unique way in which she interacted with the topocosm.

MALE AND FEMALE RITUAL ROLES

In the Yayoi period worldview, shamans addressed the needs of discontented or potentially discontented spirits in the house and nature, both ghosts and unsatisfied ancestors, while priestesses presided over fruition rites, and males most likely presided over linage rites for contented ancestors. This pattern neatly obtains in the Ryûkyûs and to some degree in Korea, with the exception that the Korean female medium appears, unlike the Ryûkyûs, to function as both priestess and shaman. In Kendall's fieldwork, Korean housewives venerate their own household spirits and ancestors, and when the need arises, they resort to the services of a female medium to direct them in their ritual practice (1985: 27). In tandem, the housewife and medium ascertain the supernatural ties of cause and effect; with the medium's direction, the housewife adjusts her practice to obtain benefits for her family (Kendall 1985: 131).[6] (The ritual practice of Mrs. Murakami, a housewife in mainland Japan's Saga prefecture, closely follows this pattern and will be examined in Chapter Six.) In the Ryûkyûs also, housewives protect the home by feeding, venerating and, when necessary, exorcising potentially troublesome spirits in the home.

Mainland Japan generally follows the same pattern, with the following exceptions:

1) *males* (Buddhist priests) officiate at important ritual occasions (reciting sutras) for contented ancestors in the home
2) *males* (both Shintô and Buddhist priests) preside in rites at which discontented "bad spirits" and ghosts are fed, offered high spirit status or sutra readings, and placated so the human community will not be harmed (as in *jichinsai* and *segakie* rituals)
3) *females* (in this case, housewives) also perform routine feeding and veneration of contented ancestors (in the former pattern, a male prerogative),
4) female shamans in rural areas, particularly Kyûshû and Tôhoku, register longings for discontented spirits, ghosts, and ancestors.

It seems that a shift occurred in the Japanese mainland where typically female ritual duties (officiating at rites for discontented spirits) were usurped by male ritual specialists. Such a development appears to represent changes effected in Japan by Ommyôdô, Mahayana, and particularly Esoteric Buddhist institutions and practices which served to marginalize and co-opt formally female prerogatives. As Blacker postulated, it does appear that after the Taika Reform in 654, the role of female mediums was removed from the court and replaced by male specialists wielding continental skills, while the female shaman was relegated to the level of a folk practitioner.

Such a male incursion on female ritual roles occurred in the Ryûkyûs, as well. Lebra indicates that between the fourteenth and seventeenth centuries, the influence of Confucian and Buddhist thought via China served to steadily erode the power of priestesses as male-centered ancestor ritual became more prominent (1966: 103, 119). In marked contrast with the Japanese mainland, in the Ryûkyûs women continued to preside over the oral, native ritual tradition, while males became practitioners of Chinese textual traditions: geomancers, Buddhist priests, and healers (Lebra 1966: 74, 85–89, 91–92). In mainland Japan, males also came to wield continental textually-based ritual prerogatives, but instead of yielding legitimate control of Shintô ritual practice to females, male priests followed Chinese forms more closely by abandoning the Yayoi order of presiding females.

In my own fieldwork in mainland Japan, women (in addition to the elderly and people in rural areas) were much more familiar with Shintô ritual and lore than were men, and in every case exhibited a natural feeling for these subjects more readily than males did. Lebra similarly found on Okinawa that belief in sorcery was most prevalent among the elderly, "women, and the uneducated" (1966: 93). Being familiar with Shintô practice, women are in a unique position to not only perceive spiritual matters but also function as directors for others in their ritual practice.

WOMAN AS THE GREAT MOTHER

Cosmogony sequences in the *Kojiki* and the *Nihon Shoki* portray the emergence of the first life forms as sprouts (*kabi*) from the young earth; Kanda Hideo (1959) claimed that these sprouts were part of a poem detailing the origin of life as sprouts at the beginning of time (Chamberlain 1981: 15–17; Philippi 1968: 47–48). The Edo period National Learning (*kokugaku*) scholar and philologist Hirata Atsutane identified the term for "sprout" or "bud" (kabi), as in the first life forms that emerged, to be "the first things to emerge into the world, extremely wonderful and mysterious" (*kabi to wa yo ni idetaru mono no hajime nite, itoto kirei naru mono*) (Hirata Atsutane zenshû kankô-kai 1977: 97). Hirata, following the work of Motoori, identifies the term for "sprout" (kabi) to be etymologically the same as the "high spirits" of mainland Japan (kami), and also as the "Ancestor of things that sprout, or bud (*moe-agaru*) [from the earth]" (Hirata Atsutane zenshû kankô-kai 1977: 95, 121).

Such metaphoric thought concerning the emergence of things from another, removed dimension was not foreign to the early mainland Japanese. In eighth century *Manyôshû* poems, poets selected *kanji* combinations to phonetically write "to bud or sprout" (*moe*, as in *moe-agaru*) that denote: "emerging eye," "growing hair," and "growing mother" (Hirata Atsutane zenshu kanko-kai 1977: 121). Hirata even claims the term for "sprouts and buds" (*me*) originates from the verb "to bud or sprout" [written: "growing mother"] (*moe*) (Hirata Atsutane zenshû kankô-kai 1977: 95, 121). These linguistic clues point to the fact that sprouts and buds were recognized in early mainland Japan as high spirits (kami), as the Ancestor that is seasonally reincarnated from the soil, and by extension, as a projection of the generative aspect of the Feminine archetype, the life-giving Great Mother (as indicated in the writing "growing mother"). In Yayoi period cosmology, the birth of offspring is pure and beneficent and is cognitively quickened by the life-giving

Ancestor that emerges from the earth as the primordial sprout. Just as ancestral spirits inhabit and are reincarnated in the vegetative features of the topocosm; ancestor spirits also lodge within the woman, and emerge from her in the offspring born to the locality. In fact, it is interesting to note that, in conversational reference to a recent pregnancy, mainland Japanese presently say the "sprout has emerged" (*me ga deta*).

The cognitive blending of woman and earth in the Feminine archetype form the living medium that receives the seed. The seed, in metaphoric terms, is analogous to the corpse that is devoured, fructifying the Great Mother, and then reemerges as the reincarnated Ancestor, in the form of offspring, vegetation, and food. Just as mountains are significant interstices in the landscape that metaphorically function as portals into the Great Mother for the life-giving high spirits, *women*, too, are major interstices. Women themselves are portals of the Great Mother.

A woman is the abode of spirits since her body exhibits changes that were awesome to witness for the Yayoi period inhabitants of Kyûshû; the powers of her body they collectively called *chi*. This ancient term indicated in the Japanese mainland a "spirit" or "elder" (Philippi 1968: 459, 622). Furthermore, it came to be used in mainland Japan to mean "great [spiritual] powers in nature that flow and move" (Kamata 1993: 3). Blood (chi) was spiritual power in ancient Japan. The "transformation[s]" of the female body revolve around the transformation and movement of blood in the processes of: menstruation, pregnancy, and lactation (Neumann 1963: 31–32). Given the metaphoric dynamics of the Feminine archetype, the seed devoured by the soil is reincarnated as the Ancestor, the "elder spirit" (chi), in offspring.

Notions concerning the role of ancestor spirits in pregnancy were not unusual in early societies; one example here will suffice. Native Australians used to attribute pregnancy to contact of a woman with some aspect of the local topocosm, such as the earth, stones, or trees; out of this contact, ancestral spirits residing in the local land were said to enter the womb, initiating pregnancy (Eliade 1958: 243, 245). Social recognition of a local topocosm, inhabited by ancestral spirits, makes such notions become a cognitive reality. But the motif of ancestor-induced pregnancy was one that would have obtained in Japan prior to the Yayoi period, even among the Jômon period hunters and gatherers.

Yayoi period experiences with horticulture and settled life fostered the development of the Feminine archetype; in particular, the planting and harvesting of seeds in the earth engendered a new awareness of the planting of seeds in the woman. The role of paternity in pregnancy became recognized when earth and female came to be metaphorically linked (Eliade 1958: 243, 256; Neumann 1963: 303).

Beyond the physical attributes that cognitively make them analogous to earth, three characteristics predispose women to be the priestesses of Feminine archetype ritual. Women: 1) possess and interpret the worldview, 2) are the source of fertility, and 3) are the physical embodiment of the Great Mother figure.

One of Rokkum's male informants, mentioning how a priestess, regardless of her age, must be reverenced explained, "This is worship of the woman . . . What we do put an emphasis on, however, is how life comes into being with the woman" (1998: 191). This man does not mention the Great Mother, neither does he speak of the Feminine archetype, but his comments do recognize the woman as a source of life and that ritual on the island reverences this fact. While this informant may not know how ideas regarding women articulate with the landscape, his remarks bear out the fact that women, and life emerging from them, are central to island ritual. Only women can officiate in the rites for the land on Dunang, ensuring its continuing fertility in the form of offspring and crops (Rokkum 1998: 42, 71, 105). Dunang priestesses must also be "fully cognizant of the sacredness of island places;" part of this familiarity includes knowledge of numerous place names in the topocosm, and a fluid ability to invoke places and their spirits in vocal prayer (Rokkum 1998: 94, 198, 212). The naming of landscape features is said to effect a unity with the spirits of that place (Rokkum 1998: 212).[7] Without a command of these skills, a woman does not become a priestess (Rokkum 1998: 198). No men become island priestesses.[8]

From at least the late fifteenth century, an elaborate court hierarchy existed in the Ryûkyûs in which men governed and women played vital sacerdotal roles (Rokkum 1998: 43). The king's court on Okinawa designated hereditary, "politico-religious" priestess positions as part of its rule in the Ryûkyûs that were dispatched even to Dunang; their title was "Great Mother" (*ôamu*) and they oversaw rituals for rich harvests (Rokkum 1998: 43–44). Island priestesses on Dunang are supposedly descendants to these positions, and when they don the yellow robe and crowns of island vegetation, local understanding recognizes that they are transformed into island "goddesses" (*kan*) (Rokkum 1998: 76, 150, 175). Sister priestesses by donning a "gem headdress" or by clutching sacred, family heirlooms, become a tutelary goddess (*bunai tidigan*) for their brothers and lineage (Rokkum 1998: 175, 198). In both of these instances when priestesses become enthused by ancestral island spirits, members of the community must stay clear; a failure to do so can be catastrophic for the offender (Rokkum 1998: 175). Rokkum explains, "The forces they [enthused priestesses] exude mix with the environment" and invoke the powers of growth in the landscape (1998: 175).

Island priestesses on Okinawa perform fruition rituals focused on birth and harvest and avoid the opposite: decay (Lebra 1966: 53, 60, 192–93). These women are held as paragons of social virtue and harmony, they have a "strong sense of duty . . . and responsibility for the" well being of their communities (Lebra 1966: 78). Island priestesses belong to a traceable lineage of descent to their priestess forebearers; it is common that the spirit of the preceding priestess serves as the directing, personal spirit in ritual duties of her successor.

As evidenced in the medium ruler Himiko and in the ritual forms preserved in the Ryûkyûs, the Yayoi period priestess figure was considered to be the personal embodiment of the Feminine archetype, a goddess, the Great Mother herself. Women were recognized as interstices of power, and were the original ritual officiants in the ritual life of Yayoi period Kyûshû. This fact is based on the cyclically creative and permeable nature of their bodies which, like the landscape itself, was a portal through which congress with the spirits from beyond was a social reality. Furthermore, as repositories of detailed knowledge concerning this particular worldview, women were also predisposed to take leading roles in the veneration of the Good Mother and the invocation of her generative life forces in the topocosm (including its landscape, animal, and human components) on behalf of lineages and local communities. Women, in ritual roles, were the natural and only persons who could invoke the high spirits, the ancestors, the bliss-bearing agents of the life-giving Great Mother. The cognitive power of the Feminine archetype bestows upon women, as was the case in Yayoi period Kyûshû, their socially recognized supernatural abilities.

NOTES

1. On the Ryûkyûan island of Dunang, the term for an interstice in time and space (*tanka*) also denotes the individual's "own physical *situation* in the family and neighborhood" (Rokkum 1998: 36, 117). This temporal/ spatial/ experiential interval in the pattern of the landscape seems to provide cognitive egress to spirits from the Unseen Realm and is analogous to the permeability of both female body and earth.

2. Blacker renders iwakura "stone altar seat" based on the *kanji* writing (*za*), but stone vessel altar seems to be a more sensitive rendering to Origuchi's insights regarding rocks and the "sealed vessel" concept (*utsubo*).

3. "Spirits of the dead are known in general as tama . . . soul. The tama is an entity which resides in some host, to which it imparts life and vitality. Thus it may dwell in the human body, in animals, in trees (kodama). . . Once let it leave the body in which it resides, however, and its host will become enfeebled and sick and eventually die" (Blacker 1975: 43).

4. Philippi indicates the likelihood of a politically-derived hierarchy of spirits; heavenly high spirits were ones venerated by the Yamato clan while spirits of other clans came to be known as earthly spirits (1968: 88).

5. These riverbed sites are found throughout mainland Japan, either at river sites or in mountains; they are said to be a boundary separating us from the world of the dead (Blacker 1975: 83). Osorezan is a particularly famous "riverbed" site (Blacker 1975: 83). In folklore, the souls of fetuses and children in limbo are marooned at these shorelines, unable to pass into the world beyond, and are frequently succored by the compassionate Buddhist savior, Jizô, whose images often are found at these and other boundary areas. At these riverbed sites, human beings can converse with the dead, often through the person of a female medium (*itako*) (Smith 1975: 64, see Katô 1992).

6. When a Korean male does function as a medium (*paksu*), he usually dresses as a female to perform ritual activities (Covell 1986: 162, 192–93, 203). On Korea's Cheju Island, considered to be "home to the purest form of Korean shamanism," females hold prominent positions as mediums in village rituals (Chang 1988: 30, 36, 38; Kim 1988: 20). These practices, reminiscent of former customs in the Ryûkyûs, acknowledge the preeminence of females as mediums. Such notions are tacit indications that the female medium is a projection of the Great Mother.

7. This vocal invocation of place, and hence spirits, represents an enduring legacy of ancient mainland Japan's word-spirit belief (*kotodama shinkô*).

8. Lebra maintains that founding ancestor/ kami are considered on Okinawa to be female, even though "descent is traced through the male line" and that women are "spiritually superior" to men (1966: 24, 140). Furthermore, the presence of males in the precincts of a High Peak shrine is polluting and offensive to the spirits on Okinawa (Lebra 1966: 50, 52). During the Ryûkyû Kingdom, this taboo prompted the custom of having males "become female" on pilgrimage to a High Peak shrine, including the king and his ministers at court, in order to avoid divine retribution (Lebra 1966: 69). Such a custom is completely at variance with Chinese forms generally, with Ommyôdô cosmology particularly, and bespeaks the incredible, socially recognized resonance of priestesses with the high spirits, and ultimately the Feminine archetype.

Chapter Four

Ommyôdô Cycles of Time

An examination of Yin-Yang Five Phase, or Ommyôdô, cosmology will provide us with prominent Chinese thought structures relating to the topocosm, the woman, and their joint relation to the Feminine archetype as they figure in Shintô ritual practice on the Japanese mainland. Ommyôdô made its way through Korea and into Japan during the sixth century (Ômori 1993: 9); this is the same century at which Hattori's linguistic analysis (1955) pinpoints the separation of Ryûkyûan and mainland Japanese dialects. In the century following, Blacker asserts that changes attendant to the Taika Reform (645) served to oust female medium figures from court, leaving them active, however, at the local, popular level (1975: 30). One indication of the popularity of Ommyôdô thought at court is that following the Taika Reform, the Chinese divinatory classic, *The Book of Changes* (Mandarin: *yijing*; Japanese: *eki-kyô*) became a standard course of study in the court university of the time (Uryû & Shibuya 1997: 230). In the two centuries following the arrival of Yin-Yang Five Phase cosmology in Japan, and continuing thereafter, a heterogeneous mixture of different, competing ritual practices were in vogue in greater society (Ômori 1993: 12–13).

Practitioners of Ommyôdô made use of a combination of "astronomy [really, astronomy-based astrology], divination, and [Yin-Yang] Five Element Theory to ply their secretive arts" (Ômori 1993: 9, 12). In China, Ommyôdô cosmology rigorously propelled advances in several fields including the "natural sciences, philosophy, and medicine," but in Japan, application of these same principles was initially limited to "divination and magical incantation" (*senjutsu*; *jujutsu*) (Ômori 1993: 9).

The influence of Ommyôdô thought in traditional Japan is vast, serving as an organizing schema for aspects of the tea ceremony, flower arrangement,

Noh, sumô, the geomantic arrangement of features in the home, the location and position of the ancient capital city, and even the placement of the impe- rial palace in Kyôto within the larger landscape (Ômori 1993: 37; also see Kiba 1997). Ommyôdô scholar Murayama Shûichi, indicates that until the end of the Nara period (794), masters of Ommyôdô (*ommyôji*) were directly employed by the imperial family (Ômori 1993: 17).[1] During the reign of the Temmu emperor (reigned 673–686), masters of Ommyôdô were made part of the central government, and placed in their own bureau at court (*ommyô no tsukasa*) (Ômori 1993: 38). The most noted practitioner in Japanese history was the Heian period master, Abe no Seimei (ca. 944–1005), who protected victims from deadly curses, employed supernatural beings (*shikigami*) on his errands, and is even said to have brought the dead back to life (Ômori 1993: 25, 29, 30). It was during Abe's lifetime that the political clout of the Fuji- wara clan reached its apex; during this period, the influence of Ommyôdô masters spread among the powerful nobles of the court (Ômori 1993: 39). The masters at court published lunar almanacs based on Ommyôdô cosmology that courtiers used for determining their own personal fortunes on a daily ba- sis (Ômori 1993: 17, 39). The influence of this variety of Chinese cosmology spread beyond the court itself and into the larger populace, cross-pollinating with other fields of ritual practice, including those strands of thought and rit- ual associated with the ancestral spirits, both inside and outside shrine venues (Ômori 1993: 37, 39). Between the Heian and Edo periods, Ommyôdô influ- ences incorporated by ritual specialists in shrines and among the populace continued to increase (Ômori 1993: 132–33, 138–43, 156–57). An overview of Ommyôdô cosmological elements at this juncture will serve to identify salient patterns of thought, particularly those relating to cycles of time that structure Shintô ritual practice.

OMMYÔDÔ WORLDVIEWS

In early human societies, the individual was not divorced from the world around them; rather, they were part of the topocosm. For modern persons, the individual lives in an environment. The distinctions for us are discrete: self and other. But in times past, there existed "an indissoluble unity" between person and world that in cognitive terms formed a "still-undifferentiated whole" (Neumann 1963: 42). This ontological understanding was based on concepts of microcosm (self) and macrocosm (topocosm), each being found in the other, and the two articulated in certain metaphysical ways. On Dunang, for example, human beings meaningfully articulate with the land- scape via the concept of life-souls which can become separated from the body in the course of mishaps (Rokkum, 1998). Spirits reside in the landscape, as they do in the bodies of Dunang islanders; because these forces interact, individuals adjust their behavior according to the prevailing worldview.

Ommyôdô cosmology is organized on this same logic of microcosm and macrocosm (Saso 1990b: 349), or an understanding of both the body and the topocosm as cosmic vessels which are interrelated in numerous ways. Such a worldview is based on the Feminine archetype in which the topocosm is the "body-vessel" of the Great Mother that contains all, and to which the individual is intimately connected (Neumann 1963: 41). In such a worldview, mystical connections between the person and the topocosm are expressed in terms of "cosmic bodies, directions, constellations, gods, demons. . . colors, regions, plants, [and] phases. . ." and are a means of creating a "magical-psychic image of the body and the outside world" (Neumann 1963: 41). In Ommyôdô thought, these connections internalize patterns of nature to the individual, and in turn, externalize patterns of individual experience onto the wider world.

TAOIST PHILOSOPHICAL THOUGHT

The Yin-Yang worldview is predicated on the general metaphysical principles of Tao, Great Ultimate, yin and yang, and the Three phenomena that unite microcosm and macrocosm. In the forty-second chapter of the Taoist classic *The Way and its Power* (*Tao-te-ching*), the cosmic order commences with the Way (*tao*), the "ultimate reality . . . the rhythm, the driving power behind all nature, the ordering principle behind all life" (Saso 1990b: 349; Smith 1991: 198). The Way, a transcendent force, underlies all life. It is ultimately unknowable, but its workings unfailingly coordinate the patterns and movement found in nature. Speaking of the Way, chapter six characterizes it as ". . . the woman, primal mother. Her gateway is the root of heaven and earth. It is like a veil barely seen. Use it; it will never fail" (Feng & English 1972: 15). In chapter twenty, the Way is identified as the "great mother" that nourishes (Feng & English 1972: 43). Huston Smith explains the Way as "Womb from which all life springs and to which it returns" (1991: 198). All life originates in and is supported by the Way.

In chapter forty-two, the Way gives birth to the One, the Great Ultimate (*t'ai chi*), also called "primordial breath" (*yuan ch'i*) (Feng & English 1972: 87; Saso 1990a: 8). Primordial breath (*ch'i*) is life force; it is energy that flows through every aspect of the cosmos. A gift of the Way, cosmic breath pulses through heaven and earth and animates everything, be they planets, mountains, or children. The Way produces and maintains creation in an impartial, disinterested, and yet minutely efficient manner, and cosmic breath is the means by which this coordination takes place. Heaven, earth, and humanity are linked together and vivified by this pulsating energy. Ommyôdô astrology was born by interpreting traces of life force through heavenly bodies and their relation to earth and its inhabitants. Geomancy (*feng shui*) emerged as energy flows were analyzed through features in the landscape and the effects these channels exerted on communities. Ommyôdô principles inspired medicine, including whole schools of meditation and exercise, herb therapy, acupuncture, acupressure, and moxibustion developed by considering energy flows in the human body. A vigorous flow of life energy underlies and defines health and good fortune; a sluggish, stagnant, or blocked flow of this force constitutes the source of disease and misfortune. Schools of practice naturally emerged to "augment" access to primordial breath, the aim being better, longer life, and even immortality (Smith 1991: 201).

Primordial breath then produced the Two, the relative characteristics of yin and yang. Just as everything is animated by primordial breath, everything possesses varying amounts of yin-ness and yang-ness. These two forces are often portrayed in the emblem called the Great Ultimate (see Figure 4.1), made up of swirling yin (black) and yang (white) in circular form. This symbol expresses unobstructed access to primordial breath that is based on an even balance of yin and yang. Early in its etymological history, yin denoted the shady side of a mountain, while yang indicated the sunny side (Noguchi 1994: 21). Nothing is completely yin or yang. These relative terms indicate two complementary aspects of life; they are only meaningful when an item is compared to others at a given time. Yin is generally characterized as: dark, cool, moist, still, receptive, retreating, the realm of the dead, and feminine. Yang is: bright, hot, dry, active, initiating, advancing, the realm of the living,

Figure 4.1.   The Great Ultimate

and masculine. So, moon is more yin than sun, and summer is more yang than winter (Saso 1990a: 3). Each force plays an important role and supplements deficiencies in the other. Balanced they create an optimal environment for life, but when mismatched, degeneration ensues. Chapter forty-two elaborates: "The ten thousand things [all parts of the cosmos] carry yin and embrace yang. They achieve harmony by combining these forces" (Feng & English 1972: 87). A balance of yin and yang produces a harmonious flow of primordial breath that fosters life and health.

The Two, yin and yang, produced the Three: "heaven, earth, and the underworld in the macrocosm, and [also] head, chest, and belly," in the microcosm (Feng & English 1972: 87; Saso 1990a: 9). The Three then gave rise to all of the cosmos (Feng & English 1972: 87). This unifying doctrine based on the Way, primordial breath, yin and yang, and the Three as origin of the cosmos was formulated and recorded sometime between the sixth and fifth centuries B.C. in China (Saso 1990a: 29).

The foundation of this cosmology is the Way which is characterized as Great Mother, the supporter, the subtle coordinator, the source and goal of all existence. Next is the Primordial Breath, originating from the Great Mother, whose circulation through the cosmos animates and binds all of existence together. The forces of yin and yang combine in every aspect of the universe, sustaining and attuning each organism to the rhythms of nature, or the Way. And finally, the Three realms in both macrocosm and microcosm bind together all disparate realms into one. In all, there are four levels of coordination that unite all parts of heaven, earth, and humanity into one great whole, an integrated system of being. At its core is the Way, the mysterious Mother that effortlessly creates, nourishes, and manages the cosmos, reminiscent of the Feminine archetype.

FIVE-PHASE COSMOLOGY

Between the fourth and third centuries B.C., another worldview called Five Phase cosmology emerged in China around the figure of Tsou Yen (ca. 305–240 B.C.); it became an additional set of lenses through which to order and connect with the cosmos (Saso 1990a: 29; Smith 1983: 23). Five Phase cosmology corresponds to Neumann's "magical-psychic image" of the cosmos; it is an alchemic system used to explain, predict, and control the transformation of matter in both the microcosm and the macrocosm. The five phases are: wood, fire, earth, metal, and water; two cycles of relationship between the phases exist: a cycle of *growth* (see Figure 4.2), and a cycle of *control* (see Figure 4.3) (Okada 1993: 123). In true alchemic form, the Growth

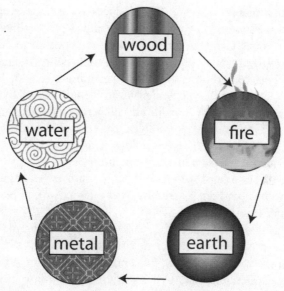

Figure 4.2.   Five Phase Growth Cycle

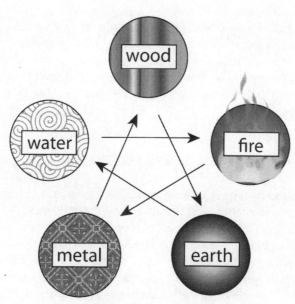

Figure 4.3.   Five Phase Control Cycle

Cycle posits that wood hosts fire, fire produces earth (ash), earth incubates
metal, metal exudes water (in condensation), and water nourishes wood (vegetation). The Control Cycle directs that water overcomes fire, fire conquers
metal, metal (tool) prevails over wood, wood bests earth, and earth subdues
water. While these relationships of themselves are not remarkable, they become so when the list of five phases grows to include sets of five directions,
colors, seasons, atmospheric conditions, planets, emotions, organs of the
body, flavors, grains, animals, vegetables, fruits, and so forth (Okada 1993:
131; Kiba 1997: 17). Five Phase cosmology is a system of thought unifying
an incredible number of phenomena through processes of "cyclical change"
(Saso 1990a: 3). Yin-Yang Five Phase thought represents a cognitive system
where relationships between macrocosm and microcosm can readily be con-
ceptualized and negotiated.

During the Han dynasty (200 B.C. to 200 A.D.) yin-yang ideas combined
with Five Phase cosmology and became collectively known as Yin-Yang Five
Phase thought (*in-yô go gyô setsu*); this amalgamated Ommyôdô complex of
understandings structured "Han dynasty court ritual" (Saso 1990a: 2).[2] Alchemic Yin-Yang Five Phase cosmology came into mainland Japan in the
sixth century and, along with the lunar calendar, this complex of time lore has
structured the temporal aspects of Shintô ritual practice ever since. Yin-yang
Five Phase cosmology is the crux of Ommyôdô as it was practiced in ancient
Japan; its theories are deeply embedded in the fabric of Japanese cultural
forms.

Yin-Yang Five Phase cosmology is based on cycles: cycles of yin/ yang
balance, and cycles of growth and control. This cosmology predisposes
Shintô ritual practice to likewise be extremely cycle-oriented. In the next section, a more comprehensive Yin-Yang Five Phase cycle that structures Shintô
ritual practice at Hakozaki will be introduced and correlated with the Feminine archetype.

THE ROUND OF TIME

The Feminine archetype is attuned to, and is a cognitive projection of, the
phenomena of unending cycles: the lunar cycle and the woman's cycle of fertility. These cycles of time represent a type of limited, circular change that
both is and is not change. Eric Neumann elaborates that Feminine archetype
imagery is focused on the cycle, or "Great Round," that combines the dual aspects of: 1) "transformation," and 2) equalizing, eternal sameness (1963: 29).

An important projection of the Feminine archetype in the tradition of Western thought is the Uroboros, literally the "tail-eater," an ancient Greek sym-

bol of a circular serpent devouring its own tail (see Figure 4.4); it is the earliest "pictorial symbol" in the literature of medieval alchemy (Jung 1953: 293). Alchemists equated this serpent image with "the world-creating spirit concealed or imprisoned in matter," as "the One, the All" that "devours, fertilizes, begets, slays, and brings itself to life again," and Jung identified it as "a symbol uniting all opposites" (1953: 293, 295, 371–72). This serpent figure of no beginning or end appears to be a projection of on-going cyclical process, embodying transformation and regression, progression and stasis. The Uroboros has neither end nor beginning, just as in the Great Ultimate diagram (yin-yang symbol); where yin ends, yang begins and vice versa. Just as the serpent both devours and begets, where yin begins to eclipse (devour) yang, at that point, yang is reborn and the cycle repeats itself.

Both the Uroboros and the Great Ultimate are projections of the Feminine archetype, for the Great Mother both generates and destroys. As expressions of the Feminine archetype, both emblems are based on the cycles of nature (earth), the lunar cycle, and ultimately, the female fertility cycle. In the course of a year, earth receives the seed and vegetation springs from the earth in the warm months, it withers in the cold. Over a month, the moon waxes in form and then wanes. In a monthly cycle, the woman's body prepares to receive the seed, and failing to receive it, her body sloughs that tissue to rebuild again.

Figure 4.4.   The Uroboros

As Margaret Miles writes, through the transformative processes of the female body, in "menstruation, sexual intercourse, [and] pregnancy," that body "loses" its "individual configuration and boundaries," it "transgresses" itself, it is continually "in the act of becoming" (1989: 153). This is also true of earth and moon cycles. At periods they are creative, at others degenerative. As a whole they constitute cognitive ideograms of the Feminine archetype, summarized in the yin-yang depiction of waxing and waning, in the generative and devouring serpent. Both the archetype and its projections embody change that follow an unchanging pattern, the Great Round; hence the preoccupation in the Feminine archetype with the cycle. The cycle of life and death, indeed of all opposites, is a summary of its unique message.

Furthermore, interstices or boundaries, already considered within the landscape, are significant phenomena in terms of the Feminine archetype because they too are indicative of change and process. They represent portals of contact with the Feminine. Boundaries are microcosms of the cycle of opposites between which the Great Mother (earth-moon-female) alternates; they correspond to the mouth of the serpent grasping its own tail, to the point in the depiction of the Great Ultimate where yin passes into yang. Interstices are the meeting of life and death, of creation and destruction, they are the mouths of the Great Mother that open wide, redolent with power and danger; hence the trepidation about departure ritual from the local topocosm on Dunang. To recklessly negotiate boundaries is always to risk having life-souls snatched, or being devoured by the Great Mother.

THE BOOK OF CHANGES

The Chinese lunar calendar dates back to the fourteenth century B.C., to inscriptions on Shang dynasty (1738–1111 B.C.) oracle bones that are also the earliest evidence of written Chinese language (Okada 1993: 141). This system of measuring time was further refined during the Chou dynasty (1111–221 B.C.) which led to the compilation of *The Book of Changes*, a classic often used for divination, that traces the permutations of yin and yang in the manifestations of the cosmos.

The Book of Changes summarizes the Ommyôdô formulation of both time and space. It depicts yin as two broken lines and yang as a whole line and identifies sixty-four hexagrams (arrangements of six yin and/ or yang lines) considered to depict all possible combinations of the two forces in the universe. These sixty-four are formed by using combinations of eight basic trigrams (arrangements of three yin and/or yang lines), that are called the Eight Trigrams (Mandarin: *pa kua*; Japanese: *hakke*). The Eight Trigrams (see Figure 4.5) will be referred to by the following names: Complying (Mandarin: *k'un*; Japanese: *kon*), Initiating (*chen*; *shin*), Leaving (*li*; *ri*), Renewing (*tui*; *da*), Advancing (*ch'ien*; *ken*),"Penetrating" (*sun*; *son*) (following Baynes 1967: 220), Threatening (*k'an*; *kan*), and Opposing (or Stopping) (*ken*, *gon*). The Eight Trigrams depict a cycle of process and change; in this study verbs, instead of adjectives or nouns, have been chosen to indicate the *action* indicative of each trigram.

Name		Attributes	Trigram	Trigram Display
1. Advancing	乾	heaven		
2. Renewing	兌	water, metal, lake cloud		
3. Leaving	離	fire, sun, light		
4. Initiating	震	thunder, electricity		
5. Penetrating	巽	wind, wood		
6. Threatening	坎	water, moon		
7. Opposing	艮	mountain, transitions		
8. Complying	坤	earth		

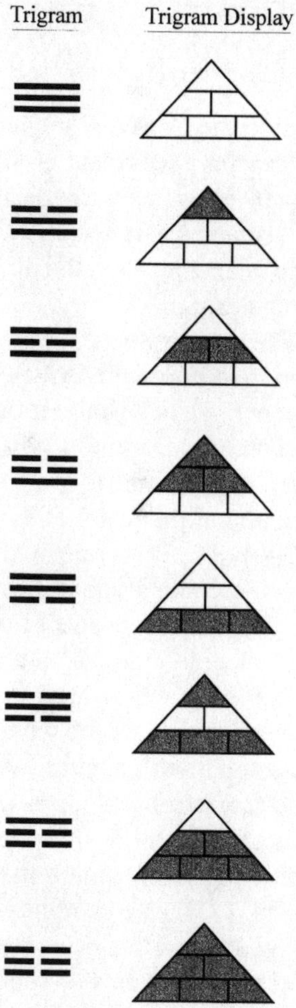

KEY yin = two broken lines or dark sections in a triangle
yang = a whole line or light sections in a triangle
These triangles and groups of lines illustrate concentrations of yin and yang in each trigram.
The bottom line of each figure is most dominant; the top line is least dominant.

Figure 4.5. The Eight Trigrams

The Eight Trigrams are arranged in two configurations that each depict a progressive cycle of transformation: the Former Heaven Sequence (*hsien tien pa kua t'u*) attributed to the mythical Fu Hsi, and the Later Heaven Sequence (*hou tien pa kua t'u*) said to be developed by the Chou dynasty ruler, King Wen, or his son, the Duke of Chou (ca. 1111 B.C.) (Liu 1986: 2; Masuda 2001: 42; Noguchi 1994: 31). The present, combined Taoist calendar and cosmology are a blending of the two systems.

The Former Heaven Sequence

The Former Heaven Sequence (see Figure 4.6) depicts the gradual, steady, and regular movement of yin toward yang and back again to yin; this earlier sequence is mostly a reflection on patterns of waxing and waning in the annual solar cycle (Okada 1993: 288). This smooth progression between yin and yang is analogous to the direct current of electricity, a constant flow between two poles.

The Former Sequence appears to have been reckoned with New Year's occurring at the winter solstice (shortest day of the year), and mid-year at the summer solstice (longest day of the year). This sequence is based on solar phenomena. Darkness (yin) is at its greatest extent at the winter solstice, when light (yang) is at its weakest. Yin is not only darkness; it is also emblematic of the realm of the dead and of spirits of the deceased (Liang 1972: 1179–1180). Therefore, in this orientation, the last quarter of the year (and the end of each lunar month) was a time of growing yin, when the forces of death were in the ascendant. In terms of the Feminine archetype, yin darkness is equivalent to menstruation and failure to obtain fruition.

In the Former arrangement of the Eight Trigrams, the last four months of the year preceding the winter solstice would have been periods of weakening solar light and gathering yin force, a time at which the powers of the dead (and the Terrible Mother) would have become increasingly threatening to the living. But extreme development of yin always beckons an inception of yang force. Yang corresponds to life forces and the realm of the living (Liang 1972: 1182–1183). The extremity of yin, cold, darkness and influences of decay at the winter solstice beckon the growth of yang, warmth, light and the powers of growth. In terms of spiritual forces, at year end the deceased would have returned, bringing the blessings of life and growth with them.[3] In terms of the Feminine archetype, the devouring phase of the Great Mother would have reached its limit at the winter solstice, which was the New Year point of the Former Heaven Sequence. According to premodern Chinese folklore preserved in Taiwan, at year end the hungry *Nien* monster (said to be the origin of the word "year") roamed the topocosm; members of the community stayed

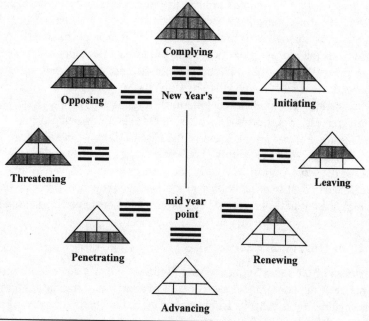

Trigram	Element	Juncture	Season
Complying	EARTH	winter solstice	mid-winter
Initiating	WOOD	Demon Gate	winter/ spring transition
Leaving	FIRE	spring equinox	mid-spring
Renewing	METAL	Wind Gate	spring/ summer transition
Advancing	earth	summer solstice	mid-summer
Penetrating	earth	Human Gate	summer/ autumn transition
Threatening	WATER	autumn equinox	mid-autumn
Opposing	earth	Heaven Gate	autumn/ winter transition

> KEY   yin = two broken lines or dark sections in a triangle
> yang = a whole line or light sections in a triangle
> *These triangles and groups of lines illustrate concentrations of yin and yang in each trigram.*
> *The bottom line of each figure is most dominant; the top line is least dominant.*

Figure 4.6.   The Eight Trigrams in Former Heaven Sequence Order

home to avoid its predation, and New Year's morning was (and continues to be in Taiwan) a time of celebration and mutual congratulation because Nien had not snatched them and life was extended. I believe that the Nien is a personification of the devouring aspect of the Great Mother; survival of her attack remains a cause for rejoicing. In ancient China, when the winter solstice was reckoned as the New Year's season, similar apprehensions concerning a Nien-like monster must have existed.

Conversely, the four months prior to the summer solstice would have been a period of waxing yang force that reached its apogee at the solstice. Even though yang is analogous to life and generative life forces, its extremity likewise beckons the inception of threatening yin forces. Here too, folk practice in Taiwan presently identifies the summer solstice as a time when threatening forces accrue and must be dispelled by ritual use of iris leaves and mugwort to prevent sickness. Even when the generative force (yang) of the Great Mother is at its greatest, a preoccupation with illness, her threatening aspect is evidenced. In the Former arrangement of the Eight Trigrams, the solstices as extremities of yin and yang, and the equinoxes (Latin: "equal night," night and day being the same length) where yin and yang are balanced were primary foci of ritual practice. It is possible that in the Former sequence, the four seasons were reckoned at the solstices and equinoxes, as in our present solar calendar.

The Later Heaven Sequence

The pattern of the Later Sequence (see Figure 4.7) is not the smooth progression between the complimentary forces of yin and yang; instead, as a cycle it still is regular, but it exhibits a bouncing pattern between yin and yang, more similar to alternating electrical current. The Later Sequence is more focused on earth phenomena (Skinner 1982: 61) and the Feminine archetype as opposed to being a reflection of solar cycles. In particular, the major points of the lunar cycle and the female cycle of fertility are central to the logic upon which the Later sequence is based.

The Later Sequence of the Eight Trigrams represents a rearrangement to reflect the prominent incorporation of Five Phase cosmology and is essential to the construction of time in Shintô ritual practice. In this ordering of time, earth is accorded a central role as medium of transmigration in the cycle; the prominent position of female/ lunar cycles in this new arrangement indicates all the more that this structuring of time is ordered in keeping with the Feminine archetype. An important shift occurred in the switch from the Former Sequence to the adoption of the Later one: while the winter solstice continued to be an important reference point for the lunar calendar (Okada 1993: 36), the reckoning of New Year's switched from the solstice (solar order) to the new (dark of the) moon (lunar order) midway between the winter solstice and spring equinox. This shift of the calendar seems to indicate a change from an emphasis on solar to a greater concern with lunar cycles, a shift from a male-sun centered system of time to a Feminine system that is focused on the cycles of moon, earth, and woman.

The Later Sequence is a configuration in which the trigrams reflect progression of the Five Phases according to the Growth Cycle (see Figure 4.2).

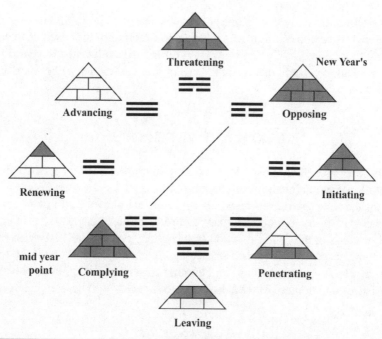

Trigram	Element	Juncture	Season
Opposing	earth	Demon Gate	winter/ spring transition
Initiating	WOOD	spring equinox	mid-spring
Penetrating	earth	Wind Gate	spring/ summer transition
Leaving	FIRE	summer solistice	mid-summer
Complying	EARTH	Human Gate	summer/ autumn transition
Renewing	METAL	autumn equinox	mid-autumn
Advancing	earth	Heaven Gate	autumn/ winter transition
Threatening	WATER	winter solstice	mid-winter

KEY   yin = two broken lines or dark sections in a triangle
yang = a whole line or light sections in a triangle
These triangles and groups of lines illustrate concentrations of yin and yang in each trigram.
The bottom line of each figure is most dominant; the top line is least dominant.

Figure 4.7.   The Eight Trigrams in Later Heaven Sequence Order

Disregarding, for the time being, the three earth phases that are not capital-ized (Opposing, Penetrating, Advancing), the progression of the phases in the Later Sequence is: WOOD—FIRE—EARTH—METAL—WATER. This is the Five Element cosmology Growth Cycle. But in the Former Sequence (and similarly disregarding the three earth phases above), the flow would be: EARTH—WOOD—FIRE—METAL—WATER. This progression does not

portray either the Growth or Control cycles. Clearly, the Later Sequence, regardless of its period of origin, represents a re-ordering of the trigrams to correspond to the Growth Cycle progression during the course of the year. This
cycle of change is best portrayed in terms of a circle (cycle), rather than as a
linear chart.

EARTH-ACTIVE PERIODS

In Yin-Yang Five Phase cosmology based on the Later Sequence, earth plays
a central role as the medium of change in the annual cycle (see Figure 4.8).
Each of the four seasons corresponds to a separate phase and to one quarter
of the cycle: spring to wood, summer to fire, autumn to metal, and winter to
water. Earth is in the center position of the cycle; its "season" is divided into
four, eighteen-day periods, each one being eighteen days preceding the four
points at which one season ends and another begins, points midway between
the solstices and equinoxes (Okada 1993: 137, 166–67).[4] These eighteen-day

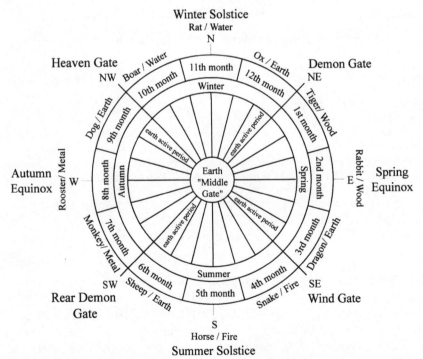

Figure 4.8.   Diagram of Yin-Yang Five Phase Cosmology

periods are called "earth active" periods (Japanese: *doyô*). In premodern mainland Japanese ritual practice imported from China, since earth was the "medium of change," movement of earth at these periods was taboo (Okada 1993: 167). Movement of earth at these special times was thought to bring the retribution of an Ommyôdô tutelary earth spirit (Japanese: *dokujin*) who was the focus of rites at these junctures (Okada 1993: 167); this being appears to be a Japanese designation for the Chinese earth spirit (*hou-tu-gung*, more popularly known in Taiwan as *tu-di-gung*) (Noguchi 1994: 156, 468–70).[5]

Earth active periods of seasonal transition are significant calendrical projections of the Feminine archetype and the Great Mother herself. These earth active periods are called "gates" (*mon*). All four gates are recognized as interstices of power in time and space, as portals of contact with spirits, both the generative and devouring aspects of the Great Mother. The four gates are: the Demon Gate, the Wind Gate, the Human Gate (or the Rear Demon Gate) and the Heaven Gate. The gate at the end of each earth active period marks the beginning of a lunar calendar season.

The Demon Gate

The first earth active period occurs at the transition of winter to spring, at the northeast quadrant of the compass; it is known as the Demon Gate (Japanese: *kimon*). The Demon Gate is an interstice indicative of the devouring Feminine archetype and is the most potent yin interstice of the calendrical cycle. This temporal gate occurs at lunar New Year's and also at the new moon. This ambiguous, dark phase of the moon is "betwixt and between," a merging of old and new, a point of transition, both the end and beginning of a lunar cycle.

In Ommyôdô thought, this transition in time was a gate through which demons, or menacing earth spirits entered and left the phenomenal world (Okada 1993: 204). The ambiguous term demon (*ki*; *oni*) denotes "spirits of the dead," including "ancestral spirits," and "invisible yin [earth] spirits" that "bring misfortune and harm to humanity" (Ogawa 1986: 1139). The yin spirits are synonymous with "mononoke" (Ogawa 1986: 1139), or "low ranking, malicious, curse-bearing (tatari) spirits" (Kamata 1993: 4) which represent the life-taking aspect of the Feminine. The demons, or low spirits of the earth, equated with this gate are dark (yin) shades; this darkness metaphorically resonates with the dark phase of the moon. This class of spirits will be more fully examined in Chapter Five.

The Demon Gate is manifest in both time and in space. *The Book of Changes* identifies the first trigram, "the Opposing," that corresponds to the Demon Gate as being analogous to: "mountain," "stones," roads, "doors and openings," "fruits and seeds," and "doorkeepers" (Baynes 1967: 278–79).

Here a profusion of transitional, interstitial images is presented. In terms of remnants of Yayoi period ritual practice, mountains (and stones) are powerful interstices for spirits and the ancestral dead. Roads and crossroads have been previously identified as the haunt of spirits and ghosts. Doors, gates, and openings are interstices pure and simple, regions at which opposites meet; keepers of these places are at the source of power. In addition, these places of physical transition delineate the spatial aspect of the Demon Gate juncture in the time/space continuum. Similarly, fruits and seeds embody the "beginnings and ends of plants" (Baynes 1967: 279). In these images, the merging of beginning and end is presented (see Ômori 1993: 42), as in the Uroboros figure devouring its own tail and the yin-yang dyad; the process of change, as both life-taking and life-giving, is depicted. The Demon Gate is emblematic of earth, which together with woman makes up the Feminine archetype. The Demon Gate is literally death (Noguchi 1994: 588) and burial of the dead in the earth.

The Demon Gate (in space and time) is also analogous to menstrual blood, the end and beginning of the female cycle of fertility, the unfertilized womb. Representing a failure to achieve fruition, it threatens the process of propagation essential to society's survival. This gate challenges society's knowledge of itself and the socially known pattern of the cosmos; it not only resists definition, it presents the creative/destructive power of the Feminine. This temporal and spatial interstice presents the terrifying image of the Great Mother, simultaneously consuming and giving birth. At Hakozaki, the Great Exorcism rite is observed at this earth active period on the last day of the old year; it will be examined in Chapter Six.

In the home, the northeast quadrant is a taboo direction for all features, and it is especially unlucky for guest rooms. A small hill (mountain) in this direction was considered lucky (Gale 1981: 44). Obviously, spatial interstices at this quadrant were thought to provide access to threatening earth spirits, and so were avoided. The Demon Gate was, in times past, identified with the hearth, or fireplace in the kitchen (Noguchi 1994: 343, 610). According to Ommyôdô ritual practice, the hearth (fire) spirit was considered to ascend to heaven on the twenty-third day of the twelfth lunar month, during the Demon Gate earth active period, and return to be received by family ritual at New Year's (Noguchi 1994: 343).

The Wind Gate

The Wind Gate (*fûmon*) is a projection of the generative aspect of the Feminine archetype; this second earth active period occurs at the transition from spring to summer and at the southeast quadrant of the compass.[6] It is associated with the third trigram in *The Book of Changes*," the Penetrating" (Baynes

1967: 220). This interstice is associated with "preparation," "expansion," and "growth;" in the commentaries for *The Book of Changes*, the Wind Gate is identified with "the flowing of beings into their forms. . . [and] the giving of life" (Baynes 1976: 680; Ômori 1993: 42). This quadrant presides over development of things and their growth "into the shape prefigured in the seed" (Baynes 1967: 270). The Wind Gate is literally entry (Noguchi 1994: 588), the planting of seeds.

During the Wind Gate earth active period, the first ritual to welcome the young, female, high field spirit (tanokami) down from the mountain and into the village takes place in Tôhoku on the sixteenth day of the third lunar month; similar spring rituals were observed in Kansai (Ôshima 1992: 162; Yanagita 1987: 407–412). This high spirit, a projection of the generative aspect of the Feminine archetype with its connection to earth, seeds, life, farming, growing, and harvest, was known in Tôhoku as the farming spirit (*nôgami*), in Kinki as the growing spirit (*tsukurigami*), in parts of Kansai as the harvest spirit (*inokami*)[7], and in the Seto region it was known as earth spirit (*chijin*) (Ôshima 1992: 183–84). In the Sendai area, sixteen round rice dumplings (*dango*) were offered to the field spirit on the sixteenth day of the third month, this being the time when this entity descended from above just prior to rice cultivation efforts; the same rite was observed again on the same day in the ninth month, in thanks following the harvest (Yanagita 1987: 412). The number sixteen is slightly past the full moon of the fifteenth night (midpoint of the lunar month), as such, the moon is no longer at the point of extreme yang (brightness, generative power) that beckons an yin reaction (darkness, sickening tendencies); at this point, yin is at its very beginning, in its weakest, most yang (life-giving) phase. This field spirit rite, observed in spring and in the fall, appears to be a ritual means of invoking the generative Great Mother.

In the home, the life-giving Wind Gate (southeast) corresponds to the gate, and is an auspicious location for a hearth, well, gate, bath, kami or Buddhist altars, and is supposed to be most auspicious for an entryway or storehouse (Gale 1981: 44, Fukuoka-ken jinja-chô 1995: 45–46; Ôshima 1992: 72–73). Identified as a generative interstice, and equated with high spirits and the reproductive Good Mother, the Wind Gate was a favored direction in space for openings into other regions, be they directed toward the outside, the other world, or the inside of even the earth itself. Influences from this region are beneficent.

The Human Gate or Rear Demon Gate

The third earth active period, known as the Human Gate (*jinmon*), is more popularly known in mainland Japan as Rear Demon Gate (*urakimon*) (Okada

1993: 204). Associated with low earth spirits (ki, oni), this interstice is a projection of both the generative and threatening Feminine archetype. It occurs at the transition from summer to autumn, is associated with the southwest quadrant of the compass, and corresponds to the full moon. A manifestation of the Great Mother, the combined woman and earth, the Human Gate is literally the womb, the interstice from which human beings emerge; it corresponds to the trigram called "Complying" which "means earth. It takes care that all creatures are nourished" (Baynes 1967: 269). This gate's images in *The Book of Changes* are: "the earth that stores all things;" "the mother;" "the kettle;" "a large wagon;" and "a cow with a calf" (Baynes 1967: 275–76; Ômori 1993: 42). In keeping with the Feminine archetype, earth and woman are paired; the image of offspring (the calf) indicates their generative manifestation. Images of kettle and wagon complete this interpretation as they portray the vessel capacity of the Feminine, its functions of bearer and nurturing agent of life. The Human Gate signifies birth (Noguchi 1994: 588), emergence of offspring from the Female. But this image of emerging life has accompanying perils.

Based on Yin-Yang Five Phase cosmology, ritual practice marked the Human Gate as a period of taboo. Cattle, as the embodiment of this earth active season, were recipients of thoughtful gestures on the first cow calendar day of this earth active period: farmers throughout Japan led their cows to the ocean, to rivers and shrines, bathing them, ridding them of insect pests, and letting them rest.[8] Given the robust corporeal nature of the cow, this animal seems an appropriate emblem of the pronounced physicality of earth and woman (and also the corresponding full moon). On the first cow calendar day of this earth-active period, humans also bathed in the sea to become as healthy as cow, or at home with iris to avoid or treat illness (Yanagita 1987: 438–40; 446–47). These ritual actions represented a petition for robust health and vitality associated with the life-giving Great Mother. In addition, on the first cow day of the Human Gate period, farmers avoided work in the fields (and hence disturbing the earth); to disregard this taboo would deprive the person of their life, or reduce them to ashes (Yanagita 1987: 438, 446–47). Taboo surrounding the earth at this juncture of life-giving energies represents an acknowledgment that the Great Mother is easily offended and can precipitously shift to snatch the life of an insensitive offender.

During this same period, taboos were observed and offerings made to water spirits (*kappa*) (Yanagita 1987: 434–40). Ritual focus on water spirits is a factor of Five Phase thought: water is the most yin of the phases, and the Human Gate interstice corresponds to the second most potent manifestation of yin among the Eight Trigrams. Attention to water spirits at this juncture denotes an acknowledgment that the Human Gate is predominantly a yin interstice. Water spirits are low spirits associated with the earth; in folklore they are mischievous and even harmful.[9] These spirits are said to snatch humans or even horses, take them into an underwater realm, drown them and extract their livers through their anuses (Amamoto 1993: 9). In the Japanese mainland, water spirits are known to be fond of cucumbers. In premodern Japan, the spirit of the Gion Shrine in Kyôto, whose shrine crest reputedly can be viewed in the cross section of a cucumber, was known as the Cowhead Heavenly King (*gozutennô*). The cucumber's dual link with the earthly cow and the water spirit seems to further substantiate their relationship to the Human Gate interstice (see Amamoto 1993: 20–21). At Hakozaki, the Great Exorcism rite, which is also conducted at the end of the summer earth active period, is related to the Human Gate interstice and will be examined in Chapter Six.

As a spatial interstice in the home, the Human Gate corresponds to the southwest and to the well; it is an unlucky direction for all dwelling features, except for gardens or trees (Gale 1981: 44–45). It is particularly inauspicious for entrances and extensions of the home (Ômori 1993: 43). It is a taboo direction, but not as greatly feared as the Demon Gate (Okada 1993: 204). According to an almanac published by the descendants of the Abe tradition of Ommyôdô, this direction "is both earth and mother. By disturbing the earth [of this direction], the mother will be harmed. [She] fulfills the role of guardian of all things" (Ômori 1993: 43). This interstice in space and time is a mixed proposition; it is equated with both the devouring and life-giving aspects of the Great Mother.

The Heaven Gate

The Heaven Gate (*tenmon*) is found at the transition from autumn to winter, at the northwest quadrant of the compass, and is emblematic of the life-bestowing aspect of the Feminine archetype. This interstice is indicative of the culmination of fertility in birth and in harvest. Associated with the trigram "the Advancing" in *The Book of Changes*, this interstice correlates to the "end of growth," "completion," fruits of the harvest (the seed), "heaven," "the gift of water" by means of which "all individual beings flow into their forms," "ancestors," "round" objects, the "father," and the "horse" (Baynes 1967: 275, 370–71; Ômori 1993: 42–43). The Heaven Gate denotes emergence (Noguchi 1994: 588), specifically, the emergence of seed in birth and harvest.

These images portray the life-giving Great Mother, producing an abundant harvest of seed. The seed is the means by which life is transmitted from generation to generation. In the woman, in light of the Feminine archetype, this seed corresponds to the seed of the man by which children are fathered.

Hence the seed corresponds to the father. This same seed fecundates the soil, the earthly aspect of the Feminine archetype. In the Yayoi period worldview previously considered, ancestors, as high spirits, inhabit the features of the topocosm. It is their power by which new life in the Great Mother (woman and earth) is quickened and passes from generation to generation. In reality, the seed itself is analogous to the ancestor (the corpse), buried in the Feminine and emerging in new life (in crops and offspring). Thus, the seed is the ancestor. In mainland Japan, these generative high spirit ancestors (kami) are equated with heaven (amatsukami), as opposed to spatial boundaries that are the haunt of threatening low spirits of the dead (kunitsukami). High spirits correspond to yang ("the Initiating," "the Advancing," realm of the living, sun [heaven], and male [father]); low spirits are indicative of yin (the receptive, retreating, realm of the dead, moon [woman/ earth cycles], and female [mother]). The sun is completeness, is constantly round, as opposed to the cycle of lunar roundness that constantly waxes and wanes. These correlations have direct application to the respective integrity and permeability of male and female bodies. But all images of "the Advancing" trigram are subsumed under the overriding image of the generative Great Mother; even as father and ancestor fecundate the collective Feminine womb, these male figures are not separate from the Mother. In Ommyôdô thought, the Way—the Great Mother—underlies, supports, produces all things, male (yang) and female (yin). Neither the father nor the ancestor stand alone in philosophical Taoism, they exist as merely component parts of the all-pervading Great Mother herself, the Way.

Ritual life at this final earth active period bears out the metaphoric fact that production in woman and field are united in terms of the Feminine archetype and are effected by means of the seed, the male principle. On the second evening of this interstitial earth period, the thirteenth day of the ninth lunar month (L 9/13), in what is now Tokushima prefecture on Shikoku, offerings of taro roots (*satoimo*) and soybeans were made to the almost full, Old Woman Moon (*ubazuki*) and to high spirits (Yanagita 1987: 566). The roundness of beans and taro invokes the completeness of the harvest cycle, initiated by the male-yang seed and culminating in the generating aspect of the Great Mother. The fruits of harvest themselves are a further indication of the triumph of the Feminine in the seed and vice versa. Finally, in the image of the old woman (in the moon), the youthful and fertile field spirit that descended into the village in spring has produced richly in the village soil; this offering of firstfruits is an acknowledgment of debt to her fecundating power. In and around Sendai, on the sixteenth day of the ninth lunar month (L 9/16) the offering of sixteen round rice dumplings is an expression of gratitude to the field spirit, sixteen invoking the most life-giving (yang) aspect of her dark (yin) nature (Yanagita 1987: 412). She is now old because her youth and vitality have been exhausted in the travail to produce crops; at harvest, as an old woman, this high spirit (of production and life) will leave the village for the winter. Yanagita points out that the spent field spirit was originally sent back to either the mountains, or to heaven (1987: 569). Mountain is the image of the next earth interstice in the cycle, the Demon Gate; heaven is the image of the Heaven Gate. Residing in the mountains, as the mountain spirit, she will be revitalized and return to the village renewed, young and fresh, once again in the spring. Her link to heaven (yang) further indicates her life-giving aspect.

An implicit metaphoric relationship establishes the Feminine archetype as the organizing criteria for ritual and language that occur at the Heaven Gate interstice in time. Ritual practice at this juncture emphasized the restoration of the tired Female through involvement with the male. In what is now eastern Ibaraki prefecture, at the Heaven Gate earth active period (L 9/13) following the harvest and at the beginning of the lunar winter, a ritual called "striking the grain head staff" (*bôchibô uchi*) was observed. Boys older than ten gathered in groups, beat the ground with plaited tuber stems while chanting, and received change and sweets at homes as they moved through the village (Yanagita 1987: 566–67). A ritual called "dealing a filling blow" (*harame uchi*) dates to at least the Heian period, and was widely observed throughout mainland Japan in the Edo period: at the lunar, small New Year (L 1/15), the man of the house chased his wife and used a stick, often phallic in shape and usually used for stirring rice gruel, to tap her buttocks or hips as a symbolic means of blessing her with children (Ohazama 1985: 20). In parts of Nagano prefecture, this same ritual was observed for women at the rice planting (Mizuhara 1981: 1: 134). In each case, males strike the Great Mother, as earth or woman. The striking of a woman with the gruel (seed) phallus is said to "impregnate" or "fill" (*haramu*) the woman with child; the striking of the earth with the grain head staff is performed to revitalize the tired soil following harvest, in preparation for it to be "filled" with heads of rice in the coming year. Both rites presage the return of the generative Great Mother to produce new life forms by involvement with the seed-bearing male.

The Great Mother's generative aspect, in addition to being equated with the harvest of seed, is also correlated with the male in other ways. For centuries, ritual practice in mainland Japan has identified the end of the Heaven Gate period (L 9/30), as the time when all the high spirits of Japan leave their various localities and go to a great meeting, during the tenth month, at the Great Shrine of Izumo (*Izumo taisha*) in Shimane prefecture. This shrine is dedicated to the Great Lord of Earthly Spirits (*Ômononushi*), also known as the

Great Earth (Topocosm) Lord (*Ôkuninushi*) (Aston 1990: 59, 81; Senge Yoshihiko 1996, personal communication). This spirit was known for "his frequent appearances in the guise of a snake and for his liking for women" (Philippi 1968: 545); in popular belief, he is known as the spirit of male-female relations (*enmusubi no kami*) and is said to play a linking role in the pairing of the sexes. Even now, the visiting spirits are welcomed at Izumo's Inasa Beach in the tenth lunar month (L 10/ 1), escorted to the shrine, and preceded by a coiled serpent arranged on a stand. When the myriad spirits return to their local areas from Izumo, they are revitalized with life energy and have determined the marriages that will take place in their areas in the coming year (Senge Yoshihiko 1996, personal communication).

Here the politics of ancient Japan influence ritual life. The Izumo clan was a fierce rival of the Yamato clan (ancestors of the present imperial family); the capitulation of Izumo in favor of Yamato temporal hegemony prompted the melding of the two groups' myth cycles into the official mythologies recorded in the *Kojiki* and *Nihon Shoki*. The chiefs of Izumo came to preside over the unseen world, precipitating the annual migration of high spirits to their Great Shrine (*taisha*). Instead of returning to the mountain or to heaven, the high spirits repair to the shrine of the Great Earth Lord.[10]

High spirits converge at the shrine of the Great Earth Lord at the Heaven Gate interstice because in the Later Sequence arrangement of the Eight trigrams, this position corresponds to the extreme of yang, to heaven, the father, and the seed, and this high spirit of Izumo is a priapic entity that fertilizes the Great Mother. The high spirits, like the old woman field spirit who is exhausted, are depleted of vitality following the harvest. Their residence at Izumo is invigorating and, being revitalized, they return to their local areas, bringing with them new life energy.[11] The presiding high spirit at Izumo is fond of women; his name, Great Earth Lord, denotes the husband of the Feminine, the provider of seed. The ambiguity of his other appellation can also mean Lord of the Great Item (mono), here again a phallic reference. His manifestation is the libidinous snake that brings thunder and rain ("the gift of water") that quickens the rice crop (the earth), that sheds its skin and is reborn (see Blacker 1975: 115–125, Neumann 1968: 187), corresponding to the phallus that brings fecundating seed to the woman, that dies in the process and is reborn.

High spirits are manifestations of the life-giving Good Mother; their travel to Izumo's virile Earth Lord, during the Heaven Gate interstice, represents the renewal of her generating aspect for the coming year. High spirits in mainland Japan are eidetic manifestations of this life-giving Good Mother complex of understandings that further the products of field and womb. This annual reinvigoration of the local topocosm's tutelary spirits at Izumo, invigorates the earth for agriculture and also provides conjugal links between men and women that will lead to the invigoration of the woman; thus fertility in both aspects of the Feminine archetype are addressed at the virile Heaven Gate.

Spatially in the home, the Heaven Gate interstice corresponds to the garden. Manifested in the northwest quadrant, it is a lucky interstice for guest rooms and gates, and is particularly auspicious for the placement of: ponds, hills, storehouses, and Buddhist or kami altars. This area is unfavorable for a well, kitchen, bath, window, or entryway into the home, and toilets or baths in this quadrant will be the source of major affliction (Gale 1981: 44–45; Ômori 1993: 43). Toilets and baths in this quadrant are particularly unlucky because, "it is as though pouring filth [waste] on the ancestors' heads" (Ômori 1993: 43).

SUMMARY AND IMPLICATIONS

Like the Yayoi period worldview, Yin-Yang Five Phase cosmology similarly represents a socially transmitted pair of lenses, but the scale and complexity of the latter system completely overshadows the former. The Yayoi period system consists of notions that are centered on spatial (landscape) and temporal (seasonal) phenomena, but these ideas constitute a schema that provides general guidelines for human interaction with the topocosm (life-souls, fruition, soil release, and so forth). The Ommyôdô system approaches the level of proto-science, it melds time and space into a single continuum (cycle) along with scores of other phenomena, accounts for positive and negative interrelations between phenomena, and makes possible endless diagnostic and corrective actions between the myriad macrocosms and microcosms in heaven, earth, and the human body. While Yayoi period ideology does persist in ritual practices at the present, Ommyôdô cosmology has made in-roads into ritual practice in the Ryûkyûs, and especially in Korea and mainland Japan. The degree to which that influence extends falls beyond the scope of this present study; the following summary of Ommyôdô time/ space cosmology is presented with the aim of pinpointing the characteristics and influence of Yin-Yang Five Phase cosmology in contemporary mainland Japan kami tradition ritual practice. Ultimately, the Yayoi period cosmological notions and Ommyôdô concepts we are considering are both predicated on the Feminine archetype. For this reason, the two systems have been able to merge and even coexist side by side; both sets of information construct and mediate the human experience of and relationship to the Great Mother.

The reckoning of time in contemporary kami tradition ritual practice is based on the Later Sequence arrangement of the Eight Trigrams. While the

Former Sequence is based on the annual solar cycle (and its influence is still evident), the Later Sequence is attuned to the lunar cycle and the female fertility cycle. In the Diagram of Yin-Yang Five Phase Cosmology (see Figure 4.8), the element of earth presides over the center and the four gates at the corners. These locations in time and space are the primary foci of ritual focused on the Feminine archetype. The four gates at the corner interstices of the diagram are points of access into the element of earth in the center. These corners and the center are all interstices at which yin passes into yang, they correspond to the mouth of the Uroboros grasping its own tail, they are the union of opposites, the convergence of seasons. These gates (corners) and the earth (center) are all interstices at which contact with the Great Mother takes place, here she both gives birth and devours. Some interstices have more threatening cognitive aspects; others have more beneficent ones. No interstice is completely one or the other, they are all relative combinations.

A preponderance of yin force denotes a threatening interstice, a concentration of yang constitutes a generative boundary, and a balance of the two energies also identifies a life-giving opening (see Figures 4.7 and 4.9). Accordingly, the three most yin interstices in the Later Sequence time cycle from first to third place are: the Demon Gate, the Human Gate, and the winter solstice (see Figure 4.9). The Demon Gate has not reached an extreme and will continue to grow more yin in nature; it is the strongest yin interstice. Because an extremity beckons an opposite reaction, the Human Gate (extreme yin) is in reality the beginning of yang life and thus the second most potent yin interstice following the Demon Gate. The three most yang interstices, in descending order of strength, are: the autumn equinox, the Heaven Gate and the summer solstice. The Heaven Gate (extreme yang) is the commencement of yin decay and therefore the second most yang interstice after the autumn equinox. Likewise, the autumn equinox is the most potent yang interstice. Interstices of balanced yin and yang are the: spring equinox (slightly more yin) and Wind Gate (slightly more yang).

The Later Sequence cycle is based on the element of earth, on lunar reckoning, and is oriented according to the fertility cycle of the woman; in other words, this time cycle is attuned to the earth and female, the Feminine archetype, the Great Mother. The Later Sequence is based on the axis of Demon Gate (end & beginning) and the Human Gate (midpoint).

The Demon Gate as the strongest yin earth active period is firmly related to the end and beginning of cycles, particularly the female cycle of fertility which, in turn, has metaphysical consequences. The Demon Gate corresponds to days 28.5 to 30 of the lunar cycle (in a 30 day cycle), and results in a new, dark phase. It relates to the *Book of Changes* hexagram "the Opposing." In a 28 day female fertility cycle, the Demon Gate corresponds to days 26.6–28, re-

The Three Most Yang Interstices in the Later Heaven Sequence

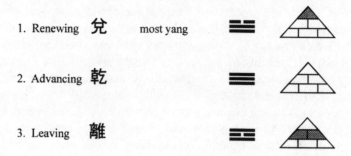

The Three Most Yin Interstices in the Later Heaven Sequence

> **KEY** yin = two broken lines or dark sections in a triangle
> yang = a whole line or light sections in a triangle
>
> *These triangles and groups of lines illustrate concentrations of yin and yang in each trigram. The bottom line of each figure is most dominant; the top line is least dominant.*

Figure 4.9. Yin and Yang Interstices

sulting in the cycle's end and the beginning of menstruation. During this period, women can experience yin conditions including: bleeding, depression (gloom), and water retention (Perry & Dawson 1988: 106–107; Peris 2002: 4).

Liminal periods abound: transitions in the lunar cycle, the female cycle, seasons, and the year. An extremity of yin force abounds: dark moon, earth spirits, and yin force gather at this interstice. Menstrual blood, indicative of a failure of seed-induced fertility, is analogous to life-threatening earth spirits (ghosts and relationless spirits) who died alone or without issue, beyond the margins of society and procreation. Demons and blood, as projections of failure to obtain fruition, menace the living and the ordered structure of society and are sources of apprehension associated with this interstice. While being female-centered, this system of time is female apprehensive, labeling the monthly period as impure and a source of spiritual danger. Since at least the founding of the capital at Kyôto (794 A.D.) (Inoue 1997: 30), the Demon Gate quadrant has been a major source of cognitive and metaphysical disquiet in mainland Japan. Ultimately, this most feared interstice, with its threatening, dark, death-related, sanguinary, opposing and stopping aspect, is the Terrible Mother who lurks at these ill-defined thresholds where life and death intermingle.[12]

The Human, or Rear Demon Gate is the second most powerful concentration of threatening yin force and also engenders cosmology based on the female cycle. A repetition of midpoints present themselves: the middle of the lunar month, the middle of the female cycle, the midpoint of the year. Opposite in the cycle to the Demon Gate, the Human Gate denotes days 13.5 to 15 in the lunar cycle, resulting in the full moon. It relates to the trigram "the Complying." It corresponds to days 12.6 to 14 in the female fertility cycle, resulting in ovulation, or release of the egg from the ovary, and a "physiological . . . increase in sexual desire" for fertile women (Perry & Dawson 1988: 100; 107). The Human Gate is the female womb, the gate from which humanity emerges. The release of an egg metaphorically corresponds to the full moon in the lunar cycle.

At this same interstice, ritual concern for water spirits from the depths (yin) is expressed to avoid being pulled into that dark realm. In folklore, water spirits eat the liver or gall bladder (*kimo*) of their victims; both of these organs correspond to: the element wood (Kiba 1997: 17), spring, due east, the Azure Dragon, and the vigorous (yang) life energy of the trigram "the Initiating," also translated as "the Arousing" (Baynes 1967: 276). Like the underwater Nira, the pull of water spirits is avoided by making food offerings (cucumbers), and by taking baths to restore one's health and vigor (yang). Yin water spirits desire vigorous life energy (yang) and cucumbers, which seem to be metaphors for the increase of female libido and desire for the male at the Human Gate interstice. The cow, in Five Phase cosmology, corresponds to earth, and the center (Kiba 1997: 17); the cow with calf, associated with the Human Gate in *The Book of Changes*, also appears to be a metaphor for the fertile female. Even so, the corporeal cow (earth) must be pampered at this gate, and work in the fields (earth) must be avoided on certain days to prevent the loss of vigor (yang/ life/ liver) for the farmer, or husband. This interstice is equated with the Terrible Mother who, like the water spirit, desires to drag the male (phallus) into the depths, desiring to receive from him his essence and vigor.[13]

These two, strong yin interstices constitute the organizing axis of the cosmological Later Heaven Sequence. The Later Sequence system is based on the Feminine archetype, more specifically on the observable cycles of woman and earth (including the moon).

The Wind Gate is a harmonious balance of yin and yang; as such it holds a unique position among the four earth interstices. It relates to days 6 to 7.5 of the lunar cycle, the first quarter. This interstice is assigned to the *Book of Changes* hexagram, "the Penetrating." In terms of the female fertility cycle, it corresponds to days 5.6–7 which mark the beginning of a five day period when women have a tendency to feel their best. The Wind Gate is the interstice at which the high field spirit descends to the village, bringing fertility. Villagers used to offer to her sixteen round rice dumplings before sowing the first seeds of rice (and again at the harvest).

Patterns of balance predominate at the Wind Gate when the sowing of seed begins. This interstice corresponds to the first quarter of the lunar cycle, a balance of darkness and light. This point in the woman's cycle is where temperature is slightly lower (yin: coolness), estrogen (yin) levels begin to rise causing the onset of positive feelings (yang), mucus production increases (yin: moisture), and according to a recent study conducted at the University of Virginia, this period (cycle days 5 to 10) was one of slightly raised libido (yang) at which women found their sexual relations the most agreeable for the entire cycle (Clayton et al. 1999: 288–289, Perry & Dawson 1988: 107). Women appear to have an even balance at this juncture, experiencing a new upswing and renewal in their monthly cycle. At the Wind Gate interstice, the young and beautiful high spirit of the fields descended from the mountains, making the soil fertile for crops (the seed) to be planted. She was offered 16 round dumplings, emblematic of the evening immediately after the full moon, the most full, light, and life-giving (yang) aspect of the waning (yin) moon. At the Wind Gate, the Good Mother presides in her generative phase bringing life and renewal.[14]

The Heaven Gate is an extremity of yang that holds within it the seeds of yin decay. The Heaven Gate juncture corresponds to days 21 to 22.5 in the lunar cycle, or to the moon's last quarter. This interstice is assigned to the trigram, "the Advancing." In the female fertility cycle, it occurs from days 19.6 to 21, a time at which women tend to feel emotionally and physically below average, or worse. In annual ritual, round firstfruits and the generative sixteen round dumplings are offered to the Old Woman of the moon; the tired field spirit is now spent and wan, in need of reinvigoration. The ritual called

striking with the grain head staff took place, a metaphoric means of revitaliz-
ing the tired earth by "filling" it with seed. Corresponding to the trigram of
"the Advancing" (extreme of yang, heaven, the father, the seed), at this juncture the tired high spirits of the earth, like the spent Old Woman, retire to
Izumo, and meet with the water-bearing serpent (phallus), the spirit of revi-
talization that dies and is reborn in the process of reviving the tired earth.

At the Heaven Gate, an extremity of life-giving (yang) force culminates in
the post-harvest (and post-ovulation) period. In the lunar cycle, the moon's
light has peaked and is waning. In a fertile woman's cycle, this point is one
where temperature is slightly higher (yang: heat), levels of progesterone rise
peaking about day 22 (yang), mucus begins to dry (yang: dryness), and "feelings of anxiety, irritability, helplessness, and depression build" as the sometimes gripping (yang) effects of premenstrual syndrome (PMS) begin to develop (Perry & Dawson 1988: 107). This period is also marked by an
incidence of "decreased libido" in women generally (Clayton et al. 1999:
290). Women also have a greater proclivity to die in the second half of their
cycle (following ovulation); in one study, 59% of female deaths (60 out of a
total of 102) occurred between days 17 and 23 of their fertility cycle (Perry
& Dawson 1988: 117–19). This occurs precisely around the Heaven Gate interstice (days 19.6–21 of the female cycle). Whereas positive feelings peaked
at the opposite Wind Gate (planting), negative feelings for women appear to
congregate around the Heaven Gate (harvest). In terms of the Feminine archetype, the image is that of the old, tired woman of the moon, the exhausted
high field spirit who has exerted herself in the production of crops in the
earth, or in the process of ovulation. This extreme exertion (yang) has produced a reaction of exhaustion (yin). At this juncture of harvest, the most
light, life-giving aspect (yang) of the Feminine (yin) is offered to the tired
Good Mother in the form of sixteen round dumplings. Phallic imagery as the
serpent that brings water, dies, and is reborn while reviving the tired Feminine, appears to prefigure the approaching Demon Gate. At the Heaven Gate,
the Good Mother is still in her generative phase, but is fatigued and in search
of access to new life energy.[15]

These last two yang interstices are cosmological portals that seem to be
based on the emotional and physiological changes of women during their fertility cycle as well as points of lunar transition: specifically, a highpoint (positive outlook—conception/ planting/Wind Gate/first quarter moon phase) and
a low point (PMS—birth/harvest/Heaven Gate/third quarter phase). Likewise, the other two points of transition, which form the main axis of the cycle, also are tied to even more significant points in the cycle of the Feminine:
a high point (ovulation—conception/planting/Human Gate/full moon) and a
lower point (menstruation—birth/harvest/Demon Gate/new moon). This cos-

mology, at first glance anti-female (and certainly one factor in the relegation of females to subservient roles in East Asian societies), is primarily a set of cognitive projections based on the collective archetype of the Feminine: woman and earth (including moon). It appears that the female fertility cycle and the lunar cycle were initially instrumental in the formulation of this Yin-Yang Five Phase worldview in ancient China. But these combined phases of cosmology became reified, and as they spread into Korea and mainland Japan, these notions, in turn, cast the role of females in a negative light, particularly producing a perception that menstruation is a defiling phenomenon, associated with failure to procreate, a manifestation of the Terrible Mother. This pejorative, Ommyôdô-influenced understanding of women, and more particularly of menstruation, is at variance with the Yayoi period understanding of this monthly event as preserved in the Ryûkyûs in which this monthly flow was an emblem of female power and fecundity, a decidedly woman-affirming interpretation.

NOTES

1. In Mandarin, this same term (ommyôji, *yin-yang-chia*) denotes a "geomancer; a sorcerer; [or] an astrologer" (Liang 1972: 1180).

2. The term "phase," as in expression Five Phases (*gogyô*), is an acknowledgment that all aspects of matter are interrelated and are but temporary phases of existence between states of transformation.

3. Okada Yoshirô notes that the winter solstice in premodern China was the point at which the solar cycle began and was the point of commencement of the lunar calendar. At this juncture, "winter solstice envoys" from neighboring countries arrived at the imperial court bearing gifts and renewing political ties with the emperor (Okada 1993: 288). This arrival of visitors from foreign regions bearing gifts parallels the ancient arrival of the deceased from the Unseen Realm bearing blessings.

4. In England, these four points midway between the solstices and equinoxes are called "Cross Quarter Days" and were defining interstices in the Celtic year (Krupp 1994: 64).

5. The Chinese earth spirit (*tu-di-gung*) is portrayed as an old man kindly in mien; folklore indicates that persons who led virtuous lives can become a local earth spirit after death. He is said to bestow wealth and rich harvests on the community. Conversely, this male spirit's wife, the earth mother (*tu-di-ma*) is said to be mean and greedy of character; she is rarely venerated (Noguchi 1994: 511).

6. According to a geomancer's compass dating from the Six Dynasties period (220–589 A.D.), the Wind Gate was identified as the "Earth Door" (*chito*) (Fong & Watt 1996: xiv; Noguchi 1994: 588; Omori 1993: 37).

7. Literally, this name is "boar spirit" (*inokami*), boar is the Chinese calendar sign corresponding to the ninth lunar month, the time of harvest. Sir James Frazer claims

that the pig was originally a symbol of a Greek goddess of dual aspect, Persephone the virgin and Demeter the mother. At the festival of Thesmophoria, pigs were sacrificed in trenches filled with serpents as women mourned the passing of Persephone into the underworld. Her return from below was later celebrated and pig remains exhumed to fertilize the new fields (Campbell 1974: 467). In traditional Japan, the maiden field spirit was welcomed to villages during the third, serpent month at the Wind Gate interstice; at the opposite point in the annual cycle, the old field spirit was sent back to the mountains for the winter during the ninth, boar month at the Heaven Gate juncture. The juxtaposition of young and old goddesses along with the boar and serpent is striking.

8. The Chinese lunar calendar functions on a sixty unit cycle when it comes to reckoning days and years. Each day (and year) is identified as a combination of one heavenly stem (*jikkan*) together with one earthly branch (*jûnishi*). Each of the earthly branches is assigned one zodiac animal of the Chinese system (see Okada 1995: 141–44). The first cow calendar day is the first day in each month that displays the earthly branch linked with the cow (*chû*).

9. In the Ryûkyûs, two varieties of minor water spirit are recognized, those inhabiting the ocean (*inkamuro*), and those in springs/ wells (*kâkaro*) (Amamoto 1993: 18).

10. Ôkuninushi is also known as the Great Lord of Earthly Spirits. The term for earthly spirits (mono) is sometimes translated "demon" or "rascal;" and while there are conceptions of spirits of this order in Japan, such a view of this high spirit of Izumo would be from a Yamato perspective. For natives of Izumo, mono simply denotes a spiritual being, not necessarily one that is menacing (Senge Yoshihiko 1996, personal communication). Earthly spirits (kunitsukami) were simply spirits reverenced in localities other than the heavenly spirits (amatsukami) of the central rulers that became peripheral after the emergence of Yamato clan hegemony (Philippi 1968:88).

11. This return of the myriad kami from Izumo bearing new life energy parallels the return of the young field spirit in the spring.

12. Darkness, blood, and destruction of social order associated with the Demon Gate surfaces in other social contexts beyond East Asia. Erich Neumann identifies this particular constellation of attributes with: the "Terrible Mother," "death mysteries," and the figure of the "old witch" (1963: 80, 83). Representative of such projections of the Terrible Female are India's figure Kali (or the Greek figure Hecate) (Neumann 1963: 80). Kali is often depicted as being dark, covered in blood, drunken with the taking of life, and raging in a manner that threatens the order of creation (Kinsley 1986: 118). The predominant images of death and destruction are central in what Neumann calls the "negative elementary character of the Feminine," in other words, the Terrible Mother (1963: 147–49). Demon Gate phenomena appear to belong to this aspect of social cognition.

13. Emphases on pronounced appetites and draining of vitality and life seem to congregate at the Human Gate juncture. Erich Neumann identifies this particular constellation of attributes with: the "mysteries of drunkenness," the figure of the "young witch" and "alluring and seductive figures of fatal enchantment" (1963: 80, 83). Pro-

jections of the young witch include Astarte (identified with the cow), Lilith, and Circe (Neumann 1963: 80). Astarte was goddess of "sexual activity, fertility, [and] maternity" that required the sacrifice of first-born animals and children (Leach 1984: 84). Lilith, according to Talmudic lore, was a succubus that seduced sleeping men and subsequently gave birth to evil spirits (Leach 1984: 622–23). In Homeric legend, Circe was a ·powerful sorceress who transformed men into beasts; bested by Odysseus, she convinced him to tarry with her for a year and gave birth to his son (Leach 1984: 234). Seduction and dissolution are defining aspects in what Neumann labels the "negative transformative character of the Feminine" in other words, the projection of young witch (1963: 80–81). Human Gate phenomena appear to be an aspect of the positive transformative level of cognition.

14. Balance, renewal, and creative potentiality seem to be associated with the Wind Gate juncture. Erich Neumann identifies this particular constellation of attributes with: "inspiration mysteries," the figure of the "divine virgin" and "the Muses" (1963: 80, 83). Projections of the muse figure include Kore, the maiden (Neumann 1963: 80). Kore, a name of the maiden Persephone, was daughter of Demeter the earth goddess (Leach 1972: 306, 858). Kidnapped by Hades, Persephone was forced to spend three (or six) months each year in the underworld; during this time, nothing grew (Evslin 1975: 177–79; Leach 1984: 306–858). This pattern parallels the time in which the mainland Japanese field spirit spent time in the mountains renewing her strength to return to the villages with fertility in the spring. Divine inspiration and fruition are defining aspects in what Neumann labels the "positive transformative character of the Feminine" (1963: 80). Wind Gate phenomena appears to be an aspect of the positive transformative level of cognition.

15. Fatigue, dryness, and a search for renewal are associated with the Heaven Gate juncture. Erich Neumann identifies this group of attributes with the "Good Mother," "vegetation mysteries," "earth goddess," and "queen of heaven" (1963: 80, 83, 125, 127). Projections of the Good Mother figure include Demeter, mother of the maiden Kore (Neumann 1963: 80). Demeter the earth goddess of harvest becomes depressed, distraught, and dresses in black at the abduction of her daughter (Neumann 1963: 318). Demeter and Persephone are essentially two aspects of the earth mother (Leach 1984: 306). Persephone is the young virgin/ earth who brings fertility in the spring; Demeter is the tired earth mother whose travail has brought forth harvest/birth. Demeter seeks and mourns for her daughter as a cognitive means of signifying that she longs to be renewed as the young, seed-receiving female of spring once again. Bearing fruit and desire for rebirth are defining aspects in what Neumann labels the "positive elementary character of the Feminine" (1963: 80, 82). Heaven Gate phenomena appear to be an aspect of this positive elementary level of cognition.

Chapter Five

Spirits High and Low

Popular notions regarding kami in Japan are ambiguous. Within the larger category of kami are the subsets of high and low spirits. There is some reluctance for researchers to acknowledge the fact that high spirits are contented ancestor spirits (see Figure 5.1). Contemporary scholars have embraced the narrow interpretation that Buddhist ancestor ritual is the *only* ancestor ritual in Japan.[1] But ancestors are the focus of both Buddhist *and* Shintô rites; rather than being exclusive sets of ritual, these two traditions represent ranges on a single continuum of behavior focused on ancestral shades. As mentioned by the Hakozaki priest in Chapter One, newly-deceased ancestors are served with Buddhist rites, but normally after the performance of Buddhist ritual for thirty-three years, the purified spirit ascends to the level of ancestor and can be addressed according to Shintô ritual forms. Buddhist ritual endeavors to shield the living from harm by placating and moving the spirit along the path toward purification and kami status; spirits successfully making this transition through the requisite ritual attention become part of the cycle of high spirits that sustain life, or Shintô. Shintô rites function to harness the purified spirit's life-granting and life-sustaining power for community benefit. Ones that do not make the transition into the cycle of high spirits become menacing low spirits attached to spatial boundaries.

The ambiguous character of low and high spirits residing in nature, both of which are recognized in Japan as kami, appears to be directly related to the complementary Chinese concept of dark spirit (*kuei-shen*; *kijin*) and bright spirit (*shen-ming*; *shimmei*, *myôjin*). Contemporary Buddhist and Shintô rites observed in Japan address the needs of the human community *vis-à-vis* low and high spirits and are an expression of a dark spirit/ bright spirit dichotomy neatly outlined by the writings of the Han scholar Wang Chung (circa 27–100) and

Figure 5.1.   Kami Beings

more completely in the philosophy of Sung dynasty Confucian scholar Chu Hsi (1130–1200). Chu Hsi's work represents the synthesis of Confucian and Taoist thought over several centuries. I assert that the historical development of the Chinese dark spirit/ bright spirit concept structures the idea of kami in Japan since both sets of spirits share the following three characteristics: 1) an early undifferentiation of spirits, 2) a later differentiation of spirits in terms of yin and yang (earth/ heaven), and 3) a further differentiation in terms of processes. The historical development of the dark spirit/ bright spirit dichotomy parallels an increasing cognitive articulation of the Feminine archetype. The Chinese term dark spirit (*kuei*) corresponds to low spirits (kami) in Japan, while the continental concept of bright spirit (*shen*) relates to high spirits (kami).

CONGLOMERATE OF SPIRITS

Analysis of spiritual beings in this chapter will be informed by Erich Neumann's Jungian theory, with slight modification. Our approach to the study of spirit beings will commence from the standpoint of Jung's "concept of projection" (Neumann 1963: 20). A cognitive projection is similar to the old time movie theater experience where the audience sees an image projected before them, but that image actually originates from (a camera located) behind (Neumann 1963: 20). Similarly, for Jung, experience of a supernatural being originated in a projection, a reflection of aspects "of the unconscious," or psychological realities from within (Neumann 1963: 20). Having been trained in the field of cultural anthropology, rather than speaking of "the unconscious," I prefer to speak of cognitive realities, or aspects of cognition resulting in the perception of spirit entities that are projections of socially-conditioned aspects of shared cognition.

In China, the term for dark spirit (or ghost) was employed long before the term for bright spirit. The first usage of dark spirit is found on specimens of the "earliest writing" (*jiaguwen*; *kôkotsumoji*), or oracle bone texts in China. Dating to the Shang dynasty (1738–1111 BC), these deer scapula or turtle plastrons were engraved with terse queries posed to ancestor spirits; a searing iron placed on the bone produced cracks that were interpreted as answers from the Unseen Realm.

Deceased spirits addressed in these texts are identified by the all-inclusive term dark spirit (kuei). We will call this Shang dynasty term, "dark spirit A" (in order to distinguish it from later definitions of the same term). The term bright spirit (shen) does not appear during this period. In Shang oracle texts, dark spirit A appears to have been the general term for all spirits of the dead. This term seems to have applied to both ancestor spirits and nature spirits equated with mountains and rivers (Mizoguchi 2001: 263). Ancestral spirits in Shang dynasty China, whose characteristics are preserved in the high spirit (kami) concept in Japan, mostly likely were thought to reside in nature and therefore were the same as nature spirits. In what Erich Neumann indicates is the second stage in the unconscious level of Feminine archetype development there is a conglomerate of polyvalent meanings, benign and disquieting, that he characterizes as the Uroboros stage (1963: 12, 20). In this study, this level of socially-conditioned cognition is one where there was an experience of the Feminine as a undifferentiated whole, an ambivalent, unarticulated fusion (Neumann 1963: 12) of waxing and waning, indicative of the Great Round, the cyclical process indicative of the cycles of earth, Female, and the moon. My assertion is that the Shang dynasty dark spirit A is a projection of an early, undifferentiated cognitive experience of the Feminine. This ambiguous dark spirit A was for persons then an expression of their ambivalent experience of the Feminine before it was identified as the Great Mother (see Neumann 1963: 12). Dark spirit A, as an expression of the latent Feminine, was a cognitive fusion of generative and devouring potentialities, an important focus of ritual behavior that I assert was expressed in the depiction of the *tao-t'ieh* figure.[2] Dark spirit A is most primordial, a combination of kindly ancestor/nature spirit (the later shen) and foreboding spirit of the dead (dark spirit B). The ambiguous term kami seems to preserve both of these characteristics.

EMERGENCE OF YIN-YANG COSMOLOGY

Articulation of the basic Yin-Yang philosophy took place during the Chou dynasty (1111–221 BC) and reached a pinnacle of elaboration in *The Book of Changes*, approximately 1000 BC (Saso 1990a: 29). Textual evidence for a further cognitive distinction between dark spirits and bright spirits occurs in the Eastern Chou dynasty (722–221), in the *Spring and Autumn Tsuo Commentary* (*Chunchiu-tsoshih-chuan*) written in 535 BC. In the *Tsuo Commentary*, dark spirits are portrayed as beings that had not successfully made the transition to ancestor status, had suffered an untimely death, and were fierce entities that wreaked havoc on the living (Mizoguchi 2001: 264). This is the emergence of the "dark spirit B" image. Development of dark spirit B's threatening aspect indicates a period of transition toward further levels of cognitive differentiation (Neumann 1963: 38). This cognitive change corresponds to Neumann's fourth stage of development of the Feminine archetype in the unconscious: the configuration of the Great Mother. At this level of cognitive differentiation, there is recognition of the Good Mother, the Terrible Mother, and the Great Mother which is a combination of the previous two aspects of the Feminine archetype (Neumann 1963: 19–21).

Articulation of Yin-Yang principles in the Chou dynasty accompanies, and itself expresses, a further cognitive differentiation of the Feminine archetype. Yin relates to the predation of the Terrible Mother and yang to the generative workings of the Good Mother. The Great Ultimate diagram (the nested, complementary yin and yang as a whole; see Figure 4.1) is indicative of the duality of the Great Mother. Emergence of Yin-Yang philosophy and terminology provided the impetus to make a finer distinction of spirit entities also. During the Chou dynasty, the emergence of the newly defined dark spirit B (an expression of yin and Terrible Mother), and the bright spirit concept (relating to yang and Good Mother) appear to be an expression of this heightened ability to differentiate the basic aspects of the Feminine archetype.

FURTHER DIFFERENTIATION IN TERMS OF YIN AND YANG

In the Han dynasty, Yin-Yang philosophy fused together with Five Phase thought, resulting in Yin-Yang Five Phase cosmology. During the Western Han dynasty (202 BC–9 AD), further cognitive developments are discernable in the identification of dark spirit B with earth (yin) and bright spirits with heaven (yang). The *Ritual Records* (*Li-chi*), probably dating to the early Han (Hucker 1994: 66), indicate: "All life must perish, and perishing must return to the earth, this [phenomenon] is called dark spirit (kuei)" (Mizoguchi 2001: 263). Here, dark spirits are equated with death and a return of physical remains to the earth. Another passage from the *Ritual Records* enumerates: "Bright spirits (shen) are beings that . . . bring about rain, wind, and clouds on hills, in river valleys, and on forested mountains" (Mizoguchi 2001: 264). Dark spirits are identified with earth and physicality while bright spirits correspond to atmospheric conditions. Another passage from the *Ritual Records* makes the terrestrial and celestial links of these supernatural entities more explicit: "At death the yin soul (*p'o*) and yang soul (*hun*) separate; the yang soul breath (*hun-ch'i*) returns to heaven and the yin soul [physical] matter (*p'o-hsing*) returns to earth" (Mizoguchi 2001: 270). Or in other words, at death, a person's yin soul (p'o) becomes dark spirit (kuei) and their yang soul (hun) transforms into bright spirit (shen) (Kim 2000: 101, 103). This dichotomy becomes operative on the individual level as a yin soul (the physical body), and a yang soul (ch'i, or life force). Ch'i is equated with breath and circulation in the body while in nature it corresponds to mist, clouds, rain, and air (Ogawa 1986: 552). The progressive, Han dynasty philosopher Wang Chung (circa 27–100 AD) articulates a view suggesting the Feminine archetype most clearly:

> Dark spirits (kuei) and bright spirits (shen) are names for yin and yang. Yin energy
> is contrary to physical objects and leads to death [and the earth], and consequently
> these are called dark spirits. . . Bright spirits are expansion, continually expanding
> and returning [to the realm of life], and if they end, [they] begin again. By means
> of bright energy (*shen ch'i*) individuals are born, and at death, again [by means of]
> bright energy they return [to the realm of life]. . . Yin and yang are called dark spir-
> its and bright spirits, the death of the individual is called [the emergence of] dark
> spirit and bright spirit (kuei-shen) (Mizoguchi 2001: 269–70).

Dark spirits and bright spirits are projections of the Feminine archetype; Wang Chung most succinctly details these spirits' characteristics as projections of the Great Mother. Dark spirits, he says, are the essence of yin energy and correspond to the dissolution of organisms and their return to the earth. This is an accurate projection of the Terrible Mother as related to the process of degeneration. Bright spirits, the essence of yang energy, are equated by Wang Chung with "bright energy" and the continual emergence of life forms. Here the generative auspices of the Good Mother are identified. Finally, Wang Chung labels the death of individuals as the creation of both dark spirits and bright spirits. His implication is that death embodies the processes of both disintegration and emergence of new life. Wang Chung's observations foreshadow Chu Hsi's work that did not appear for another eleven centuries.

LOW SPIRITS AND THE MARGINS OF COGNITION IN JAPAN

Owing to Yin-Yang Five Phase cosmology, there is a predominant concern in traditional East Asian thought with the threatening aspect of yin forces, and particularly with death taboo. As mentioned in Chapters Three and Four, low spirits in Japan are equated with menstrual blood and are indicative of a failure to obtain fruition and thus cognitive elements that threaten to disorder the structures of social thought. As the Chinese antecedent to Japan's low spirit concept, dark spirits are projections of similar apprehensions. From an Ommyôdô perspective, yin corresponds to the Unseen Realm (*yin-chieh*), and to disembodied, dark spirits (kuei) inhabiting that realm that lack ritual attention from the living. In Japanese folklore, these lurking spirits of the dark seek to rob the living of vitality (Uryu 1997: 84–86); ultimately, these spectres are projections of the Terrible Mother. From an Ommyôdô perspective, females belong to the realm of yin; as such, women, being yin by gender, have an immediate cosmological affinity with low or dark spirits (kuei).

In East Asia, yin phenomena represent cognitive margins that are potentially harmful to shared thought structures of the human community. These phenomena must be controlled to assure the continuity of cognitive structures upon which social order is predicated; this control also includes ritual management. Representing untidy margins of thought, yin phenomena always run the risk of being manipulated by structurally weak members of society to further their own ends at the expense of social integrity. The conceptual significance of yin is made clearer by considering the Japanese term "backside" (*ura*). Backside denotes matters that are private, hidden, and closed off from the public eye. They can be "informal" and "relaxed" (see Hori 1994: 23–25), but also inside, shady, opposite, contrary, wrong, and even illicit realities that challenge the cognitive structures of society and social order. The backside cognitive orientation will divulge new insights about yin, yin spirits, the Unseen Realm, and the female medium tradition.

Yin and backside phenomena are indicative of the amorphous reality of disintegrative change and are the cognitive building blocks of mediumistic ritual practice. In the Shintô worldview of northern Kyûshû, boundaries of all varieties are indicative of the meeting of yin/ backside realities together with yang influences. Owing to Ommyôdô cosmology, the winter solstice together with the Demon Gate and Human Gate interstices at the Hakozaki Shrine are treated as being more yin than other annual interstices in time; these interstices will be covered more thoroughly in Chapter Six. Earth is a yin reality and spatial boundaries, interstices on the earth, are uniformly perceived as the haunt of dark (yin) spirits; at Hakozaki, thresholds, crossroads, and corners are particularly so. Known as Great Yin (*taiin*) in Ommyôdô thought, the

moon with its ceaseless cycle between light and dark embodies the three aspects of the Feminine archetype. Its light phase corresponds to the Good
Mother, its darkness to the Terrible Mother, and the entire cycle is indicative
of the Great Mother. The moon's ambiguous nature, both light and dark, typ-
ifies the cycle orientation that structures all ritual practice in the Shintô
worldview. As the most immediate human yin equivalent, woman also
evinces constant change in her monthly cycle of fertility.

Hair, nail pairings, and effluvia of all kinds, moving from inside the body
outwards, embody change and are yin in nature. They are yin because they
pass from the realm of the Unseen into the seen. These substances are sense-
less, sloughed physical matter that has been used in human societies in secret,
mediumistic ritual as magical items that can control the body from which they
originated. Emerging from an Unseen Realm in the body, these substances
represent vulnerable margins of the individual, part of the yin soul (p'o) presiding over life, the body, and the will to live (Jordan 1972: 31, Kim 2000:
224, Mizoguchi 2001: 267) and can be manipulated to injure and kill their
originator. These items become cognitively powerful due to their traversing
the boundaries of the body (see Douglas 1992: 120–21).

Yin or low spirits in Japan, corresponding to the Chinese dark spirit
(kuei), in folklore change their shape and range in behavior from playing
pranks, to robbing the living of their senses or lives. Low spirits in Japan
are known by a variety of category names including: transformed-object ap-
parition (*bakemono*), changeling (*henge*), demon (oni), changeling spectre
(*yôkai*) and evil spirit (mononoke, mamono). These strange beings are projections of social apprehensions regarding anomalous times, places, and effluvia. For example, changeling spectres or transformed-object apparitions
often appear in the uncertain light of dusk and dawn (Nomura 2000: 820).
They are identified most prominently with ambiguous locations not fre-
quented by and unnerving to the living: remote features in the natural environment, deserted locations with no other people, or the precincts of Buddhist temples (Williams, forthcoming manuscript). In folklore, these
changeling spirits are generated from matter out of place: from toothpicks
improperly disposed, from tools lost or abandoned, from deserted and di-
lapidated human habitations. Ommyôdô influence in Japan has influenced
the portrayal of demons (oni) as having cow horns and a tiger skin draped
around the loins (Shinmura 1969: 314); the conjunction of cow and tiger
symbolism denotes precisely the Demon Gate cosmological juncture (see
Figure 4.8).[3] Demons in Japan are projections of social apprehensions surrounding yin phenomena: menstrual blood and an inability to achieve
fruition. Demon lore thrives in Korea, too. Korean demons (*tokkaebi*) are
also equated with deserted locations, can transform their shape, cause mis-

chief, and can be spawned from tools (such as old pestles), particularly ones that have been stained with female blood (Ito 2000: 325).

Apprehensions about dissolution (the process of transition, disintegration, and decay) produce socially-conditioned, cognitive projections of the Terrible Mother, in the form of yin, low, and dark spirits; in Japan, these spirits are identified in folklore as agents that trick and waylay mortals. Apprehensions about dissolution are focused on transitional, "liminal" phenomena (Turner 1995: 94–95, 108–9). In Japan, these apprehensions surround: 1) ambiguous areas in classificatory systems, and 2) deceased spirits who lack requisite community ritual attention to attain beneficent status. Identifiable matter out of place, items that do not fit neatly into discrete, socially-defined patterns of cognitive order, challenge these systems of social knowledge (Douglas 1992: 38–40, 94–97, 115). For example, effluvia are redolent of danger to socially-scripted definitions of the world; as such, they represent anomalies that can challenge and redefine a society's system of cognitive order.[4]

From the perspective of Ommyôdô thought, the Demon Gate juncture is equated with the final disintegrative event: death. Demise of the individual forcibly attacks and dissolves all of society's cognitive categories. It is change that defies control, and yet human societies hedge death about with concepts of pollution and taboo as a means of controlling it. Death transition produces projections of suspect spirits, entities that are marked by society as transitional, and out-of-place. Ritual in mainland Japan focuses on the deceased person's spirit and taboo focuses on the survivors. By binding surviving family members to the spirit in the performance of mortuary ritual, social order is preserved by moving the spirit through successive realms of purity to benefit the soul and its descendants. Ritual practice transforms a dark, suspect spirit (kuei) into a bright spirit (shen; kami). But when mortuary ritual is *not* performed for the dead, or when the individual dies in the bonds of rancor and refuses to be mollified, the twice anomalous case of transformed human ignored (or unmoved) by the human community creates an unhappy, low spirit bearing ill-will.

In addition to cognitively anomalous phenomena, the range of low spirit entity concepts preserved in Japanese folklore also include projections of socially-generated apprehensions about the relationless dead, so often held to be a source of affliction to the living. The cognitive position of these low spirits is equivalent to the combined social apprehensions focused on menstruation, death, ambiguity, and disintegration that threaten to subvert and destroy society's structures of cognition. At least two lines of argument substantiate these claims. First, the origin of these spirits is equivalent to the mistreatment that relationless spirits receive from the human community. These strange, deformed (characteristics indicative of their cognitive incompatibility with social order) low spirits (such as, changeling spectres) originate from items (tools, habitations, blood) that are improperly placed, disposed of, or forgotten by the living. This mistreatment of things is directly analogous to the abandonment, in terms of ritual attention by the living, of relationless low spirits. Both object apparitions and low spirits have been left out of the regular order and pattern of life.

Second, the manner in which low spirits act toward the living is analogous to the cumulative effect they exert on cognitive systems. Low spirits play pranks on the living, disorient them with illusory experiences, or weaken mortals with illness, or death. These spirits range from transformed object apparitions to more threatening entities. One-eyed apparitions (*hitotsume kozô*) or shiver-from-behind spirits (*ushirogami*) and their ilk startle and unnerve unsuspecting mortals (Mizuki 1989: 56–57; Mizuki 1991: 63). Shape-shifting foxes transformed into beautiful women intoxicate and seduce mortal men, until these men come to their senses in a strange state of affairs (Piggot 1984: 120–21; Smyers 1999: 106; Tyler 1987: 116–18). Roaming epidemic spirits (*ekibyôgami*) congregate in areas bringing illness and death in their wake (Ômori 1993: 10–11). And cognitive projections like the Snow Woman (*yukionna*) or the nighttime demon procession (*hyakki yagyô*) usually bring quick death to unlucky mortals encountering them (Mizuki 1991: 460; Uryu 84–86). These cognitive apprehensions of dead spirits stuck in a limbo state without ritual attention, as projections of matter out-of-place confuse, weaken, or destroy the structures of social thought. Japanese folklore records the ongoing match of wits between mortals (projections of social thought structure), and low spirits (projections of anti-structure). Quite often, but not always, by cleverness or use of talismans the forces of anti-structure (low spirits, dissolution, the Terrible Mother) are thwarted. Low spirit ritual, other than exorcism, (for example, *segakie*) represents a bid to manipulate the margins of social thought structures to obtain individual or community benefits. This manipulation of cognitive margins for personal gain forms the basis of shamanism.

HIGH SPIRITS AND THE
STRUCTURES OF COGNITION IN JAPAN

According to Yin-Yang Five Phase cosmology, yang is indicative of the seen realm (*yang-chieh*) and corporeal existence. In Japan, high spirits are equated with the fruits of harvest, the birth of offspring, and the life-granting powers of yang. In Japan, this constellation of cognitive projections serves to uphold and protect the thought structures of society. High spirits are cognitively linked with heaven and sun, and freely circulate in the Shintô life cycle bringing life to the human community; as such, they are projections of the Good Mother. From an Ommyôdô standpoint, the male corresponds to the yang realm. As such, males have come to dominate the realm of high spirit ritual in mainland Japan given their cosmological affinity with bright or high spirits (shen, kami).

In Japan, yang corresponds to the term "frontside" (*omote*) that provides new perspectives on yang (high) spirits, the seen realm, the male priest tradition, and shrine-centered ritual practice. Frontside indicates open, public, social matters that tend to be formal affairs. Frontside phenomena are outside, proper, conforming, right, and legitimate. Not surprisingly, this realm of phenomena serves to maintain cognitive structures of thought and social order. Yang and frontside phenomena correspond to generative development and are the cognitive features essential to the construction of the male priest ritual tradition at Hakozaki. In the Shintô worldview of northern Kyûshû, boundaries of all varieties are indicative of the conjunction of yin/backside forces together with yang/frontside phenomena. Structured according to Ommyôdô cosmological principles, certain temporal boundaries are more indicative of yang (explication of these yang interstices will take place in Chapter Six). Heaven is the predominant yang cognitive feature and at Hakozaki, annual interstices in time which correspond to points of solar and lunar balance (i.e. the equinoxes and Wind Gate/ Heaven Gate axes) are the yang axes around which male priest ritual focused on high spirits is observed. The sun, or Great Yang (*taiyô*) according to Ommyôdô principles, also exhibits a cycle of light and dark phases. The equinoxes are points when life-giving, high spirits, corresponding to the Good Mother phase of the Feminine archetype, visit the seen world. The solstices are points of solar extremity (short or long days) when apprehensions about demons and sickness are preserved in East Asian folklore; these ideas correspond to the disintegrative influences of the Terrible Mother. The four cross-quarter day transitions (Demon Gate, Wind Gate, Human Gate, and Heaven Gate) are more ambiguous interstices, corresponding to the dual-nature Great Mother. The cross-quarter day interstices are mixtures of beneficial and menacing influences; this having been said, the Demon Gate and Human Gate are more yin and sinister in character while the Wind Gate and Heaven Gate are on a whole more yang and beneficent.

Food and drink, entering the body from without, are stimuli that embody a yang effect on the individual. These life-giving, sense-producing phenomena are the basis of life and social interaction. Food and drink are the prime items employed in the society-affirming, male priest-led rituals at Hakozaki and in many shrine contexts in Japan. Food and drink particularly represent reincarnated high spirit life energy having reemerged in the seen world and cognitively corresponds to the auspices of the Good Mother. Ritual manipulation of this produce represents gratitude to high spirits for fruition and a petition for their continuing support of the mortal community.

Analogous to the bright spirits (shen) of Chinese ritual life, yang high spirits (kami) in Japan are identified in the popular imagination as anthropomorphic beings. Their most common manifestation (to those who can see) is reported by Blacker to be the Old Man (*okina*) or a snake (1975: 35–37). Paired together with the Old Woman (*ôna*), the Old Man was identified by Yanagita as the collective ancestor who lived in the local land and prospered the fortunes of descendants (Nomura 2000: 565, 570–71). Yanagita claimed that the high spirit (kami) concept originates from the phenomena of familial ancestral spirits (Blacker 37; Nomura 1998: 151; Yanagita 1970: 59, 128, 132, 149). This elderly couple, or more often the figure of the Old Man alone, is the most common iconography associated with high spirits. The Ancestor couple, bearers of life energy, represents the spiritual element from the Unseen Realm that produces crops and offspring. The snake manifestation emphasizes the link between ancestor spirits, reincarnated into the seen realm as crops and offspring, and the phallus.[5] The snake (phallus) bearing the seed is emblematic of the physical element from the seen realm that fertilizes field and female.

The phallic icon most prominent in high spirit (kami) ritual is the pillar. High spirits are counted by the counter word "pillar" (*hashira*); for example, "There are three [literally, pillars of] kami enshrined here," (*Koko ni wa san-bashira no kami ga matsurarete imasu*). The pillar is emblematic of high spirits because it is indicative of creative, life-giving forces: the planting of the seed (in procreation and sowing) and its re-emergence (in birth and harvest). Spirit Trees in Shintô ritual life, function as nature's pillars. The Old Man and Old Woman are portrayed in Noh theatre as the high spirits of Sumiyoshi and Takasago, respectively (Tyler 1992: 279–80, Shinmura 1969: 1356). Made famous by Zeami's play, the Takasago couple are high spirits united by their two spirit pines in the precincts of the Takasago Shrine in Hyôgo prefecture (Tyler 1992: 279–80, Shinmura 1969: 1356). By means of their united trees, the Takasago spirits [Good Mother designation] in Zeami's play are said to be linked to the seen world by "spirit intercourse" (*kamikatarai*), the planting of seed that beckons the return of high spirits (Sanari 1982: 1879). The Old Woman and Man are ancestral spirits (ciphers for yin and yang) whose materializing-medium (*yorishiro*) is the phallic pillar of the Spirit Tree that plants the seeds culminating in birth and harvest. The pillar is a sign of the vivifying Ancestor life force re-emerging from the Unseen Realm.

Hakozaki's Spirit Tree is the living manifestation of Hachiman's role as high spirit of fruition. As the point of heaven (yang, male, Ôjin ritual) and earth's (yin, female, Tamayorihime ritual) conjunction, the Spirit Tree is emblematic of endless emergent life triumphant over the threat of disintegration and death. Elderly parishioners and visitors to the Hakozaki Shrine, in addition to priests at ritual junctures, habitually bow at the gate of the spirit fence that surrounds the Spirit Tree when passing before it. This Spirit Tree is the cognitive center of generative life-force at Hakozaki; its eternally-celebratory boughs are indicative of successive generations of descendants.

At Izumo and in the inner and outer precincts of Ise, Japan's most exalted high spirit shrines, the power source activating each Main Hall is a "central spirit pillar" (*shinnomihashira*), partly buried in the earth below the Main Hall. These pillars occupy an important cognitive position in the quelling of the threatening aspect of the Feminine: according to Yin-Yang Five Phase cosmology, the center point, where the pillar is placed, is indicative of the menacing aspects of the Feminine archetype. At Ise, due to the rebuilding of the shrine every twenty years, the pillars are objects of special ritual attention: for eight years prior to their being placed in the earth beneath the new Main Halls in the Outer and Inner Shrines, both spirit pillars are wrapped like a bale of rice, and stored together with rice dedicated to the high spirits (Nitschke 1993: 17). The placing of the pillars in the earth is the most important aspect of the entire reconstruction at Ise (Nitschke 1993: 17). In previous times the pillars were placed in the ground "immediately after the earth-quietening rite (*jichinsai*) . . . before the actual reconstruction work [on the shrine structures] started" (Nitschke 1993: 17). After the planting of a pillar, generation-invoking words (*norito*) "celebrate" the spirits of the four corners of the shrine earth (Nitschke 1993: 17). Placement of the pillar, analogous to planting the seed, renders the threatening Feminine benign and life-granting; the celebratory generation-invoking words emphasize this positive change has taken place. During the eleventh through the thirteenth centuries, the spirit pillar was only partially buried in the earth; now in Ise's Inner Shrine, the pillar is completely sunk in the ground (Nitschke 1993: 17–18). In the Outer Shrine, presently less than half of the pillar is sunk in the earth (Nitschke 1993: 18). The pillar at the Outer Shrine, emerging more from the ground than being sunk into it, is cognitively more consistent and most likely is the older placement pattern of the two.[6] The emerging pillar emphasizes the triumphant return of the Ancestor/high spirit/seed from the earth. In both the Inner and Outer Shrines, the sacred mirror is placed inside the Main Hall, directly above the pillar and seems indicative of both sun and the emperor (Nitschke 1993: 18). The pillar is emblematic of the male principle that fecundates the Female/earth and brings about new life.

The pillar image appears to be the male principle dominated by the Feminine. Scattered about the precincts of Ise's Inner Shrine are numerous stone platforms, each standing about thirty centimeters in height, surrounded by a rice straw festoon (*shimenawa*). From the middle of each of these platforms emerges one broad, phallus-shaped rock some twelve centimeters above the top of each platform. Although priests at the inner shrine seem largely reticent on the subject, one priest in 2003 explained that these emerging rocks on the platforms are "kami of the earth/place" (*chinokamisama*). Although the male principle is clearly indicated by the stone pillars, their cognitive linking with earth and place seem to make the phallus a possession of the Feminine archetype. The Shintô cycle of the perennial return of high spirits/seed is cognitively dependent on the Female earth. The male principle is never completely free of the Female, he is part of her never-ending cycle.

At Hakozaki, cooked rice pillars (*jukusen*) are employed at Rites of Celebration (see Photo 6.18). These rice pillars are emblems of the male principle, similar to Ise and Izumo's life-giving pillars that quell devouring earth influences. Cooked rice pillars represent the Ancestor/high spirit/phallus/seed and are presented before the Main Hall at three solar cycle rituals near the spring equinox, the autumn equinox, and the winter solstice. In addition, they are offered at one rite on New Year's Eve and one on New Year's morning. These rice pillars are offered by Hakozaki's male priests, in the central male-controlled ritual space (before the Main Hall), at the balance of yin (night, darkness, female) and yang (day, light, male) at the equinoxes. These two points are times of invigoration of the female by the male: the spring equinox is the planting of the seed (sowing and procreation) while the autumn equinox is its return (in harvest and birth). At these two times, Hakozaki's male priests celebrate and invoke the fertilization of the Feminine by the male, signified by the rice pillar. Rice pillars are offered at the winter solstice, the third most potent yin interstice in the Yin-Yang Five Element cosmology (see Figures 4.8 and 4.9), to counteract the growing length of night (yin) at the expense of day (yang). Here the male principle of seed is offered to offset the growing yin and to usher in the growth of yang, warmth, and light. In a similar manner, cooked rice pillars are offered on New Year's Eve at the Demon Gate juncture and again on New Year's morning just past this cognitively threatening juncture. These offerings invoke the Ancestor/high spirit/phallus/seed at the most powerful yin juncture in the Yin-Yang Five Element cosmology, a point at which threatening Feminine influences are at their greatest. At this point in the cycle, Hakozaki's priests officiate in their central ritual space, presenting their answer to the menacing Feminine in the shape of a rounded, well-formed, pillar denoting the male, seed, and the sun as a petition to the life-granting contented high spirits, the collective Ancestor. Similar to the quelling of Ise's cosmologically threatening center point at the Main Hall with a pillar, ritual at Hakozaki ultimately invokes the Good Mother, the cognitive foundation of high spirit phenomena, and is calculated to promote life in general and social cohesion in the local community specifically. Rites of Celebration at Hakozaki together with their cosmological implications will be more thoroughly discussed in Chapter Six.

CHU HSI'S INFLUENCE ON JAPANESE RITUAL LIFE

Bright spirits in China (shen) and high spirits in Japan (kami) are contented ancestral spirits, and are projections indicative of social cohesion and community integrity. Dark spirits in China (kuei) and low spirits in Japan (mono), the malcontent dead, are cognitive phenomena that are ill-defined and challenge social systems of order.

When travelers from the Chinese state of Wei visited the late Yayoi period, Yamato kingdom in Japan, they mentioned in *The Chronicles of Wei*, dated 297 A.D. (Brown 1997: 97) that Himiko the medium-queen practiced shamanism, or literally, "the Way of Dark Spirits" (*kuei-tao*; *kidô*) (Mizoguchi 2001: 264). Dark spirit in this instance may have been used in an undifferentiated sense (dark spirit A), generally denoting spirits of the dead. Dark spirit in this instance may also have been employed in a pejorative manner, denoting alien ritual practices, or even female-led ritual that already was suspect given the disquieting cognition surrounding yin phenomena in China (dark spirit B). Since the level of differentiation resulting in the dark spirit B concept had emerged by the Western Han dynasty (202 BC–9 AD), it seems more likely that the Chinese travelers had this idea in mind when referring to the ritual practice of Himiko. From their continental perspective, what other type of spirits could a woman possibly be addressing? However, as a practitioner of the female-affirming, Yayoi period female medium tradition that survives in the Ryûkyû Islands, Himiko most likely ritually managed both high and low spirits.

During China's Northern and Southern dynasties (439–589), the religious Taoist tradition became increasingly interested in the ritual management of dark spirits (kuei-shen) (Mizoguchi 2001: 266). Details regarding their realm of existence, methods of blocking their unhealthful influence on the living, and ritual means by which these dark, low spirits could be redeemed became popular topics of inquiry (Mizoguchi 2001: 266–67). From an orthodox Confucian standpoint, this raging Taoist preoccupation with disembodied spirits was a wholly superstitious venture.

The T'ang dynasty (618–907) became an era in which China experienced new heights of achievement in many fields, including a revival in interest in the early classic texts. The Confucian scholar Kung Ying-ta (574–648) and others in his coterie were at the forefront in the textual interpretation of bright and dark spirits (Mizoguchi 2001: 266). Kung identified dark spirits with yin ch'i and bright spirits with yang ch'i, as had Wang Chung (Mizoguchi 2001:

266). "Matter is produced by coalescence, and by dispersal it dies. This all is the work of dark and bright spirits" commented Kung (Mizoguchi 2001: 266). In addition, he equated ghosts and spirits with "changes in the four seasons, and the production of all creation" (Mizoguchi 2001: 266).

Ch'eng I (1033–1107), a Confucian scholar of the Northern Sung dynasty (Kim 2000: 1) went a step further, equating dark and bright spirits with a Creator, perhaps even a Great Mother figure. Ch'eng writes, "Bright spirits and dark spirits are the operation of Heaven (yang) and Earth (yin), the traces of Mother Nature (*tsao hua*)" (Liang 1972: 1102; Mizoguchi 2001: 269). The term "Mother Nature" is an appropriate English translation of "creative change," the creating and nourishing of all aspects of the cosmos, and the Wielder of those powers (Ogawa 1986: 999). From a Confucian perspective, this Creator should be a completely impersonal force, thus the distant term "creative change." From a Yin-Yang cosmology (Taoist) perspective, however, as mentioned in Chapter Four, this coordinating force in the natural world is the Way (Tao). For Lao-tse in the *Classic of the Way and its Power*, this Creator is decidedly Female and is characterized as the great and primal Mother. Ch'eng I articulated aspects of the Feminine archetype in a cool, unimpassioned manner. But, his intellectual descendant Chu Hsi subsequently articulated the dual character of the Feminine archetype even more accurately although from a similarly detached, Confucian perspective.

Another predecessor of the Chu Hsi's work was the Northern Sung, Confucian philosopher, Chang Tsai (1020–1077) (Kim 2000: 6). Chang defined dark spirits as being "the principle of retreating and shrinking" yin force, while bright spirits he linked with "the principle of emerging and expanding" yang energy (Mizoguchi 2001: 269). This interpretation closely presages the philosophical contributions that Chu Hsi would make.

Chu Hsi (1130–1200) created a powerful dichotomy based on the concepts of dark spirit and bright spirit, the ramifications of which still permeate thought in East Asia. His Neo-Confucian worldview presented the realm of nature as simply being dark spirits and bright spirits (Mizoguchi 2001: 269). Chu Hsi interpreted natural phenomena, a thunderstorm, for example, as being a combination of dark spirit and bright spirit realities (Mizoguchi 2001: 269). Natural phenomena emerging from the Unseen Realm denote bright spirits; concluding events of return are dark spirits (Mizoguchi 2001: 269). Elaborating on Wang Chung's observations made eleven centuries earlier, Chu Hsi articulated a vital dichotomy based on dark spirits and bright spirits that exercised great influence over the development of the notion of kami in Japan.

Chu Hsi's dark spirit concept influenced the development of low spirit notions in Japan. Dark spirits are associated with the yin soul (p'o), or the gross physical matter comprising the human body. They are equated with the earth and the return of the physical form to the earth in death. Having returned to the Unseen Realm, low spirits are indicative of shrinking and withdrawal. Low spirits are associated with inauspicious rites that are focused on the grave site (Mizoguchi 2001: 270). On the other hand, bright spirits become high spirits in Japan, macrocosmic manifestations of the yang soul (hun), and the circulating ch'i associated with breath in the body. High spirits represent heaven and emergence from that Unseen Realm in birth. Yang spirits are equated with arrival and expansion, and are addressed in auspicious rituals that, in China, focused on the familial ancestral hall (*miao*) (Mizoguchi 2001: 270).

Chu Hsi's definitions had far-reaching ramifications on ritual life in Japan. In short, Chu Hsi's dark spirit concept has greatly influenced Buddhist ancestor ritual in Japan. In Japanese mortuary ritual, managing 1) the physical remains of the newly, familial deceased and 2) the spirits of the relationless threatening dead, particularly since the Edo period, has become the provenience of Buddhism and temples (La Fleur 1992: 79–82). Non-celebratory (*medetakunai*), funeral events are hedged about by taboos, and have little to do with kami ritual or shrines. As noted earlier, performance of Buddhist rites, at the grave and in the home, ushers the deceased spirit forward in a process toward a state of greater purity: the state of high spirit. Buddhist rites in Japan, memorial services for relationless spirits (*segakie*) for example, are designed to deliver these beings from their state of limbo and concomitantly are calculated to negate the menace they present to the mortal community. Ultimately, apprehensions surrounding dark and low spirits, projections of the Terrible Mother figure, are, in turn, a projection of apprehensions surrounding disintegration of physical form and return to the earth. Boundaries and change are particularly indicative of relationless (unvenerated) low spirits that are identified in Japan (and East Asia) with forces that threaten both the individual and society.

In Japan, rituals performed at life-enhancing, celebratory (*medetai*) rites of passage have become the prime responsibility of Shintô shrines. For Chu Hsi, birth and other rites of passage indicative of emergence are phenomena linked to bright spirits (shen). In Japan, high spirits (kami) are equated with and petitioned at these types of life course events. Purified by means of Buddhist ritual, spirits of contented ancestors in Japan are incorporated into the cycle of high spirits that emerge into and animate all features of the seen realm. Rather than at the familial ancestral halls of Chinese ritual form, high spirit ritual in Japan is observed at shrines or in other Shintô ritual contexts. Regardless, rituals focused on China's bright spirits and Japan's high spirits address entities equated with heaven that bless the living, and both sets of ritual serve to reconfirm community and familial solidarity. Well-defined phenomena and constancy are cognitively linked in Japan with the content ancestral, high spirits that are beneficial to life and the maintenance of social ties and order.

NOTES

1. This is most certainly an outgrowth of the overwhelming emphasis placed by the Tokugawa shôguns on Buddhist ancestor and funerary rites as an institutional means of thwarting Catholic influences during the Edo period. (see La Fleur 1992: 79–82)

2. The name tao-t'ieh signifies a "legendary ferocious animal," or a glutton (Liang 1972: 1234). The name is associated with a composite, stylized motif found on Shang ritual bronze vessels (Cheng 1986: 84–90), said by some scholars to be a "baleful demon" and "guardian of boundaries," or by others to be a representation of all creatures fused into a single entity (Blunden 1998: 60, 73, 76,). Mizoguchi theorizes that the tao-t'ieh figure was a mask worn as a means of representing ancestral spirits for purpose of offering rites to them (2001: 263). Joseph Campbell asserts that the tao-t'ieh is indicative of the Feminine principle equated with earth, a "symbol of the consuming power of Mother Earth" shown devouring the life she created (1975: 120–21, 126–27, 128). I concur with Campbell that this motif emphasizes the Feminine's devouring aspect.

3. Japanese demons (oni) are graphically displayed with aspects of both cow and tiger symbolizing the Demon Gate, which according to Ommyôdô cosmology is the conjunction of the earthly branches corresponding to cow (twelfth lunar month) and tiger (first lunar month). See Figure 4.8.

4. Profane language in English, for example, revolves around effluvia, sex, death, and deity. Verbal manipulation of these four marginal realms represents socially-confrontational action that places the speaker on the margins of civil confines in an attempt to privilege the individual's position *vis-à-vis* the cognitive structures of social expectations. Such action represents a bid to disintegrate structures of social order in order to acquire for the speaker added prestige and access to benefits the person feels lie beyond their reach within the normal (temporary or long-term) pattern of society. Social presentation of profane language is an action calculated to convert (disintegrate) social power into individual power. The individual's own perceived state of weakness, and thus desire to augment their personal position by use of profanity, are positively correlated.

5. Joseph Campbell interprets the serpent and pillar as emblems of transcending death, either through endless physical "reincarnation" as found in the lunar cycle, or through a "leap from Moon to Sun consciousness" where physical limitations are left behind in a realm of "undiminishing light" (1974: 22, 298–300). The first, lunar pattern seems in keeping with the female medium tradition of Japan, while the latter image of sun centeredness is more indicative of the male priest tradition that presides at Hakozaki. Serpent and pillar are signs that signify transcendence beyond the duality obstacles of life and death, spirit and matter (Campbell 1974: 89, 298, 300).

6. At present, the placement of the Grand Ise Shrine's central spirit pillar (shin-nomihashira) in the earth takes place after all construction is finished, but this is a relatively new development (Nitschke 1993: 17–18). At some point in history, the pillar at the Inner Shrine was completely sunken in keeping with the cognitive image of inside, as opposed to the image of outside for the Outer Shrine.

Chapter Six

Hakozaki's Spirit Tree

Founded in 921 A.D., the Hakozaki Hachiman Shrine located in the East Ward of Fukuoka has endured for more than a millennium (see Photo 6.1). As a center of ritual practice, it has enjoyed periods of prosperity and decline, rebounded from the shocks of two attempted, thirteenth century Mongol invasions, and weathered the Second World War. According to shrine priests, the present era is a more precarious age than any heretofore known. For centuries the Hakozaki Shrine maintained its unchallenged position as a cognitive center for the local community. But, in the present Heisei era, the pace of life has quickened. High rise apartment buildings have heralded a new urban restructuring of the locality. Intergenerational families are no longer the norm. The demand for priestly rituals is not as strong as in the remembered past, juvenile delinquency and crime rates have increased, and fewer persons seem to identify with the composite worldview the shrine presents. The challenge of maintaining the local public's economic support of the shrine is a matter that weighs heavily on the minds of the present-day Tamura lineage of priests whose family has managed the shrine for 52 generations.

Their family name originally was Hata, a powerful Korean clan that immigrated to Japan in the late third century (Papinot 1988: 144). At a later date, this name was changed to Murata. In 1336, during a military campaign pursued by Ashikaga Takauji in Kyûshû, the Chief Priest Murata Shigenari at Hakozaki sent reinforcements to the nearby Tatara River and helped Takauji prevail over the Kikuchi clan (Hirowata 1999: 89). As a gesture of gratitude, the first Ashikaga shôgun Takauji awarded the shrine new landholdings but inadvertently reversed the order of the characters in the family name, turning "Murata" into "Tamura." Coming from the hand of this powerful warrior, even though the new name was a mistake, the family became Tamura.

Photo 6.1.   The Hakozaki shrine grounds

Under ideal circumstances, all kami shrines have a physical lane of access to a region symbolic of the Unseen Realm. These lanes of access, typically either a path or approach, link a shrine with a sacred mountain, cave or tumulus, ocean or any other remote region which cognitively serves as an interstice leading into the Unseen Realm. At Hakozaki, this interstitial location is marked by the "other dimension shrine" (*otabisho*). At Hakozaki, the prime lane of access to the Other World is the shrine approach that connects the shrine precincts with the sacred beach on Hakata Bay. A permanent feature on the shrine beach is a large wooden plaque engraved with the inscription, "[This is a] sacred place" (*shinsei-dokoro*) (see Photo 6.2).

SPIRITS ENSHRINED AT HAKOZAKI

The Main Hall is Hakozaki's central shrine structure, a ritual stage controlled by the male priesthood (see Photo 6.3 and Figure 6.1). In the center bay of the Main Hall is enshrined Emperor Ôjin's mother, the female warrior, Empress Jingû. Residing in the right bay, on the west end, is Tamayorihime. In the extreme left bay, on the east end, lodges Emperor Ôjin (see Figure 6.2). Both legend and ritual surrounding the triad of deities enshrined at Hakozaki appear to be firmly structured in terms of Ommyôdô cosmological principles. In fact, Hakozaki's three

Photo 6.2.   The shrine beach

main spirits bear more than a passing resemblance to three directional deities popular in early China. Emperor Ôjin appears to be related to the Chinese King Sire of the East (*Tung-wang-kung*), the androgynous Empress Jingû corresponds to both the Lord of the Northern Dipper (*Pei-tou-hsing-chun*) AND the Mother of the Northern Dipper (*Tou-mu-yuan-chun*), and Tamayorihime seems to be a Japanese variant of the Queen Mother of the West (*Hsi-wang-mu*). For this particular shrine in northern Kyûshû, the influence of Taoist cosmology is marked.

Emperor Ôjin

The formulation of Hakozaki's Ôjin lore and ritual are squarely based on the worldview of Ommyôdô; in short, Ôjin appears to be a personification of the second of the Eight Trigrams, "the Initiating." According to the Later Heaven Sequence, "the Initiating" corresponds to east, dawn, eldest son, rabbit, the spring equinox, and wood (Baynes 1967: 274, 276; Okada 1993: 137). In terms of yin and yang, *dawn* is the point of growing yang force, in other words, of increasing light and warmth. In similar fashion, *spring equinox* is also a time of waxing warmth and light that heralds the emergence of new life from the earth. East is the direction from which the sun, the "great yang" emerges at dawn. Emerging yang force is further indicative of a male, the Emperor Ôjin. From an Ommyôdô perspective, the Emperor's birthday is of

Photo 6.3.   The Main Hall

Figure 6.1.   Hakozaki Shrine Precincts

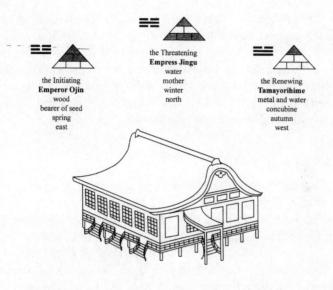

the Initiating
Emperor Ojin
wood
bearer of seed
spring
east

the Threatening
Empress Jingu
water
mother
winter
north

the Renewing
Tamayorihime
metal and water
concubine
autumn
west

KEY yin = two broken lines or dark sections in a triangle
yang = a whole line or light sections in a triangle
These triangles and groups of lines illustrate concentrations of yin and yang in each trigram.
The bottom line of each figure is most dominant; the top line is least dominant.

Figure 6.2. Hakozaki's Three Main Spirits

prime significance: according to the *Nihon Shoki* (Aston 1972: 232), and also according to shrine legend at Hakozaki, Emperor Ôjin was born on the fourteenth day of the twelfth lunar month (ox month) in the year 200 A.D (metal dragon year). This point in the lunar cycle (14th day) is the maximum point of continuing yang development before the fifteenth day when yang light reaches its extreme and begins to wane. Given this shrine-transmitted day of birth, Emperor Ôjin is an embodiment of maximal yang fruition that is still gathering strength. This and vigorous, waxing corporeal development as signified by the fleshy ox (his birth month), and dragon (birth year) also indicates flourishing life energy (see Okada 1993: 137).

A major Rite of Celebration, Hakozaki's First Rabbit Rite, takes place just prior to the spring equinox. This ritual celebrates the ascendancy of Empress Jingû's *eldest son*, Ôjin, as bearer of seed and fecundator of earth and womb. Finally, relating to *wood*, Ôjin is also equated with the shrine's divine pine tree, the Box Pine (*hakomatsu*), where legend says that his placenta and umbilical cord were buried following his birth. Priests and parishioners venerate the tree as sacred; this ritual attention is recognition that Ôjin is represented in this living wood.

Emperor Ôjin is also equated with New Year's and the spring equinox. Rites of Celebration at theses times are rituals directed by Hakozaki's male priesthood, focused on major junctures in the annual solar cycle that extol the virile, yang-bearing Emperor Ôjin as bearer of seed that initiates abundant births and harvests. Later in this chapter, in the section devoted to the spring equinox observance of the First Rabbit Rite, Emperor Ôjin's correlation to the trigram "the Initiating" will be explored further.

Empress Jingû

Empress Jingû, the mother of Emperor Ôjin, appears to be a personification of the last of the Eight Trigrams, "the Threatening." Legends surrounding Empress Jingû bear out her unusual affinity with and power over water; Hakozaki myth relates that this is due to her having been granted the "ebb and flow jewels" by Ryûjin, dragon king of the sea (Hakozaki-gû 1928: 44, 46). Following her husband's death, Empress Jingû levied troops, crossed the ocean, and subjugated the Korean state of Silla thanks to the intervention of kindly sea spirits (Philippi 1968: 262–63). Before departing Kyûshû for her military conquest in Korea, the Empress discovered by divine oracle that she was with a male child who legend relates she kept from being born on her expedition by tying stones around her abdomen (Philippi 1968: 260, 264).

The First Rabbit Rite, observed just prior to the winter solstice marks the ascendancy of threatening yin, darkness, and water equated with Empress Jingû. This rite, celebrates the relationship of Empress Jingû as mother, bearer of the baby Ôjin. At this juncture, too, the Box Pine receives ritual attention as the location where the placenta and umbilical cord uniting the dark mother and life-bearing son rest. Empress Jingû's connection with "the Threatening" trigram will be examined further in the section of this chapter devoted to the winter solstice observance of the First Rabbit Rite.

Tamayorihime

Residing in the right bay, on the west end, is Tamayorihime whose name means the "Female (*hime*) [from whom the] spirits (*tama*) come (*yori*)." Yanagita Kunio identifies this name as an epithet for a female medium (Blacker 1975: 118), but Tamayorihime signifies much more. Priests at Hakozaki explain that they do not know why this kami is enshrined at their shrine, but some feel that she was originally a sea spirit (*uminokami*) that was anciently served at this locality and was superseded by the advent of the Ôjin tradition. The use of sacred beach sand at Hakozaki, which will be outlined in the following annual rituals, is strikingly similar to the use of birth-soil in

Dunang. It is this similarity that allows for a connection to be made between the sea spirit Nira in the island of Dunang and the sea spirit Tamayorihime at Hakozaki. The evidence for this connection is overwhelming.

According to *Kojiki* and *Nihon Shoki* accounts, Tamayorihime is a daughter of the chief sea spirit and came to land from beneath the waves, from the Other World of Tokoyo (see Philippi 1968: 157). She served as the wet nurse for her sister, Toyotamahime's son born on the beach; Tamayorihime later married this foster child and bore him five sons, including the Emperor Jimmu (see Philippi 1968: 157, 159). The names of her four sons, recorded in the *Kojiki*, are each related to food production.[1] While this union of aunt and nephew created great moral furor in some quarters during the Edo period (Philippi 1968: 159), Tamayorihime is first and foremost a projection of the Feminine archetype, simultaneously nourishing and procreating with mankind; her ocean origin is an indication that she is the Great Mother. Tamayorihime is routinely petitioned for: marriage, safe birth, bringing good luck and averting disaster, and safe sea travel (Abe 1992: 185). Including the food production indicated by the names of her sons, she presides over the essence of Yayoi period ritual concerning fruition (medetasa): 1) agricultural production and 2) offspring, both made possible by the reemergence of life-giving high spirits (kami/ ancestors). In keeping with the aim for which birth-soil is ritually used, Tamayorihime is also petitioned for good luck and protection from mishap, in day-to-day life. Like Nira, she is equated with the ocean, and grants safety to travelers in her realm of waves.

Although the formally enshrined aspect of Tamayorihime appears to be beneficent and indicative of the Good Mother, the peripheral shrine complexes at Hakozaki indicate she possesses a more sinister side, too. The peripheral shrine complexes are divided into two parts, the East Shrine and the West Shrine. The East Shrine corresponds to the east bay of Hakozaki's Main Hall: the male, Emperor Ôjin. The West Shrine is cognitively linked to the Main Hall's west bay: the female Tamayorihime, the Female archetype in both its Good and Terrible aspects. Tamayorihime appears to be a personification of "the Renewing;" this will be explored further at the end of this chapter.

Peripheral Shrine Spirits

Behind the main hall are peripheral shrine complexes which are divided into two parts, the East Shrine and the West Shrine (see Photos 6.4 and 6.5). Shrine priests have used Ommyôdô cosmology in the organization of the Main Hall and peripheral shrines to accentuate Yayoi period ritual concerns; this knowledge is crucial to understanding the ritual universe at Hakozaki. Both shrines are cognitively constructed to grant petitions related to *both* fruition and protection (the

Great Mother possesses a dual nature); but the East Shrine, corresponding to yang, male offspring, deals more prominently with issues of fruition while the West Shrine, corresponding to yin and the Terrible Mother, is slightly more devoted to protection concerns.[2] The threatening aspect of the Feminine archetype is further evidenced in the West Shrine since petitions that might excite the devouring aspect, including childbirth and illness, are not located in the West Shrine, but instead in the life-giving East Shrine. Furthermore, the West shrine's focus on protection involves a cognitive entreaty to the Terrible Mother to grant safe passage across boundaries, the very areas at which her threatening powers are encountered.

There are five bays in each of the peripheral shrine complexes, and a directory before each structure records the names of the kami enshrined and delineates the petitions each spirit grants. In total, nineteen spirits (eight female and eleven male) are enshrined in the bays of the East Shrine and twenty-five (ten female and fifteen male) in the bays of the West Shrine. Both East and West Shrines contain even numbers of enshrined female spirits (eight in the East and ten in the West). Odd numbers of male kami outnumber the females in both shrines (eleven in the East and fifteen in the West). Even numbers are indicative of yin and odd numbers emblematic of yang. Obviously, Ommyôdô ideas are in evidence in the peripheral shrines, both in the numbers *vis-à-vis* the gender of kami, and also in the majority of male spirits which denote petitions for a preponderance of life and fruition (yang).

Photo 6.4.   The East peripheral shrine complex

Photo 6.5.   The West peripheral shrine complex

While no overtly threatening entities are housed in the East Shrine complex, the West Shrine contains three spirits that are potential sources of disquiet, indicative of the Terrible Mother. Emperor Chûai, the father of Emperor Ôjin, is enshrined in the West. According to the *Kojiki*, Chûai sought the will of the kami in his expedition against rebel states, but upon receiving an oracle, he pronounced the words deceitful and was immediately struck dead (see Philippi 1968: 257–58). His untimely demise, having the potential to make him an unhappy spirit, seems indicative of the easily offended, dangerous nature of the Terrible Mother. Enshrined in the West, Izanami, the female kami who with her husband Izanagi created the islands of Japan by their procreative endeavor, early on displayed qualities of the Good Mother. But following her untimely death, and being offended by her husband in the underworld, Izanami becomes the vengeful "Great Kami of the Underworld" who takes the lives of the living each day (see Philippi 1968: 61–66). Izanami most clearly presents the duality of the Great Mother within ancient Japanese myth: on the one hand, beautiful agent of fruition, but on the other, the heartless snatcher of souls.

The third entity, Magatsukami, is the most sinister being yet to be considered in the West Shrine. Following his return from the underworld and divorce with Izanami, Izanagi bathed, and from the impurities on his person came into existence two terrible kami, the "Abundant-Misfortune-Working-Spirit" and the "Great-Misfortune-Working-Spirit" (see Philippi

1968: 69, 544, 640–41). For priests at Hakozaki, the name Magatsukami is used to indicate both of these threatening spirits. Whereas Yayoi era ritual focuses on fruition and protection from injury, Magatsukami is identified at Hakozaki as the cognitive source of all misfortune. From a mythological standpoint, originating in the impurities of the underworld, Magatsukami seems to be the embodiment of weakness, blood, and injury that excite the predatory aspect of the Terrible Mother. But given the significance of the name Magatsukami itself, this entity appears to be the unmitigated terrible aspect of the Great Mother herself. The term "misfortune" (*maga*) in this name literally denotes: twisted, bent, crooked, awry, warped, perverted, wicked, evil, vicious; as a verb (magaru) to oppress, to persecute, to entrap, and to ensnare (see Ogawa 1986: 492). For priests at Hakozaki, the Terrible Mother is recognized as the lurking evil spirit, Magatsukami — the twisted, or evil spirit, a malevolent kami born from impurities when Izanagi washed his body after return from the underworld (see Philippi 1968).

ANNUAL RITUALS AT HAKOZAKI

Kami tradition ritual at the present is a product of both Yayoi period and Ommyôdô cosmologies. Both tension and synergy characterize the relationship between these sets of ideas. At the Hakozaki Hachiman Shrine, three classes of rituals are focused on reducing apprehension regarding the Feminine archetype and are structured according to Yin-Yang Five Phase cosmology as it relates to temporal interstices: 1) Rites of Major Exorcism, 2) Yang Earth Rites, and 3) Rites of Celebration. These rituals preserve three aspects of Yayoi ritual concerns: a) soil release, b) ransom, and c) celebration/invocation of fruition (i.e. abundant crops and offspring).

In terms of the Feminine archetype, Rites of Major Exorcism (*ôharai*) are events at which extreme rituals of separation sever ties with the Terrible Mother and ransom the human community from her grasp at the two most threatening temporal interstices in the Yin-Yang Five Phase cosmology: the annual Demon Gate and Human Gate. Yang Earth Rites serve to ransom and protect the local community by creating links with the Good Mother at four Yin-Yang Five Phase cosmology interstices: near the monthly Demon Gate (first of the month) and Human Gate (fifteenth of the month) junctures, and also at the spring and autumn equinoxes. Rites of Celebration function as celebratory petitions for the bounty of the Good Mother at the following Ommyôdô calendar junctures: near the annual Demon Gate, the winter solstice, and the spring and autumn equinoxes.

It seems clear that interstices in time, as determined by Yin-Yang Five Phase cosmology, are marked with major rituals at Hakozaki; but on a deeper level, these shrine rituals are based on the Yayoi period Feminine archetype, a mixture of both the reassuring and the unnerving. For this reason, kami rites always employ exorcism to cognitively dismiss all that is disquieting before invoking the beneficent. Quite often, informants speak of these menacing and protective influences as being bad spirits and good spirits (kami), or as simply misfortune or blessing, but all of these concepts arise from the major cognitive constellation of Great Mother, which in turn is comprised of the joint aspects of the Feminine archetype: earth and female.

THE GREAT EXORCISM

The Great Exorcism is conducted to dispel major apprehensions that threaten to overturn the entire male-centered, Ommyôdô cognitive system. It is observed at the annual Demon Gate conjunction, the last day of the old year (S 12/31, originally L 12/30), and at the annual Human (or Rear Demon) Gate point, the last day of the first half of the year (S 6/30, originally L 6/30) (see Photo 6.6). As the termination of temporal cycles, they represent significant junctures at which human beings, since ancient times, have

Photo 6.6.   Priests gather before the Great Exorcism

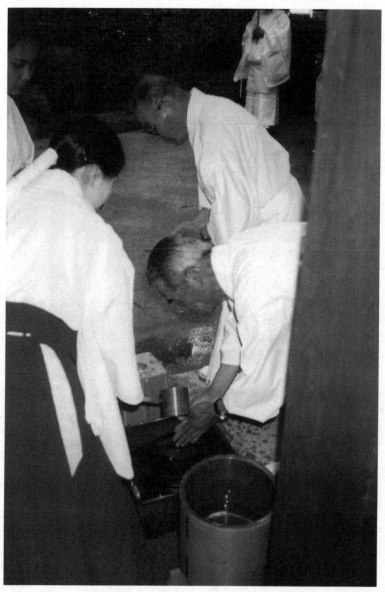

Photo 6.7.   Purification at the Great Exorcism

ritually "fought for and won" the renewal of both time and topocosmic life energy (Gaster 1961: 23, 37–38). The Great Exorcism represents a ritual form of "emptying" (*kenosis*) by means of which the human community seeks to purge itself of collective impurity as a means of assuring renewal of time and the topocosm (Gaster 1961: 23, 25). According to the Later Heaven Sequence of the Eight Trigrams, year-end and mid-year Rites of Major Exorcism at Hakozaki represent the greatest concentrations of yin force (*kegare*), junctures in the annual ritual cycle at which the pull of the Terrible Mother is at its strongest. These rituals are some of Hakozaki's most tersely constructed and efficient, severing relations with the threatening Feminine aspect in a manner that preserves Yayoi era concerns with a strong Ommyôdô component (see Photo 6.7).

The main approach leading to the precincts of the Hakozaki Shrine originates at a small beach facing Hakata Bay. The sacred sand (birth-soil) of this beach is an extremely important ritual feature at Hakozaki. It fulfills an important function at the Great Exorcism which priests at Hakozaki explain has the effect of clearing away all the impurities committed within the shrine parish during the preceding six months. The Great Exorcism, unlike most other priest-led rituals which occur before the Main Hall, is conducted *outside* of the inner shrine enclosure, in the partitionless Hall of Votive Tablets (*emaden*). This rite is regularly attended by roughly forty individuals consisting of priests, parishioners, and shrine maidens.

The ritual is impressive because of its brevity and simplicity. First, a small handful of sacred beach sand wrapped in a packet of crisply-folded, thick, white Japanese paper (*washi*) is distributed to each of the attendees, beginning with the priests and ending with the shrine maidens. Next, after rising from their camp stools the attendees bow their heads as a priest pronounces "words of respect" (*haishi*) to the kami.[3] This text is known as the Words of Great Exorcism (*ôharai no kotoba*). All but the priest delivering "generation-invoking words" remain silent during the recitation, except at two points during the delivery when the priest intones a low, cadencing "oh" and the audience echoes this cry in unison. Once more, at the text's conclusion, this echoing exclamation is repeated. Everyone is then seated.

At the conducting priest's signal, all arise. Each participant then opens the packet of birth-soil, and loosely sprinkles the coarse sand over his or her own body. Having done so, some lightly brush off their bodies with their hands; others simply retake their seat. The sprinkling of sand over oneself and then brushing it away is stunning in effect; for me, it brought about a feeling of being newly cleansed and refreshed.

Another priest rises, and from the ritual table on the west of the hall, removes a large, beautifully symmetrical branch of sakaki evergreen. From the branch hang slender, zigzag streamers of cut paper (*shide*) whose shape is vaguely reminiscent of bolts of lightning. This branch is also tied with hemp fibers. All arise. Facing the ritual table, the priest first bows, then holds the branch in front of his body and snaps it to the left, to the right, and then back to the left in quick succession, using the branch to perform an exorcism. He bows again toward the ritual table. Next, coming near the assembled group and facing the northeast, Demon Gate direction, he repeats the sakaki ever-green exorcism. He then uses the wand to exorcise the priests who stand as a group and lower their heads before he begins. Next, the parishioners and shrine maidens stand and lower their heads before receiving the exorcism. The sakaki evergreen is then replaced in an upright position in its ritual stand as the group resumes its seats. A priest then collects the empty paper wrap-pers that held the sacred beach sand, placing them on a wooden ritual offer-ing stand (*sambô*), which he then returns to the ritual table.

A priest moves to the front of the ritual table and bows toward it in a pre-cise manner. From under the stand he removes a wooden chest (*karahitsu*). He removes its top. Into this receptacle he deposits the empty paper wrappers. Then, taking the sakaki evergreen branch from the ritual stand and holding it in front of and parallel to his body, suddenly and deliberately, he rips the branches from it, turning it until they are all removed. When only the bare wand remains, he breaks it forcefully in half, depositing all of the remains in the open chest. From a wooden ritual offering stand on the ritual table he re-moves a long, folded, white paper packet. Unfolding it, he removes a long length of bleached white cloth (*sarashi*). Holding the cloth in front of his body in both hands, he pauses. Then, sharp, ripping sounds are heard as the cloth is torn asunder eight times. The shredded cloth is then returned to its folded paper envelope, which he places into the wooden chest. After replac-ing the top, he sets the chest back underneath the ritual table. He arranges the ritual offerings stands in an orderly manner near the center of the table, un-hurriedly bows toward the table, and then returns to his seat.

A young priest then rises and approaches the Chief Priest of the shrine (*gûji*), who is seated in the position nearest the ritual stand, and escorts him from the hall. The priests in order of their rank follow the Chief Priest out of the hall in a single line. The parishioners then join the line, followed closely by the shrine maidens. They all make their way back to the enclosed area at the formal entryway to the shrine office where all the attendees had assem-bled before the rite began. Assuming the same order in which they stood prior to the rite, the chief priest offers his formal greetings to the group. After this, shrine maidens, standing under the purple, ceremonial bunting emblazoned with the sixteen-petal imperial chrysanthemum crest hanging in the main en-try, pour rice wine (*omiki*) that had previously been offered to the kami. The maidens also distribute pairs of red and white, dry rice flour sweets (*higashi*) to the parishioners before they leave the shrine grounds to return home; with this, the Great Exorcism comes to an end.

The Great Exorcism: 1) addresses boundary apprehensions which originate in the Yayoi period worldview and also in Yin-Yang Five Phase thought and 2) employs a set of ritual practices structured in terms of both traditions. In keeping with Yayoi period cosmology, earth ritual is central to the Great Exorcism, and to ritual life at Hakozaki in general. Birth-soil is the permeable body of the Great Mother, the substance employed to effect a soil-release from misfortune.[4] It symbolizes high spirits and the Good Mother who gives birth to all life—an image in direct opposition to the devouring quality of the Terrible Mother. As in Dunang, proper soil ritual must be performed at interstices to pacify the Mother, to cleanse, to legitimate passage, and to avoid predation. Individual life-souls are a significant cognitive factor unifying persons with the matrix (the overarching spiritual conglomerate) of the Feminine archetype. Although the existence of life-souls is not explicitly recognized by practitioners at Hakozaki, rituals of soil release, or permission to negotiate boundaries, employing birth-soil (*oshioi, ubusuna*) are performed at particularly threatening junctures in time (and space). These rituals are recognized as a means of invoking the protection of good kami (the influences of the Good Mother) and as an exorcism of misfortune (the Terrible Mother). At the most serious rituals at Hakozaki, sacred beach sand signifies a rebirth. Parishioners of the Hakozaki Shrine, like residents of Dunang, carry birth-soil with them when traveling abroad. Doing so invokes the protection of the local kami and maintains a link with the Good Mother of the topocosm; maintaining this link avoids her transformation into a hungry presence that desires to prematurely reincorporate them into the locality. The Hakozaki Shrine is conspicuously linked to Hakata Bay and, even though local persons do not presently speak of a Nira-being of the depths who preys upon the living, birth-soil rituals appear to serve a pacifying and ransoming function as do similar rituals in the Ryûkyûs.

Following ritual use of local birth-soil, sakaki evergreen exorcism is employed to further rid the community and topocosm of impurities that would make it a potential prey for the Terrible Mother. A bough of evergreen assists in ridding the topocosm of decay and represents a petition for continuing vibrant life energy. Evergreens are credited with this power because anciently evergreens were known as "eternally celebratory trees" (tokiwagi) (Matsumura 1987: 831); this name suggests the image of unabating life and development. With this evergreen, the most cognitively threatening feature according to Yin-Yang Five Phase cosmology is cleansed: the spatial equivalent of the Demon Gate, the northeast quadrant of the compass. Senior priests at

Hakozaki recognize this practice to be an Ommyôdô means of exorcising yin earth spirits which threaten at the year-end and mid-year Demon Gate and Human Gate, the most significant interstices of the entire annual ritual cycle, in terms of ritual apprehension. Being the most dangerous boundaries, they constitute the highest magnitude of threat, which in turn, dictates the Great Exorcism be held *outside* of the normal ritual space before the Main Hall. This separate, temporary location signals the different nature of the Great Exorcism and the delicacy of the situation.

The Great Exorcism is fraught with rituals of separation from low (yin earth) spirits, the influence of the Terrible Mother, and with dissolution. All that is not life-promoting (yang) is purged with words of respect, the use of birth-soil, and with the bough of the eternally celebratory (evergreen) tree. The evergreen bough, sullied with adhering impurities, is destroyed lest the accumulated life-sapping (yin) forces of anti-structure that threaten social order combine and continue to function unthwarted. The white cloth is torn asunder a total of eight times (in kami ritual practice, eight signifies myriad, or infinitude), thereby purging the countless improprieties of the community. In terms of homonym suggestion, the exorcism (*harau*) is also sweeping away of impurity; and the eight-fold rending (*saku*) signifies manifold levels of separation. Together with the orderly garnering away (*osameru*) of the spent items which is emblematic of order preservation, the integrity of yin earth spirits is sufficiently compromised and all ties with the threatening Terrible Mother are ritually severed. This separation is further emphasized by the complete lack of food offerings during the Great Exorcism. All other rituals at Hakozaki include the presentation of food offerings to appease the beneficent kami and to seal a joint relationship with the shrine community. No food is offered at the Great Exorcism in a deliberate bid to break ties with the influence of the Terrible Mother.

A meal of rapport (*naorai*) at the end of the Great Exorcism takes place visually and spatially removed from the location where the main rite took place, signifying a break with the threatening forces that were the focus of exorcism. Instead, the meal cements a relationship with life-promoting, high spirits, projections of the archetypal Good Mother and generative life energy. In keeping with Yayoi period practices, rice wine, an embodiment of the life-giving ancestors, is partaken of to renew an ongoing relationship with these sources of corporeal vitality. The white and red rice flour sweets, on the other hand, are Ommyôdô talismans of good fortune; white signifies yin and red stands for yang. Paired together, they are emblematic of a balance of these complementary forces. According to Ommyôdô thought, a balance of yin and yang denotes the optimum, a state of health and harmony. The cakes are each formed in the shape of the sixteen-petal chrysanthemum, the Japanese emperor's crest (the privilege of using of this crest is due to the fact that Hakozaki's enshrined spirits include imperial family members, Empress Jingû and Emperor Ôjin). This yin-yang symbolism combined with the chrysanthemum (traditionally associated with long life) might suggest a petition for the longevity of yin-yang balance, a petition for the longevity of imperial reign, or even a petition for the parishioner's own longevity to be like that of Japan's continuing imperial line. At any rate, these sweets embody the three pillars of the kami tradition: they establish a relationship with the ancestors (kami), they are made of the ancestors' essence (rice), and they bear the crest of the "ancestor manifest in human form," the emperor.

YANG EARTH RITES

A second class of ritual at Hakozaki, Yang Earth Rites, are occasions of intermediate exorcism that reveal tensions between the Emperor Ôjin-focused, Ommyôdô structured rites and the even earlier traditions preserved at Hakozaki. The earlier ritual tradition is focused on a) the two peripheral shrine (*massha*) complexes located behind the shrine's main hall, b) the "other dimension shrine" (otabisho) near the shrine beach, c) the shrine beach, and d) earth, moon, and the Feminine archetype—a cognitive combination of both the disquieting Mother image in the West Shrine and the Good Mother associated with the East Shrine. The Ôjin tradition is oriented in terms of a) Hakozaki's Main Hall (*honden*), and b) heaven, sun, and the male Emperor Ôjin—associated with the Good Mother image in the East Shrine (as in Hatsu-u celebrated at the First Rabbit Rites at the winter solstice and spring equinox). At Hakozaki and in northern Kyûshû, at least, mainly male-centered, Ommyôdô rituals are conducted by male priests in prominent shrine complexes that politically, socially, and economically occupy significant and legitimate status in the community (see Photo 6.8). Women's rituals as observed in this section, on the other hand, while patronizing the male-dominated shrines and ritual, also preserve Female-centered rituals in more peripheral shrine locations, structured in terms of a more Yayoi period mode of cognition, one which addresses issues of female fertility on the first and the fifteenth of the month.

Yang Earth Rites are a mixed bag; they contain phases of Ommyôdô interstice apprehension, acknowledged in the figure of malevolent spirit, Magatsukami, in addition to the celebration of rising yang forces and the harmonious balance of yin and yang. This pattern obtains because the lunar month's first day (the new, dark moon) is a celebration of successful Demon Gate passage, and yet, is so near to this concentration of yin force that great celebration is

Photo 6.8.   Offering a petition before the Main Hall

still premature. The lunar month's fifteenth day is celebratory since this is the
extremity of yang light (full moon), but from this point, life energies will begin to decline with the waning moon.[5] Yang Earth Rites, observed at the first
and the fifteenth of each month, and also at the spring and autumn equinoxes
are times at which the sites associated with Tamayorihime—the beach, the
other dimension shrine, and the peripheral shrine complexes—become active.
The following Yang Earth Rites will be examined: 1) the gathering of sacred
beach sand at the spring and autumn equinoxes, 2) shrine-sponsored rites on
the 1st and 15th of each month, and 3) popular, non shrine-sponsored rites that
occur at the shrine or in the home on the 1st and 15th of each month. Bear in
mind that *all* the rituals we will examine in this section were previously observed according to the lunar calendar.[6]

Gathering Sacred Beach Sand

Birth-soil from the shrine beach is an important feature in ritual life at
Hakozaki. Not only does it figure prominently at the Great Exorcism, but also
during the equinoxes and at two points in the lunar cycle. Near both the spring
and autumn equinoxes, the rite of "gathering sacred beach sand" (*oshioi-tori*)
is observed. The day on which these rituals will occur is decided according to
the lunar calendar and is the closest yang earth (*tsuchi-no-e*) day to the spring
and autumn equinox. On these two special days each year, the sand is particularly sought after by practitioners for its power to avert accident and disaster. Incidentally, kami tradition practitioners most numerously gather birth-
soil, at the spring equinox and the 1st of the month (which will be examined
in the next section), times when yang forces are markedly in the ascendant
(see Photo 6.9).

At five o'clock on the morning of the rite, a short ritual is performed at the
beach by priests of the shrine. A large branch of sakaki, the preferred evergreen tree of kami ritual, is inserted near the top of a large cone of sand on
the beach, sand that will be distributed among parishioners who will arrive
throughout the day. One priest explains:

> That [branch of sakaki evergreen] is the kamisama. First, at five in the morning
> the kamisama favored us by descending [to the pile of sand] as we held a festi-
> val called "the rite of kami descent" (*kôshin-no-gi*). The descent and taking up
> abode here [on the sand] by the kami begins this festival. Then at about five this
> evening we will conduct "the rite of kami ascent" (*shôshin-no-gi*), at which time
> the kami will return to where they originated.

In 1996, during a typical spring gathering of sacred beach sand, both the
beach and grounds were thronged with visitors who had come to receive the

Photo 6.9.   Gathering birth-soil at the beach

sacred earth. Several of them were more than willing to share insights on the
tradition. A lady in her eighties had this to say:

> Today is the "birth-soil" day and it only happens one day in both spring and au-
> tumn. Down there [at the beach] there is sacred sand that the priests have exor-
> cised and purified which we humbly receive and take home. Then, when we go
> out of the house we sprinkle it [on ourselves] so there will be no mishap. And if
> we sprinkle it on plants, they will grow quickly. It only occurs once on a day in
> both spring and autumn, this festival. . . And there are small baskets made from
> bamboo to carry the sacred sand; you hang those at the entrance to the house
> (*genkansaki*) and before you go out, you sprinkle some on yourself. That's so
> there won't be any accident. If you use the sacred sand, it will smash all mis-
> fortune (*sainan*). This is a custom from long ago.

All other informants' explanations concurred, and some commented further that the beach sand averts evil and could be used for purification. One informant, when asked about the effectiveness of gathering and using the sand,
indicated that birth-soil day (shanichi) is found in the almanac (*koyomi*). Re-
spondents routinely identify birth-soil collected on life-promoting (yang)
earth days as a ritual means of avoiding: "accident, calamity, injury, misfortune, and mishap." Cognitively speaking, they use birth-soil in order to escape the predation of the Terrible Mother that lurks to maim and reincorpo-

rate the living. Spatial boundaries, such as the threshold to the home (where birth-soil is regularly used by practitioners), and even entrances to the main shrine grounds (see Photo 6.10), are cognitive portals of direct contact with the Terrible Mother. As such, they represent areas of existential danger, her "mouth" that gapes wide open. According to Ommyôdô thought, interstices are points where yin passes into yang, where the forces and realm of death merge into the realm of the living. The influence of the Terrible Mother is also exorcised by the Chief Priest at Hakozaki as he recites generation-invoking words on these mornings and which read in part, "Grant that there be no influence of the evil spirit Magatsukami in either our bodies or our homes, but rather with sound minds and healthy bodies encourage and increasingly stimulate each and every livelihood of the people." Pilgrims to the beach on these days also receive exorcism. Furthermore, a petition is offered that health, vigor, and safety may guard the local populace.

The gathering and use of sacred beach sand mimics the use of birth-soil in Dunang, and therefore hints at the existence of a female entity of the depths, an ambivalent Nira-like spirit. I assert that kami ritual at Hakozaki was centered on such a spirit, perhaps in the figure of Tamayorihime, before the enshrinement of Emperor Ôjin. Tamayorihime is an embodiment of the Feminine archetype; she is the Great Female that presides over the Other World. That other realm is a cognitive conglomeration of the womb, the field, and particularly at Hakozaki, the ocean depths; they all are inhabited by ancestor spirits (kami) that enter the everyday world, sometimes via the person of the medium—herself a microcosm of the larger Other World.

Hakozaki's shrine beach is a sacred place precisely because it represents the shrine's main point of access to the Unseen Realm from which the kami originate. Hakozaki's Yayoi period Other World lies beneath the waves. From an Ommyôdô, male priest perspective, visitation by the kami from the Unseen Realm at the equinoxes imparts power to the birth-soil at Hakozaki. The opening of the doors to the east and west peripheral shrine complexes behind the Main Hall, and the other dimension shrine near the shrine beach further signals this arrival of powers from beyond. On these yang earth days, the doors to the Other World are open.

The selection of these yang earth days near the equinoxes must have been carried out by priests who were much more familiar with the Ommyôdô structured calendar than many kami tradition practitioners are at the present. Birth-soil, representing the body of the Good Mother, may not always be life-giving, but gathering it on yang earth days (when the beneficent aspect of the Feminine is predominant) assures that only its life-giving and life-preserving aspects are active.[7] The equinoxes also add significance: yin and yang meet and are balanced at the equinox since night and day are of equal length. In

Photo 6.10.   Birth-soil near the entrance of the Hakozaki Shrine

terms of daily time, according to Yin-Yang Five Phase cosmology, the spring equinox is equated with east and six o'clock AM, sunrise; the autumn equinox to west and six o'clock PM and sunset. Shrine priests at Hakozaki welcome the kami to the beach at five o'clock AM, just before the "daily" spring equinox (6:00 AM), and they see the kami off from the beach just prior to the "daily" autumn equinox (6:00 PM). Additionally, at the equinoxes, sunset and sunrise occur precisely from the cardinal directions due east and due west. All of these combinations signify the life-bestowing properties of balanced yin and yang.

This harmonious meeting of yin and yang as evidenced at the equinoxes is cognitively central to kami tradition ritual practice and is labeled by the Japanese term *musubi*. This meeting of yin and yang is not insignificant; by kami tradition practitioners, it is held to be a synergistically creative phenomenon. "When the relative forces of yin and yang combine harmoniously, without fail, there will arise some new phenomena" (Kakuda 1972: 194). A focus on life-giving production (*medetasa*), arising from the congress of yin and yang (musubi), is the prime characteristic, function, and goal of Japan's kami tradition rituals; the beneficent aspect of the Great Mother is herein implied. This meeting of opposites at the equinoxes—of night and day, of west and east, of ocean and land, and of the ancestors and the living—makes available to the living the blessing of the kami, the life-extending powers of the Good Mother in the birth-soil at Hakozaki's shrine beach. This is the way in which practitioners consider and speak regarding Hakozaki's birth-soil.

Unique to Japanese Buddhism is the popular belief that ancestor spirits return to visit the living at the equinoxes (ohigan) (Okada 1993: 106–7). Japanese Buddhist thought identifies the equinoxes as "other shore" periods, other shore being the realm of the ancestors as opposed to "this shore" (*shigan*), the realm of the living. The equinoxes represent times at which the spirits from beyond, be they venerated according to Buddhist or kami tradition rites, reenter the world of the living. In Japan, three schools of thought appear united in outlook in this instance: Ommyôdô, Buddhist, and Shintô.

Shrine-sponsored Rites on the First and Fifteenth of Each Month

With the exception of the first morning of the New Year, priests at the Hakozaki Shrine hold a ritual called the "monthly ritual" (*tsukinamisai*) on the morning of the first and fifteenth of each month. This ritual, in previous times, was held at the new moon and the full moon junctures according to the lunar cycle. The new moon, as the juncture just past the monthly Demon Gate interstice of most threatening yin influence, represented the very beginning of yang development and the successful negotiation of the Demon Gate; the full moon represented the point at which yang light had reached its maximum. The monthly ritual is now observed according to the solar calendar on both the first and fifteenth; it is led by male priests in the central ritual space before the Main Hall.

This ritual is simple, lasting about thirty minutes, like many other rituals performed at the shrine. One feature that sets these bimonthly rites apart is that the exorcism which takes place prior to the ceremony does not originate in the space between the Veneration Hall (*haiden*) stage and the Main Hall, as is routine. Instead, a temporary place of exorcism (*oharaijo*) is set up under the eaves of the northeast portion of the gallery which separates the inner precincts from the rest of the shrine grounds (see Photo 6.11). In the eaves the priests, a shrine maiden, and parishioners line up in that order, right to left. Two priests advance to the ritual table set up in the gallery eaves; one takes a large exorcism wand (*haraigushi*) of zigzag paper strips, the other a receptacle of salt. The two priests, wearing footwear made of wood coated by shiny, black lacquer, make a crunching sound as they cross the wide interval of gravel separating the gallery from the front of the Main Hall. Arriving before the Main Hall, one priest waves the wand while the other priest flicks salt; they exorcise the offerings of food and drink, the evergreen offering branches (*tamagushi*), and the parishioners sitting between the Veneration Hall stage and the tower-gate doorway. Walking back across the expanse of gravel, they exorcise the priests and the shrine maiden, and finally the parishioners in the eaves. Following this rite of exorcism, the priests as a group cross the gravel in single file while the shrine maiden leads the parishioners around under the eaves; both groups then sit in folding camp seats in the space between the veneration hall and the main shrine. The only other time that the preliminary exorcism originates from the eaves is at the rituals which occur near the spring and autumn equinoxes, on the mornings at which sacred sand is gathered from the shrine beach.

In generation-invoking words delivered by the Chief Priest, petition is made to the kami of fruition for protection from the influence of Magatsukami. These generation-invoking words are presented before the shrine's Main Hall, the central ritual arena associated with yang, the male Emperor Ôjin, and with fruition:

> May our children and grandchildren continue for countless generations, grant us peaceful prosperity, abundant harmony in our homes, faithfully and assiduously assist the livelihoods of the people, may there be no pernicious influence of Magatsukami (*Yaso-magatsu-hi*) in either our person nor our homes, but rather grant us [thy] benevolence and protect all who serve [thee] both night and day.

Photo 6.11. Northeast corner exorcism site

After the presentation of offerings and delivery of the generation-invoking words by the Chief Priest, the priests and parishioners file outside and proceed to line up in front of the Box Pine (*hakomatsu*). There they bow once in unison, clap twice, and bow once more. From there, they continue single file to the peripheral East Shrine complex and then to the West Shrine, where they bow and clap in unison again, and the Chief Priest delivers generation-invoking words at each location, asking, among other things, that the local community be prospered and spared from the machinations of Magatsukami.[8] On the first and fifteenth days of the month, as at the equinoxes, the inner doors to the individual shrines within the peripheral complexes, as well as the doors of the other dimension shrine near the beach, are all open, revealing the white, zigzag paper offering wands (*gohei*) inside.

Yang Earth Rites at Hakozaki are organized according to two cosmologies: 1) priestly ritual emphasizes an Ommyôdô set of concepts, while 2) popular ritual observed at the shrine coalesces around a characteristically Yayoi period frame of reference. Priest-led ritual at Hakozaki at the equinoxes and on the first and fifteenth of each month acknowledges close contact with the Great Mother in the opening of the shrine doors at: 1) the peripheral East and West Shrines, and 2) at the other dimension shrine near the beach. The opening of these doors at these interstitial junctures in time identify these times as boundaries at which the power of the Feminine spirit of the depths,

Tamayorihime, erupts into the space and time of the local community. For male priests following a Ommyôdô mode of thought, this Female presence is suspect. Ritual before the central Main Hall associated with Ôjin-centered veneration commences with exorcism originating in the peripheral northeast, Demon Gate quadrant of the inner enclosure. No spatial quadrant compass is more indicative of yin, life-threatening, low spirits than is the Demon Gate. This peripheral exorcism could just as appropriately be performed at the peripheral shrines East and West, or at the beach. Its performance in the eaves of the inner enclosure is a function of convenience, but the northeast quadrant makes its purpose clear. This special exorcism is directed at the Female-centered apprehensions that obtain at these points in time.

Most succinctly, the Demon Gate corresponds to the "red impurity," menstrual blood, corpse phenomena, and other impurities that excite the predatory aspect of the Great Mother.[9] While priestly ritual at these junctures serves to harness the life-giving power inherent at these times, the first order of business is to cleanse all that would lead life-enhancement energies awry. The lone shrine maiden that stands in the eaves of the special exorcism area on these days, wearing her red divided skirt (*hakama*) appears to effectively express this male-priest apprehension regarding "red impurity." This threat is further acknowledged by the Chief Priest's generation-invoking words delivered before both the Main Hall and both peripheral shrines as he petitions for a ransom from the ravages of Magatsukami, the embodiment of the underworld impurities and the epitome of the Terrible Mother. Obviously, Feminine apprehensions are ritually foremost in the agenda of priestly ritual at these junctures. This tendency is further accentuated by the fact that *no* birth-soil ritual, this being the body of the Great Mother herself, takes place *inside* the Main Hall compound. Birth-soil appears to be too redolent of the Great Mother to be used before the male-heaven centered ritual of the Main Hall. The only time shrine priests employ this ritual tool is at the Great Exorcism, when Female-centered impurities and threatening powers are at their most potent. And then, birth-soil is used *outside* of the Main Hall enclosure, in a separate, spatially peripheral location in the shrine precincts.

But, from the perspective of priestly ritual, occasions of Yang Earth Rites do not represent an unmitigated threat to the community, as does the Great Exorcism. The equinoxes, the first and the fifteenth of the month *are* ritually marked by priest coordinated ritual. And also unlike the Great Exorcism, food offerings (the bounty of land and sea) are made before the Main Hall. This fact brings to light three points. First, a mutual relationship between the high spirits and the shrine community is reaffirmed and renegotiated. Second, presentation of the bounty of land and sea highlight the petition of continuing fruition. Furthermore, the presentation of life-sustaining produce also acknowledges the central role ancestral high spirits (yang, central, life-giving bright spirit) in the production of food. The high spirits equated with the Main Hall are both offered the community's gratitude for their bounty while being implored for continuing protection from devouring influences (yin, peripheral, threatening dark spirit). Finally, these offerings are made at the central-heaven focused Main Hall, the locus of high spirit ritual, and not at Hakozaki's peripheral shrines. On New Year's morning, the only time when offerings are presented at the peripheral shrines, they are much simpler in composition and smaller in size.

Birth-soil ritual is never observed by priests or others within the Main Hall's inner enclosure. This sacred sand belongs to the realm of Hakozaki's peripheral shrines, to the domain of the local spirit of the depths, Tamayori-hime, and to the mainspring of sacral Female power. The only times that priests employ birth-soil are the junctures which are most dangerous for the Ommyôdô-influenced male priesthood: the annual Demon Gate and Human Gate junctures. These two interstices in annual time represent the most prominent points at which unmitigated Female power is concentrated, during menstruation and ovulation. At these two points in annual time, the Yayoi era Feminine archetype threatens the male dominated cognitive order; at these times, *outside* of the Main Hall enclosure, the male priesthood uses *dry* birth-soil to exorcise impurities, to avoid the predation of the Terrible Mother lurking at the annual cycle's end, and to effect a renewal of time for the local topocosm. This desperate juncture when the male is confronted by Feminine powers is negotiated by Hakozaki's priests by resorting to using the very source of Feminine power against itself—her yang aspect made fertile by the male, the life-granting Good Mother, is pitted against the life-snatching Terrible Mother. The Great Exorcism, ritually speaking, fights fire with fire.

At and around the Main Hall, priests control the use of birth-soil because it represents the prime embodiment of Feminine power that is potentially subversive to male-oriented Ommyôdô cosmological principles. Hakozaki's priests coordinate the gathering of this sacred soil at the yin and yang convergence at the equinoxes. This conjunction of Female (yin) and male (yang), or musubi, from an Ommyôdô perspective is indicative of conjugal union and beckons the emergence of ancestral spirits from the earth-womb, in the form of vegetation and offspring: fruition. The predominant image is that of the Female (earth and woman) being fertilized by the male (seed and man). The results are the life-granting aspect of the high spirits, and ultimately the Good Mother. For priestly ritual, the Great Mother's life-giving bounty is brought about by relations with the male; therefore, the cognitive pairing of male and female, and the fruits of that union, are regularly invoked in ritual observed before Hakozaki's Main Hall. Male priests only direct and advertise birth-soil gathering at the equinoxes when yin (Female, darkness) and yang (male, light) are balanced (musubi), when the Female is made fertile by the male. Ommyôdô cosmology bristles at cognitive points of overt Female power, menstruation and ovulation. Women, seemingly devoid of apprehensions at these times, gather life-giving "birth-soil" at points in the monthly cycle that relate to both menstruation and ovulation, as outlined in the next section.

Popular, Non-Shrine Sponsored Rites Observed on the First and Fifteenth of Each Month

Popular Rituals at the Shrine

On the first of each month, compared with other mornings, there are appreciably larger numbers of visitors that clap, bow, and offer petitions before the shrine; the fifteenth of the month usually sees a smaller number of these extra visitors. The majority of them, on both days, are women (with an occasional, elderly man), which correlates with the fact that two-thirds of the individuals who care for the memorial tablets in the home are women, as reported by Smith (1974: 118).

Popular, non-priest coordinated Yang Earth Rites at Hakozaki, rather than being focused on the heaven, male-centered Main Hall, are organized around practices that are more spatially peripheral and Female-centered. Independent of the male priesthood, these practices are carried out on the first and fifteenth of the month by individual women whose prime objective is visiting the shrine beach to gather birth-soil. A priest at the shrine explains:

> Birth-soil is always available at the beach here; some people come and gather sacred beach sand on the first of every month, others come on both the first and the fifteenth. They gather it at the beach, and then bring it and offer a little here [before the tower gate entrance to the Main Hall enclosure]. People sprinkle birth-soil on themselves when entering their home in order to perform exorcism; and some sprinkle it about themselves as they leave the house so that they might go and come without accident.

These women do not gather dry sand high on the beach; instead, they gather birth-soil at the waterline where it has been moistened by seawater. Practitioners explain that salt from the seawater makes birth-soil even more effective in repelling injury and misfortune. The inclusion of salt in birth-soil appears to be a ritual bid to block the predation of the Terrible Mother.

After collection, the wet sand is offered at Tamayorihime's peripheral shrine at the beach (see Photo 6.12)—the other dimension shrine—and also before the Main Hall (see Photo 6.13). There, they take a small amount of the wet sand, shape it into a small cone, and place on the top of the money offering box before the sanctuary (see Photo 6.14). Tossing in a couple of coins, or placing offerings of salt or rice wine on top of the box, they offer a short petition. The cones of sacred sand are eidetic representations of fruition, that is the emergence of sprouts and buds, of produce and offspring, of high spirits and ancestors—the bounty of the Good Mother. These cones are petitions to the Good Mother for her protection and continued generation of life, and when offered before the Main Hall, acknowledge and petition the role of the male (and seeds) in this process of fruition.

Just as the official opening of the peripheral shrine doors on the first and the fifteenth of the month acknowledges that contact with the Great Mother obtains at these junctures, gathering of birth-soil by local women on these days also indicates that the life-giving powers of the Female spirit are in the ascendant. While priest-sponsored ritual at Hakozaki identifies the Ommyôdô calendar's yang earth days nearest the *solar* equinoxes, themselves junctures of yin (night) and yang (day) balance, as times at which "birth-soil" is optimally gathered, women at Hakozaki observe an additional set of gathering practices. Women also gather the life-promoting soil on days commemorating the beginning and the midpoint of the *lunar* cycle. These women indicate by their practice that the first and the fifteenth are also yang earth days, and in terms of the lunar cycle they are the beginning of waxing yang, and

Photo 6.12.   Offering birth-soil at the beach shrine

Photo 6.13.   Carrying birth soil to the shrine

Photo 6.14.   Birth-soil cones offered on the 15th of the month

maximum of yang light. Peripheral to the male dominated priesthood, calendar, and ritual, women gather earth according to the lunar cycle at the threshold into the Feminine Other World: Hakozaki's beach. This female practice is peripheral to the rites of male ritual space, and yet, these women acknowledge the high spirits of the Main Hall and create an affinity with and invoke their life-promoting auspices by offering cones of their birth-soil before the central ritual arena. But the cognitive difference between priestly and female ritual appears in the respective postures of male priests and female parishioners; while male priest ritual is focusing on exorcising the threatening aspects of the Feminine archetype, women are availing themselves of the life-giving power of the beach's birth-soil.

Women at Hakozaki gather this earth at two times in the lunar cycle that are indicative of two defining points in their own cycles of fertility: menstruation (or birth) and ovulation. These two interstices in the lunar cycle, for women at Hakozaki, are junctures of life-giving Feminine power equated with fruition. Male-oriented, Ommyôdô cosmology labels these junctures as the Demon Gate and Rear Demon (or Human) Gate, redolent with female power associated with the Terrible Mother. But from a Yayoi period cognitive standpoint, successful negotiation of the Demon Gate threshold is cause for celebration: the cycle has recommenced. This renewal is indicative of fruition and all the nuances of meaning associated with the term medetai (see Glossary): the emergence of sprouts and buds, emergence from an interstice, womb emerging, and the emergence of high spirits. All of these cognitive images denote the life-giving auspices of the Good Mother. From this Yayoi period perspective, women are not Demon Gate phenomena as they are labeled according to Ommyôdô cosmology; instead, together with the Good Mother, women are sources of fruition.

Popular Rituals in the Home

The first and fifteenth of each month are ritually important times for Mrs. Murakami. She was born into a branch family (*bunke*) and was brought while still a small infant to be reared by her relatives in the main house (*honke*) of her familial clan. It was only when she was in junior high school that she found out that her biological mother was actually the "relative" who came to the main house everyday to help with the chores! Mrs. Murakami eventually married the eldest son born into the main house. With her mother-in-law and father-in-law now deceased, she is a support to her husband who, as the eldest son, took over the family's kimono retail business and also assumed the responsibilities as head of the main house. The Murakami's have a daughter and a son. They live in a small township near the city of Karatsu in Saga prefecture.

Mrs. Murakami, now in her mid-fifties, explains that much of the ritual that she observes at her family's Buddhist altar (*butsudan*), venerating the ancestors, as well as the veneration of several household kami (*ie no kamisama*), is due to her maintaining the customs that were formerly observed by her late, foster parents. Every morning she first performs ritual before the main household kami altar, located in a long shelf next to the ceiling, over the entry into the main hallway that roughly bisects the house. This long kamidana contains a large amulet-tablet (*ofuda*) from Ise, half a dozen amulet-tablets from Dazaifu Tenmangû for family safety and prosperity in business, and also a handsome, dark wooden statue of the popular kami Ebisu. "Ebisu is a misfortune-dispelling (*yaku-yoke*) kamisama," says Mrs. Murakami. Next, she performs ritual for the ancestors at the Buddhist altar.

In addition, she maintains three other shrines for household kami. In the kitchen, on a shelf near the ceiling is a kamidana dedicated to the veneration of Kôjin-sama, kami of the hearth. Outside in the garden, located on the east side of the house, is a stone shrine at which O-inarisama, kami of rice cultivation and business prosperity, is offered obeisance. And finally, although there is no actual shrine structure there, one more kami is placated inside the family store. Some years ago there was a well on the family property but, in order to enlarge the kimono shop, the well was covered up. A priest from the local, Gion shrine was summoned to perform an exorcism at the sealing of the well, and now a pipe provides air for the covered well, in order to allow Suijin-sama, kami of water, to breathe, explained Mrs. Murakami. The site of the old well has become a narrow hallway inside the shop. Offerings to Suijin-sama are placed on a table that permanently rests over the site of the old well.

Although the long kamidana in the main hallway of her home receives daily veneration and offerings, Mrs. Murakami presents offerings to the spirits of the hearth, rice, and the well only twice a month, on the first and fifteenth, according to the solar calendar. These offerings of rice wine, uncooked rice, salt, and water, each being placed in its own tiny glass receptacle, are placed on a small tray on the small veranda-under-the-eaves (*engawa*) connecting the house and garden (see Photo 6.15).

Mrs. Murakami has faithfully followed this routine of presenting offerings on the first and fifteenth of each month for many years now. She explains that the form of this ritual was suggested to her by a family friend, an elderly female spiritualist who often imparts advice. Mrs. Murakami continues to perform this rite on the first and fifteenth of the month so that she and her family might "enjoy safety, health, and good relations with the land" on which they live.

On the first and fifteenth of the month, Mrs. Murakami in a Yayoi period manner makes offerings to placate the Great Mother. She offers foods at a

Photo 6.15.   Mrs. Murakami makes offerings on the 1st of the month

cognitively peripheral location in her home, the veranda, a point midway between the inside and out. Here again, a spatial boundary surfaces: a transitional area between inside and out indicative of the threat of the Terrible
Mother. But instead of using birth-soil, Mrs. Murakami offers rice wine, raw
rice, sea salt, and water. Water, equated with the well and soon to be discussed, ensures continuing life. Rice is the ritual food *par excellence*, and as
the reincarnation of ancestor spirits, provides the living with spiritual power
and represents the triumphal return of ancestor spirits from the earth. Salt
blocks the development of death and decay. Obviously, at the points corresponding to menstruation and ovulation in the female cycle, Mrs. Murakami
is making a petition for continuing fruition. She corroborates with this conclusion, explaining that this ritual ensures her family "health, safety, and good
relations with the [local] land."

Mrs. Murakami equates the Great Mother with house kami of the garden
soil, the well, and the hearth. Spirits of these same three places are the focus
of soil release rituals on Dunang Island. On Dunang, soil is the body of the
Great Mother; wells are passageways into her depths and sources of protection of priestesses, and by extension, their families. The spirit of the hearth
(fire), venerated on the first and fifteenth of each lunar calendar month, is
a paired male-female entity indicative of the wife and of women and is a
place of Female power that can deliver life, conjugal bliss, and particularly

protection for women in Dunang (see Rokkum 1998: 99–100, 157, 177). Mrs. Murakami is cognitively connecting with the Feminine archetype by means of Yayoi period cosmological concepts. These three ritual loci—soil, well, and hearth—emphasize the corporeality and sexuality of women; ritually addressed at times corresponding to menstruation and ovulation, they represent the Great Mother who is the overarching cognitive foundation of Yayoi period female-centered ritual practice. Mrs. Murakami's bimonthly offerings represent a petition for continuing fruition (medetasa), and even a ransom to the Great Mother to grant her family safe passage at these female-centered temporal interstices, all as a means of forestalling the threat of the Terrible Mother, echoed in the presentation of decay-preventing salt. In keeping with Yayoi period cosmological notions, Hakozaki's birth-soil ritual is a petition for furthering growth and life, Mrs. Murakami's monthly offerings echo this same theme. Both rituals use salt to block all influences that would hinder continuing corporeal development. Both rituals are focused on fostering positive relations with the local soil—this pointing to the Great Mother, the cognitive pairing of earth and female.

Mrs. Koga, who lives in the small hamlet of Hanami, about thirty kilometers west of Fukuoka, also explains that the first and fifteenth of the month are times at which ritual ought to be performed. She is a housewife in her mid-forties with two boys; she enjoys attending classical music concerts in Fukuoka and practicing her English conversation skills. She says that her mother often tells her to scatter salt in the four corners of her land on the first and the fifteenth of each month. "I do it if I happen to think about it," she says, implying that this ritual is much more important to Mrs. Koga's mother than it is to her. "Things like salt, rice spirits, uncooked rice, kelp, and dried squid are offerings that belong to shrines (jinja)," she explains.

Mrs. Koga's monthly ritual of scattering salt in the four corners of her home site (land) on the first and the fifteenth of the month represents a much more Ommyôdô-influenced exorcism along the lines of the male-centered Great Exorcism. Here again, ritual focus on earth and salt obtains, but like the Great Exorcism, no food offering is made—hence, no overt relationship is established nor maintained with the Good Mother on the first and the fifteenth. The net effect of Mrs. Koga's bimonthly exorcism is an unmitigated ousting of yin low spirits, and the predation of the Terrible Mother. While the ultimate aim of this practice may indeed be exorcism to pave the way for fruition, the complete lack of ritual aspects that either affirm or establish links with the positive aspects of the Feminine archetype appears to lack any Yayoi period characteristics.

Keiko, a fourteen-year-old junior high school student who lives in the small community of Wada, immediately southwest of Fukuoka, explains that

her family customarily eats celebratory red rice on the first and the fifteenth
of each month and also offers some on the family's kami altar on these days.
She giggles and says, "We call these times 'red rice days' (*sekihan no hi*)!"
Keiko's mother, as well as grandmother, say that offering and eating red rice
on the first and the fifteenth is a means of offering thanks to the kamisama.
Smith notes that many of his informants also made offerings at their family,
kami altar on the first and the fifteenth of each month (1974: 137).

Keiko's family, in a Yayoi period bid for continuing fruition and protection,
renew ties at the family's high spirit altar by offering and consuming red rice
to receive the blessings of the Good Mother. Red rice consists of rice, usually
glutinous, cooked together with small, red azuki beans that impart a reddish
hue to the rice. Sprinkled with roasted sesame seeds and salt, this dish is decorated with a sprig of nandina (*nanten*) and, at the present in Japan, is eaten
at celebratory (medetai) occasions. The negotiation of all boundaries brings
affected parties into cognitive contact with the Great Mother, with both her
beneficent and threatening aspects.

Originally a ritual food eaten at funerals in the Kyôto area ("Sekihan no yurai," 2003: 1), my claim is that like the consumption of rice balls in Dunang
Island, red rice is an Ommyôdô-influenced ritual means of restoring life-souls
to the body, or as a means of preventing life-souls from separating that would
initiate the on-going predatory drag of the Terrible Mother. Azuki beans are a
yang food item (other beans are yin in character); their inclusion in red rice is
a petition for strengthening and life-giving energies to be in the ascendant.
Rice itself embodies the life-giving energy of reincarnated high spirits; as
such is used as a sacramental means of receiving new vitality. Red rice is offered and eaten at defining points of the female fertility cycle, and is also a
common ritual means of celebrating a young woman's menarche in the Japanese mainland.[10] Equated with these times, red rice appears to be a ritual
marker that celebrates the strength of Feminine reproductive power and
fruition emerging from the earth-womb Other World. But salt and nandina
signal the apprehension also equated with boundaries and the Terrible Mother
who also lurks there. Salt effects exorcism and prevents decay. Nandina is
commonly explained by informants to signify the phrase "diverting misfortune" (*nan wo tenzuru*). Therefore, red rice ritual in a Yayoi period fashion
celebrates fruition; simultaneously, in a more male-centered Chinese fashion,
the threat of the Terrible Mother of the depths is exorcised by means of salt
and nandina.

These four popular rituals observed by women on the first and the fifteenth
of the month represent a continuum of cognitive responses *vis-à-vis* the Feminine archetype that bridge both male-centered Ommyôdô and female-
centered Yayoi period worldviews. Each of these women's rituals revolves

around soil, salt, Feminine cognitive markers, and boundaries. On the other hand, priest led ritual focuses on the centrally located Main Hall at Hakozaki, is preoccupied with apprehensions regarding points of Feminine power—menstruation and ovulation, and ritually seeks to curtail Feminine symbols in a bid to maintain Ommyôdô forms and male-centered control of ritual practice.

Women gather birth-soil mingled with salt water at the lunar junctures corresponding to menstruation and ovulation. Rather than a Main Hall, Ôjin-centered observance, gathering birth-soil is an expression of peripheral shrine ritual practice focused on the Female spirit of the depths, Tamayorihime. Small cones of birth-soil, indicative of the emergence and sustenance of life from the Female Other World of the depths, are offered at Tamayorihime's peripheral shrine at the beach (the other dimension shrine) and also before the Main Hall, locus of the Great Mother's fertilization by the male. The gathering of birth-soil by women at Hakozaki appears to be an outright declaration, in a Yayoi period fashion, that menstruation (the first of the month), particularly, is a yang, life-giving event which bestows on birth-soil the cognitive power capable of crushing the threat of the Terrible Mother inherent at threshold boundaries. From this Yayoi period perspective, women are not Demon Gate phenomena as they are labeled according to Ommyôdô cosmology; instead, together with the Good Mother, women are sources of fruition.

RITES OF CELEBRATION

Lastly, Rites of Celebration hail the emergence of yang energies (*hare*) at New Year's, at the spring equinox, at the winter solstice, and in the harvest at autumn equinox. Rites of Celebration are events at Hakozaki when the pairing of yin and yang, of female and male, is invoked as a petition for and celebration of emergent new life (medetasa). A primary Yayoi period ritual concern, fruition, is the focus of Rites of Celebration that are directed and performed by priests according to Ommyôdô cosmological principles at Hakozaki's center ritual arena, before the Main Hall. Three of the five temporal interstices thereby marked were and are events of the annual *solar* cycle: the spring and autumn equinoxes, and the winter solstice.

Rites of Celebration are high rites of fruition (medetasa), and as such are invocations of the bounty emerging from the Good Mother made fertile by the male. Unlike the Great Exorcism these are not severe rites of severance. Unlike Yang Earth Rites, there is no mention made in generation-invoking words of Magatsukami, no removed "place of exorcism" in the northeast is employed, and no birth-soil ritual is observed. Celebratory rites before the Main

Hall do include brief salt exorcism, but this is an acknowledgment that the Great Mother always presents a threat that must be subdued. Rituals of Good Mother invocation at Hakozaki belong to the realm of Ommyôdô cosmologically-oriented, Ôjin-centered ritual focused on east, yang, and fruition.

The Rites of Celebration that will be examined are 1) the Divine Placenta Rite; 2) New Year's rituals, which include The Rite of Three Origins, amulet-seeking pilgrims, and popular rituals in the home; 3) Rites of the First Rabbit Calendar Day; and 4) the Life-Freeing Rite.

The Divine Placenta Rite

On the evening of December 31st, a ritual takes place in which red rice, shaped into the form of a placenta, is offered in front of the Box Pine at Hakozaki. This red rice placenta suggests the legendary burying of Emperor Ôjin's placenta and umbilical cord at this very location. This event was not merely the disposal of waste; it is commemorated at every major, priest-led ritual at the shrine.[11] The placenta offering at Hakozaki has three cognitively significant aspects.

First, Ôjin's placenta buried at Hakozaki serves as a petition for fruition and development for the locality in general. Above the placenta was planted the Box Pine (hakomatsu) (see Photo 6.16), the eternally celebratory tree that is emblem of both flourishing life energy through all seasons, and represents the joint veneration of the Mother of earth and ocean, Tamayorihime, and the heavenly son sent to rule the islands, Emperor Ôjin.

Second, burial of the imperial placenta near the beach at the annual Demon Gate, the yawning mouth of the Threatening Mother, was presented to be a calming offering (*shizume-mono*), as in soil pacification rites (jichinsai). This event has also been interpreted as a pacification of the female spirit of the sea, in order to obtain her permission for the advent of the Ôjin-centered rites to be housed at Hakozaki. Nevertheless, this sacrificial offering placed in a round box (*hako*), first and foremost appeased the Great Mother of the depths so that safe travel on the ocean could take place. Hence the place name Box Cape (*hakozaki*) came into being. Control of the ocean depths, and water in general, is a central ritual aim at Hakozaki, and evidence of Hakozaki's function to provide safe sea travel endures to the present day.[12] In Japanese folktales, the human pillar (*hito-bashira*), or human sacrifice to the local water spirit, is a common motif that is required to quell the fierceness of water and grant the integrity of water-related construction projects including bridges, dikes, and dams.[13] With great frequency, this human pillar offering results in the immolation of a mother and her infant son and is linked with various local Hachiman shrines (see Iijima 1992: 320–21). I assert that the archetypical

Photo 6.16.   Hakozaki's spirit tree

placenta sacrifice of mother/ son to quell the predation of Tamayorihime at Hakozaki spread along with Hachiman veneration into other regions of mainland Japan to similarly deal with unruly spirits of water in other localities. The victory of the Minamoto clan, devotees of Hachiman, over the Taira (who, incidentally, venerated the female sea spirit variously associated with Benten and the three Munakata females enshrined at Itsukushima) most certainly played a prominent role in the rise of the Hachiman-centered ritual tradition. I claim that during the Kamakura period the imbuing of this particular cosmological significance to the burial of Ôjin's placenta at Hakozaki was a prime reason why Hachiman came to be identified as a Buddhist savior figure, a bodhisattva.

Third, the offering of red rice (*sekihan*) in a placenta shaped form on the last day of the year at the Divine Placenta Rite (*o-enasai*), presents again the life-preserving ransom and renews its effect at the Demon Gate juncture, where apprehensions concerning the Female and low spirits are most conspicuous. According to shrine legend, the placenta of the imperial child, born on the fourteenth day of the twelfth lunar month, was not buried until the *thirtieth* day of the twelfth lunar month: the moon's dark phase, the last day of the lunar year, the Demon Gate juncture. The Demon Gate is the gaping cognitive interstice where the ominous earth-womb realm exerts its strongest pull upon the living. At Hakozaki, it is where the darkest aspect of Tamayorihime, as the viciously twisted spirit of impurity Magatsukami, lurks to trap and devour mortal beings. This ransom to calm the Terrible Mother was buried in the local earth of Hakozaki beach, then known as Ashizu-ga-ura, which is itself a cognitive threshold leading into the underwater Other World presided over by the ambivalent female spirit equated with Tamayorihime.[14]

It is precisely at spatial interstice locations, such as the Hakozaki beach, where the devouring aspect of the Feminine archetype is most keenly felt. During the fifteenth century in Japan, the afterbirth was commonly buried under thresholds, below the floor, at crossroads, at graves; at locations that serve as cognitive points of contact with the Other World; quite often, a pine was planted above the place (see Yokoi 1988: 42–48). The Terrible Mother is often cognitively equated with these interstitial areas as evidenced by the appearance of transformed-object apparitions (bakemono) emerging from these places, examples being the folktales "Chatsubo" and "Ichikamme Taro." These fearsome beings, entities that have begun to slip from the seen realm into the Unseen are manifestations of the destructive aspect of the Feminine archetype.

The initial burial of the imperial placenta at Hakozaki was a ritual to insure the healthy growth of the child. But for later generations concerned with Ommyôdô cosmology, this offering of human flesh (of jointly mother and son) at the beach on the Demon Gate juncture of the last day of the year represented a ransom offered to appease the predation of the hungry Terrible Mother of the depths. The Box Pine itself is the nexus of Emperor Ôjin centered rituals and the earlier Tamayorihime centered complex of understandings. The Box Pine is emblematic of a unique ransom which ensures continuing fruition and protection, in effect, sealing the devouring aspect of Tamayorihime, the Terrible Mother. In Yayoi era terms, the Box Pine represents the triumph of fruition over destruction; in Ommyôdô terms, it indicates the continuing reign of Yang light and development over the lurking threat of Yin darkness and dismemberment.

New Year's Rituals

The Rite of Three Origins

The designation Three Origins comes from the conjunction of the beginning of new year, month, and day all on the same morning. This new morning represents a successful negotiation of the Demon Gate juncture on the last day of the old year, cognitively an interstice redolent with the influence of yin, life-taking spirits and the Threatening Mother, these entities being the focus of the Great Exorcism. The Rite of Three Origins (*sangen-sai*) is a ritual means of fanning the spark of hope after crossing the most potent yin juncture in the annual cycle, the Demon Gate. As the commencement of a new day, month, and year, in Ommyôdô terms, yang (life-giving energy) is in the ascendant; the Rite of Three Origins' high level of auspiciousness derives from this threefold conjunction and from its representing a celebratory new lease on life and time.

This is a ritual performed by priests and is noteworthy for the ideal of fruition evidenced in the morning's offerings. This rite commences at dawn and is briefer than some because offerings are not presented at all three bays of the Main Hall; only one joint set of offerings is placed before the central bay dedicated to Empress Jingû. Among offerings that collectively represent the bounty of land and sea, there is "sea cucumber mochi" (*namakomochi*), prepared the evening before (see Photo 6.17). This is the only time during the ritual year at Hakozaki that sea cucumber mochi is presented as an offering. Incidentally, on this morning all of the doors to the east and west peripheral shrine complexes are open, and new offerings of miniature mirror-mochi, each topped by a single bitter orange (*daidai*), lay at the top of the steps in front of each shrine bay. Given its symbolic and metaphorical significance, the entire sea cucumber mochi offering is worthy of closer examination.

The sea cucumber mochi offering is an emblem of the paired male and female, indicative of male-induced bounty that will emerge from the Good Mother. On a light-colored, wooden offering stand, rests a pair of thick, round

Photo 6.17. Sea cucumber mochi

mirror-mochi, one round placed on top of the other. Mirror-mochi, a common form of New Year's decoration throughout mainland Japan, are symbolic. A woman in her forties explained that mirror-mochi (*o-kagami*) denote "front" (*omote*). When asked about the significance of front, she said, "New Year's is the front, the beginning of the year (*toshi no hajime*)." Later in the same interview, she said that mirror-mochi is "celebratory" (medetai) because it represents husband and wife (*fûfu*). Another informant, a female in her mid-twenties, stated with a great deal of confidence that the two mochi represent the "sun and the moon put together." Such an answer seems to imply that the two mirror-mochi offered at New Year's are representative of Ommyôdô cosmology, the designation for sun in Japanese being the Great Yang (taiyô) and an old designation for the moon is the Great Yin (taiin). Since mirror-mochi signifies both sun and moon, *and* husband and wife, this ritual decoration does seem to be representative of yin yang duality. Not only that, the two round mochi, one resting atop the other, also symbolize the beginning of the year. This pair of mochi, equated in kami mythology with beginnings and sources of all types, most especially with the generation of the natural world by their procreative activity, are emblematic of Izanagi and Izanami. As emblems representing yin and yang, the two mochi would then embody an infinite set of dualities: cold and hot, moon and sun, wet and dry, earth and sky, to mention but a few. According to Ommyôdô cosmological principles, combinations and permutations of these two dualities are the basis and origin of all creation.

The earliest written records in Japanese are myths regarding beginnings and the kami. The *Kojiki* and *Nihon Shoki* both contain accounts of the primal couple of creation, the male kami Izanagi and the female kami Izanami, while still in her life-giving aspect. This first couple who created the islands of Japan, including all of their animate and inanimate features, did so by their joint procreative activity. Although the myths identify this male and female as kami, these accounts do not provide a picture of omnipotent nor omniscient beings. In the beginning, Izanagi and Izanami were child-like in their simplicity and naiveté. Their first recorded dialogue is a discussion of their own bodies. The male, Izanagi, asked Izanami the question, "How is your body formed?" Izanami answered that her body was well-formed, but that one place that she called the "source of womanhood" (*me-no-hashi-me*) was formed in deficiency. Izanagi rejoined that his body was likewise well-formed, but that one place, his "source of masculinity" (*o-no-hashi-me*) was formed in excess. According to one account, Izanagi then suggested that they unite the "source places" (*hashi-me-no-tokoro*) of their bodies; Izanami acquiesced. And so circumambulating the "central pillar of the land" from opposite sides they met on the opposite side and became united as husband and wife (Kuroita 1966: 6). They met as husband and wife at a pillar, emblem of the reincarnated ancestor from the earth-womb Other World, or in other words, fruition.

The lower mirror-mochi rests on two types of evergreen leaves: fern (*urajiro*) and transfer leaves (*yuzuriha*). The leaves of this particular fern grow in pairs on a single stem; in Japanese they are thought to "face one another" (*aitai suru*). This metaphorical characteristic of facing each other is probably responsible for another name for this fern, "two facing together" (*moromuki*). "Because its two leaves face one another, [this fern] is a symbol of conjugal harmony (*fûfuwagô*). The white underside of its leaves [the color of hair when elderly] is a metaphor of husband and wife growing old together; furthermore, since it is a flourishing evergreen, it is a "celebratory" (medetai) plant, as well" (Mizuhara 1981: 1: 184).

Transfer leaves are also an evergreen that grows west of central Honshû. The old leaves of this tree fall to the ground only *after* its new foliage has emerged in the spring. "Transfer leaves are used in New Year's decorations because they are an auspicious item signifying the succession of one generation from its predecessors (*fushi sôzoku*) and also an abundance of offspring (*shison hanei*)" (Mizuhara 1981: 1: 184–85). The fern and transfer leaves underneath the mirror-mochi echo the symbolism of male and female in the mirror-mochi.

On top of the upper mirror-mochi rests the thick slab of sea cucumber mochi. In front of the mochi offering sit ten flattened and dried persimmons (*hoshigaki*) on a long wooden skewer that overhangs the edges of the offering stand. The placement of persimmons on the skewer is important: there are six persimmons arranged close together in the middle of the skewer, flanked by a pair of persimmons on each side. This arrangement is not unique to the Hakozaki Shrine; in fact, mirror-mochi are similarly decorated by dried persimmons in households all over mainland Japan. The six persimmons in the middle are referred to by the native Japanese counter for six (*muttsu*). A priest at Hakozaki explains that muttsu (six) conjures the somewhat phonetically similar term *mutsu* which means friendly, intimate, harmonious, or affectionate. An expression for conjugal harmony also utilizes this term (*fûfu ga mutsumajiku*). The pair on either side of the six in a row are "two and two" (*nikoniko*), a homonym, he explains, for (*nikoniko*), to smile, to beam, to have a smiling face. Furthermore, he added, the pair on either side can also be expressed as two and two (*futasu-futatsu*), sounding like and standing for husband and wife (*fûfu*). So the complete message that the dried persimmons convey is something like: "May husband and wife smile in harmony and be happy with one another." Or in other words, this particular arrangement of persimmons expresses the wish that conjugal harmony may prevail. Again, the symbolism of male and female is revealed; in terms of the earliest mythology associated with the kami tradition, that male and female are the primal couple Izanagi and Izanami. In the much broader terms of Ommyôdô cosmology, the petition represented is that yin and yang may converge and harmoniously produce all aspects of the cosmos.

A senior priest at Kashii Grand Shrine in Fukuoka explains that such emblematic representation of yin and yang, "functions to make the relation between male and female, yin and yang, smooth. If this relationship is not a good one, then nothing is good. If it only rains, or it is only sunny, this causes problems. The goal is to have conjugal harmony (*fûfu emman*)." Such an offering represents, "a petition [at New Year's] for the smooth interplay (*umaku chôwa*) of yin and yang. . . As a result, the world should become extremely whole, peacefully dynamic, and smoothly functioning (*heiwa*)." Within the same statement, this priest speaks using the terms yin and yang, female and male, interchangeably; obviously, one set of terms is a cipher for the other set.

In front of the persimmons are three bars of white agar gelatin (*kanten*). Responding to an inquiry about the meaning of the agar gelatin, an assembled group of priests at Hakozaki said that it and the other produce offered together with the sea cucumber mochi are representative of the bounty of the sea (*umi no sachi*) and the bounty of the mountains (*yama no sachi*). Finally, a bitter orange (daidai) sits atop the offering; this name is a homonym for "from generation to generation" (*daidai*). Informants explain that this fruit is often used in New Year's decorations because it expresses the wish of numerous and prosperous descendants (shison hanei) from generation to generation.

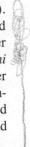

The primordial couple Izanami and Izanagi, presented as manifestations of yin and yang, are indicated on the offering stand by such items as the mirror-mochi, the paired leaves, and the dried persimmons, offering the eidetic image of male/female procreative endeavor resulting in fruition. The joint creation of the parent kami, including the bounty of land and sea, are further emphasized by transfer leaves, the bitter orange, and the produce of mountain and sea. The sea cucumber mochi, produced on the evening the infant Ôjin's placenta was buried, appears to be indicative of the infant Emperor Ôjin, and more generally, of every aspect of the topocosm (offspring) that emerges from the union of the abstract forces of yin and yang. However, rather than simply abstract representations of yin and yang, given the frequency with which couple and offspring imagery are incorporated into this offering, a conjugal pair is indicated. The cognitive combination of rice (cake), imperial offspring (Ôjin), and the bounty of land and sea present all three pillars of the kami tradition (kami, rice, and emperor) and communicate the insight that high spirits (kami) are the vital life force that make all generation, including procreation, a viable reality. The sea cucumber mochi offering, as all food offerings are before the kami, additionally expresses gratitude for the bounty of life, and represents a petition/ incantation for continuing corporeal development. The paired male and female, symbolically represented on the offering stand, are emblematic of the planting of the seed, (agriculture and procreation) the means by which the high spirits experience resurrection from the earth-womb.

This priest-crafted offering, embodied by the mirror-mochi, the Emperor Ôjin (sea cucumber), and the bounty of the earth-womb have all been symbolically arranged on the ritual offering stand and represent the return of ancestors from the underworld. In this instance, this dualistic symbolism delineates the temporal boundary known as the Three Origins. Just as kami and spirits of the dead are equated with passage across spatial boundaries, they are also are considered to visit at the New Year. By emphasizing life-giving tendencies fostered by high spirit intervention, the existential threat of negotiating a major conjunction of temporal boundaries is mitigated at Hakozaki by priestly ritual.

Amulet-Seeking Pilgrims

In addition to priest-led rituals on this morning, crowds of New Year's visitors flock to the Hakozaki Shrine to claim for themselves new extensions of life and fortune, as well.[15] For many New Year's shrine pilgrims, the purchase of protective-talismans (*o-mamori*) and amulet-tablets (*ofuda*) are part of the reason for their visit. At the Hakozaki Shrine, as is the practice at many other shrines too, a temporary reception area for old amulets and talismans is set up. The old items are placed in either of two long wooden chests which sit under a tent. At each of the four corners of the tent stands a green stalk of bamboo with leaves; a rice straw festoon (shimenawa) strung from the bamboo marks off the eaves of the temporary structure.

The popular idea exists that amulets and talismans are only effective for the year in which they were bought. At the end of the old year, these ritual items must be returned to the shrine to be burned; the purchase of new ones ensures happiness, or at least peace of mind, during the coming year. Junki is a 14–year-old middle school student, the younger of two children; his father is a medical doctor with a successful practice in Fukuoka. Junki explains:

> At the first-pilgrimage we take the evil things from last year and leave them at a temple or shrine, and we take home with us things which will make this year happy and lucky. *Like what sort of things?* Like protective-talismans, demon-crushing-arrows (*hamaya*), and amulet-tablets. These things protect you from evil. But they only protect you for one year; after one year, they lose their ability to protect people from evil things. Evil spirits possess (*tori-tsuku*) them, so they [the talismans and so forth] are burned.

The annual exchange of shrine amulets: 1) carries the ritual struggle for life in the new year to the family/ individual level, and 2) serves to synchronize the pattern of new life to the emerging annual cycle of the Feminine archetype. In keeping with Gastor's claim that initially human communities ritually fought for and won new extensions of time and life energy within the topocosm, the purchase of amulets at the threshold of New Year's expresses this existential struggle on a household level to lay claim over a new extension of life within a new, annual cycle of time. It is a petition to the high spirits, and ultimately the Good Mother, for an extension of life and vitality.

In addition, amulet return cognitively effects a soil release, to avoid the predation of the Terrible Mother. Return of the previous year's amulets signals the end of the old annual cycle; their being deposited at the shrine also signifies the return of these "tickets to ride" through the old cycle at the "gate" of the new. Passage into a new cycle of annual time not only makes old amulets void, their surrender to shrine priests avoids the wiles of low (yin) spirits that some informants say come to infest old amulets in the new year.[16]

Soil release rituals, previously considered in Chapter Three, involved negotiation of *spatial* boundaries, and were performed to cognitively reaffirm an on-going relationship with the Great Mother, thereby avoiding her predation. Return and purchase of amulets at New Year's also effects a similar soil release only, in this case, *temporal* boundaries are being negotiated, and the "currency" of exchange, rather than being birth soil, consists of amulets. Cognitively, the Great Mother is not a static entity; she is the epitome of process, of change, of an ongoing, unchanging cycle. The cognitive interstice of the year threshold embodies all of the apprehension and power embodied in spatial interstices; at these times (and places) social knowledge dictates that cognitive contact is made with both high, life-giving spirits (equated with new amulets) and life-threatening spirits (identified with old ones). These two classes of spirits, are cognitive projections of the Good Mother and the Terrible Mother. Instead of utilizing Yayoi period earth ritual (female-centered practice) as is common at spatial interstices (birth soil ritual observed at the threshold of the home in Hakozaki, for example), the medium of negotiation at this major temporal interstice becomes amulet exchange, this being a more typically Ommyôdô ritual form (male priest coordinated practice).

Popular Ritual in the Home

New Year's ritual observance in the Murakami family's household is coordinated by Mrs. Murakami and, compared with priestly ritual at Hakozaki, contains a more Yayoi period emphasis on ritual observed at spatial interstices as portals of contact with the Great Mother. On New Year's Eve, when the season's decorations are displayed, Mrs. Murakami presents offerings at locations in her home that fall into one or more of the following categories: 1) sites of physical entrances and exits, 2) cognitive interstices between the seen and Unseen realms, equated with spirit entities, and 3) objects that are receptacle-like in form/ function. Receptacles and containers generally are objects of ritual focused on the Great Mother; when these objects are also linked with the earth, they are even more strongly affiliated with the Feminine archetype. Eight main areas in the Murakami home are sites of New Year's ritual and will be considered as they relate to the categories outlined above: the entry to the home, the hearth, the garden shrine to Inari, the well, the toilet, the main kami altar, the ritual alcove, and the Buddhist altar.

Two small arrangements of pine, bamboo grass (*sasa*), and nandina, an ornamental plant with red berries are tied on a single pillar on the front porch. Mrs. Murakami says that these are gate-pines (*kadomatsu*) and should be placed on either side of the entry, but since they have just one pillar, they put the two together. Mrs. Murakami explains that the three plants in the arrangement represent pine, bamboo, and the flowering plum are used at celebratory (*iwai*) occasions. The pine, she says, represents flourishing and thriving (*sakaeru*), the bamboo, prosperity (*hanei*), and the nandina is an auspicious (*engi ga ii*) plant. Each of the gate-pines is bound near the base with thick, white Japanese paper that is tied in place with red and gold "water-applying knots" (*mizuhiki*), which Murakami explains are like lengthened-abalone ornaments (*noshi*) used at celebratory occasions. Water-applying knots include a petition for purity, long life, and fruition and also serve the general social function of delineating an interstice in space, time, or in the life course. She explains that black and white water-applying knots are used at funerals and are not appropriate for New Year's.

Just past the gate-pines, hanging over the front door of their home is an entry-decoration (*shimekazari*), an elaborate type of rice straw festoon (shimenawa) used in Japan during the New Year's season. The entry area (genkan) to the home (the home being a large container) is site of physical entrance and exit, and as a spatial interstice, cognitively can function as a location at which contact with the Other World and beings associated with that realm. On top of the thick straw festoon are fastened a bitter orange, a red plastic lobster, and two small Japanese flags. Mrs. Murakami explains that the lobster signifies longevity (*chôju*), but she was unsure of the significance of the bitter orange. She adds that at the end of the New Year's season, they will take the shime-decoration to the local shrine to be burned. "People with [proper] qualifications (*shikaku*) must burn things like this or amulet-tablets (ofuda)," she explains.

A single gate-pine arrangement of pine, leaf bamboo, and nandina, each resting in a small vase, is placed at the main kami shrine in the hallway, and also before the shrines of the hearth spirit, the well spirit, and the rice/earth spirit in the garden. Receptacles, such as the small vases in which the gate-pine arrangements are placed, are related to the Feminine archetype (Neumann 1963: 43–4), as outlined in the practices of Dunang priestesses and Korean women in Chapter Three. As a special New Year's variant to vases of sakaki evergreen placed at kami shrines, the Murakami family's gate-pines, emerging from ceramic vases, appear to be petitions to the high spirits and Good Mother for continuing life, health, and protection at the home's Feminine interstice shrines. Such receptacle-employing ritual of a Yayoi period priestess persuasion, integrates this ritual practice in northern Kyûshû with related practices in East Asia.

A small pair of mirror-mochi is offered at each of these shrines as well. Each pair of round, white mochi rests on a pair of fern and transfer leaves resting atop a sheet of thick, white Japanese paper which lies on the stand or tray on which the offering is presented. A bitter orange sits on top of each pair of mirror-mochi. Finally, a pair of flasks containing rice wine is placed in front of each of the shrines.

The well, the hearth, and the toilet are all based on the three phases of earth, fire, and water. An additional reason why these phases are associated with Great Mother ritual could also originate in the fact that all three are great sources of creation and destruction; thus all three embody the dual character of the Feminine archetype. The well, being a shaft leading into the earth, is container-like in form. It is a physical interstice at which exit of water takes place and as examined earlier in Chapter Three, particularly in Dunang (Rokkum 1998: 157, 161) and mainland Japanese ritual practice (Oshima 1992: 72) has functioned as an important portal into the realm of spirits. The hearth, particularly the traditional hearth (*kamado*), was a huge clay vessel within which the fire was built; it functioned as the fireplace where fuel was spent and food created and, in terms of Yayoi period and Ommyôdô ritual practice, was considered a site where tutelary spirits came and went (see Rokkum 1998: 155, 177–79; Noguchi 1994: 343).

Mrs. Murakami says that she places the mirror-mochi offering on a shelf near the toilet as a gesture of gratitude (*osewa ni naru kara*). "Sometimes, people put amulets in the restroom, and if you either build or move a water closet, exorcism is a necessity," she explains. She says that the mirror-mochi offered in the restroom is the only one which the family will not eat at the end of New Year's. Another informant said that in their W.C., along with mirror-mochi, they also offer a small branch of pine at New Year's. The toilet, a receptacle leading into the earth, also functions as a route of physical exit from the home. In the traditional Japanese home, the privy was considered to be inhabited by a spirit that would grant strong children to women who kept this fixture of the home clean (Fuji 1996: 118–20; Oshima 1992: 73–74).

There is evidence that the rice/ earth spirit called Inari, venerated in the garden of the Murakami home, belongs to a strain of tutelary ancestral spirits linked with the peregrinating Field Spirit and Mountain Spirit who brings fertility to the fields and insures the harvest of rice (Oshima 1992: 174–75, 181, 184). Inari is popularly equated with the fox. Folklore from China initially identified the fox as a shape-shifting, ambiguous, trickster figure (Smyers 1999: 90–91, 127–28). I find the fox, a messenger of Inari, to be a cognitively appropriate companion for high ancestral spirits who re-cycle (shape-shift) into the seen realm as the life force that animates the rice crop (or offspring). In my opinion, Inari is the "spirit of rice" (Yamaori 1989: 21), or in other words, a cognitive projection of a high spirit host that inhabits the earth, vivifying the processes of rice, and other agricultural endeavors. Ultimately, Inari is an earth spirit. The earth is the supreme receptacle, which together with woman, forms the cognitive basis for the Feminine archetype. Earth both consumes and produces life forms, in addition to being the fertile cognitive locus for a wealth of the spirit entities heretofore considered. Given Inari's function as tutelary, ancestor spirit of the local soil, it seems no idle comment by Mrs. Murakami that the rituals she performs on the first and fifteenth of the month are observed with the goal of "enjoy[ing] safety, health, and good relations with the [local] land." The foci of her ritual practice are life-granting earth spirits, including Inari, which as a fruition-granting earth host, seems to belong to a Yayoi ritual reality.

Another pair of mirror-mochi is offered at the Buddhist altar; here, however, there is no offering of rice spirits, nor is there an arrangement of pine, bamboo, and nandina. Mrs. Murakami explains that these offerings are not appropriate offerings for ancestors (*hotoke-sama*). Flowers are offered on the Buddhist altar, instead; flowers, rather than sakaki or other evergreens, are the appropriate plant offering for ancestors according Buddhist ritual, explain several informants, including Mrs. Murakami. The Murakami family's offerings match closely with the types of offerings reported by Smith (1974: 90–91), with one notable difference being that the mirror-mochi are offered by the Murakami family at their Buddhist altar.

The main kami altar, the ritual alcove (*tokonoma*), and the Buddhist altar in the Murakami home each serves a receptacle function in that they hold amulets, ritual items, spirit tablets, works of art, and so forth. The kami altar and Buddhist altar are interstice areas that are both cognitively considered by the family to serve as a point of access to the Unseen Realm; in a similar fashion, the ritual alcove is said to be a "psychological center of the home" (*ie no seishin teki na chûshin*). It is in this alcove in the main living space that the most elaborate offering of mirror-mochi is placed. This mirror-mochi has a red, plastic lobster (like the one over the front door) and two alternating red and white zigzag paper streamers (shide) which emerge from under the mochi and hang over the front of the offering stand. A scroll painting of the wedded Old Man and Old Woman hangs on the wall of the alcove, behind the mirror-mochi. In the painting, the Old Man and Old Woman, a high spirit couple that figures prominently in the Noh drama "Takasago," stand next to an enormous pine tree which is growing on a sandy beach. Far out at sea, the morning sun begins to rise on the horizon, out of the wide expanse of ocean.

In summary, all of the locations mentioned in this section, with the exception of the Buddhist altar, are Feminine container-interstices where contact with the Great Mother is made. At these locations Mrs. Murakami performs two sets of ritual: 1) fruition rites, to beckon the life-promoting influences of high spirits and the Good Mother, and 2) exorcism rites, to quell the ire of local spirits and prevent inadvertent invocation of the Terrible Mother. While the Murakami's do not speak of a cognitive Great Mother figure, they do speak of spirits linked with places in the home and register concerns or anxieties about particular times and situations which affect these ritual spaces.

For ease in writing, the following letters will be used to designate ritual loci in the Murakami home:

A. entry to the home (genkan)
B. hearth
C. garden shrine to Inari
D. well
E. toilet
F. main kami altar (kamidana)
G. ritual alcove (tokonoma)
H. Buddhist altar (butsudan)

Four examples of ritual practice focused on fruition delineate these Feminine shrines as junctures at which the generative influences of the Good Mother may be obtained. First, gate-pine arrangements, specifically containing pine and leaf bamboo and bound with celebratory red and gold water-applying (mizuhiki) knots, are placed by the Murakami family at features A, B, C, D, and F. Second, these plant arrangements (with the exception of the entryway) are placed in vases. Third, offerings of mirror-mochi are presented at features B, C, D, E, F, G, and H. Finally, offerings of rice wine are presented before features B, C, D, F, and G. Offerings are presented at Feminine interstice shrines as a means of providing energizing life-energy of the high spirits embodied in rice to the spirits of each place.

Exorcism at Feminine interstice shrines in the Murakami home occurs at two junctures, at the negotiation of: 1) spatial boundaries, and 2) temporal boundaries. These examples of exorcism are evidence that Feminine archetype interstice features are not just cognitive features associated with high spirits and the Good Mother; exorcism itself indicates that disquieting phenomena, including low spirit and Terrible Mother influences, are also associated with these portal spaces—particularly at the negotiation of significant spatial and temporal interstices.

The important temporal boundary in this instance is the annual Demon Gate. Apprehensions concerning evil spirits and the attendant drag of the Terrible Female on the living at these spatial interstices occur at the temporal Demon Gate. At this most threatening annual juncture in terms of Ommyôdô cosmology, the Murakami's gate-pines are placed at Feminine interstice shrines as a ritual means of exorcising misfortune and pollution. Additionally, on the evening of December 31st, Mr. Murakami gathers birth-soil with salt water at the nearby beach and uses it to perform an exorcism of features A, B, C, D, and F. These five locations relate to the five gates of Yin-Yang Five Phase cosmology. Mr. Murakami's use of birth-soil to exorcise the main Feminine interstice shrines of the home, including the entry as is routine at Hakozaki, further emphasizes the gravity of the Demon Gate juncture and the potentially noxious influences it can cognitively exercise on Feminine interstice shrines. In this instance, Mr. Murakami's exorcism parallels the Great Exorcism of Hakozaki's male priests at on the last day of the old year. This is an expression of the male-centered apprehensions regarding the Feminine archetype as expressed in and propagated by Ommyôdô cosmological principles.

Negotiation of spatial interstices consists of building new or modifying existing Feminine interstice shrines. Such events require the expertise of a shrine priest to exorcise disquieting influences, and might involve the installation of an amulet at the place to invoke the good graces and protection of a tutelary entity. As previously mentioned, Mrs. Murakami indicated that building, moving, or changing the features of E necessitates exorcism performed by a shrine priest, just as the family did in the past when covering feature D. Presumably, modification of other features A-F would require similar exorcism. Mrs. Murakami also mentioned that some individuals place an amulet in feature E. The Murakami family does have amulets at features B (Sanpô Kôjin), C (Inari), and F (Ise Jingû and Dazaifu Tenmangû). And finally, on December 31 (Demon Gate interstice) gate-pine arrangements which include nandina sprigs and white, Japanese paper wrappings, are placed at features A, B, C, D, and F. According to folk practice, nandina (nanten) is a homophone for "diverting misfortune" and therefore is a symbolic means of performing an exorcism. White Japanese paper (washi), since it contains fibers of hemp that anciently was used for exorcism, is also a ritual means of purifying pollution, impurity, and defilement (kegare).[17]

Rites of the First Rabbit Calendar Day

The remaining three Rites of Celebration observed by Hakozaki's priests occur near significant solar cycle junctures: namely the winter solstice, the spring equinox, and the autumn equinox. The Rite of the First Rabbit Calendar Day (*hatsuusai*), or First Rabbit Rite for brevity in writing, is conducted preceding both the spring equinox and the winter solstice. At both times this non-public rite is carried out at night, by the light of two bonfires which illuminate the inner courtyard area before the Main Hall. Given the origin of its name in the Chinese calendar, the First Rabbit Rite is a ritual situated in terms of time (and intent) according to Yin-Yang Five Phase cosmology and calculated to elevate the position of male priests and males cosmologically, for it casts the male in the role of triumphant fruition bearer over the darkness and decay of yin earth spirits and the Terrible Mother. Yoshino Akiko, in her work on Ommyôdô cosmology in Japanese ritual contexts, has cogently identified that the joint relationship between the trigrams "the Threatening" and "the Initiating" are a prime cosmological axis around which ritual revolves in shrine contexts (2002: 213). Such cognitive organization definitely obtains at Hakozaki.

The Chinese lunar calendar designates each day (and year) as a combination of both a heavenly stem and an earthly branch. The ten heavenly stems serve mainly as calendar signs, and each of the twelve earthly branches corresponds to one of the twelve animal signs of the Chinese animal zodiac (Okada 1995: 133–39). In premodern Japan, before the adoption of the solar calendar, the winter ritual's day was conducted on the first day displaying the earthly stem for rabbit in the eleventh lunar month. The eleventh lunar month falls generally during our solar calendar month of December and the winter solstice occurs on December 22 or 23. Therefore, according to the lunar calendar fixing of the date, this ritual took place some 10 to 22 days prior to the winter solstice. But at the present, the day of the First Rabbit Rite is fixed on the first rabbit day in November which could fall anytime between the first and twelfth days of this month. So, the ritual today will occur anywhere from approximately between 42 and 52 days prior to the winter solstice.

At this writing, *only* the day of the springtime rite is determined according to the lunar calendar, and takes place on the first day displaying the earthly stem for rabbit in February. Therefore, the spring First Rabbit Day could fall anytime between the first and twelfth days of February. The spring equinox falls on either March 21 or 22, so the spring First Rabbit Rite presently takes place anywhere from approximately 38 and 49 days *prior* to the spring equinox. In premodern Japan, the interval would have been much shorter, only 10 to 20 days. Slightly longer spaces of time now occur between the times when each ritual takes place and the arrival of the next major solar cycle event. This distinction is important, because the ritual was primarily calculated according to the old calendar, and in Ommyôdô cosmological terms, to bring both lengthened days and an increase of new, vivifying yang life energy to the topocosm.

The Spring Equinox Observance of the First Rabbit Rite

The origin of the First Rabbit Rite, and the rise of Hachiman veneration as recognized by priests at Hakozaki, is found in a document that was abridged in the late Heian period, entitled *An Abbreviated Record of Japan (Fusô-ryakki)* (Hakozaki-gû 1928: 47; Nakano 2002: 67). In the thirty-second reign of Emperor Kimmei (571), an elderly priest named Ôga no Higi, after three years of prayer, beheld a vision of the three-year-old child Ôjin standing on the tops of leaf bamboo proclaiming, "I am Honda Sumera-mikoto (or Emperor Ôjin) the great, transcendent king and savior [*bosatsu*, or bodhisattva]" (*Ware wa honda-sumera mikoto nishite daijizai-ô bosatsu*.) (Nakano 2002: 67–68). This vision is said to have taken place at the triple conjunction of the earthly branch rabbit: year of the rabbit (571), month of the rabbit (second lunar month), and day of the rabbit (Hakozaki-gû 1928: 47; Hakozaki-gû 1993: 40).[18]

In this account of divine revelation, Ôjin is presented in the role of high spirit of fruition, that is as an agent granting abundant crops, offspring, and generative life energy. There are at least four lines of evidence that support this conclusion. First, the calendar sign for rabbit, according to Ommyôdô calendar lore signifies dense and luxuriant growth of plants (Okada 1993: 137), and since Hachiman was revealed on the triple conjunction of luxuriant growth, this image is multiplied—indicating that this spirit's visitation brings abundant life. Expounding the significance of the rabbit calendar sign, the early first century B.C. Chinese classic, *Annals of History* (*Shih-chi*) records, it "signifies luxuriance; the flourishing of all life," while the commentary of *The Book of Changes* adds, "In the second [lunar] month, all life ventures to emerge from the earth. [It expresses the action of] Opening [of the earth]" (Yoshino 1993: 87). Ôjin is here initially identified with a profusion of life and the emerging of new life from the Unseen Realm of earth and female, or the combined features of the Feminine archetype.

Second, the sign of the rabbit, in terms of Ommyôdô calendar lore, corresponds to dawn, the trigram called "the Initiating," east, spring, wood, and the dragon. In terms of dawn and east, Hachiman becomes linked with the images of sunrise, increasing light, and warmth. This set of images indicates growing yang, or life-promoting, active influence. The two junctures of the First Rabbit Rite fall at two times when light is markedly in the ascendant: winter solstice and spring equinox. The image of spring accentuates this, combining increasing light and warmth with the emergence of new buds and sprouts from the earth. The flourishing rabbit sign also is an expression of the phase wood, indicative of all plant life in general, but at Hakozaki corresponding to the shrine's cognitively central, eternally celebratory, luxuriant evergreen, the Spirit Tree. Finally, the earthly branch of rabbit also is linked with the dragon, spiritual guardian of the east according to Ommyôdô cosmology. Yoshino Akiko cites ritual in the Hiroshima and Shimane area of western Japan, particularly the Kôjin Kagura rites, in which the dragon is specifically identified as the embodiment of ancestral spirits, after observance of the requisite 33 year period of mortuary ritual by the family (1993: 132–35). These ancestral dragons are said to wrap themselves around the trees of the forest of ancestral spirits (Yoshino 1993: 135), there to serve as tutelary spirits of the locality. Ôjin is the tutelary spirit of Hakozaki, and as such, is the high spirit agent of light, and continual emergent new life as embodied in the evergreen boughs of the living manifestation of the ancestral, vivifying presence: the shrine's Spirit Tree.

Third, the numeral three repeated thrice in the account of Hachiman's initial revelation, indicative of the triad of male, female, and offspring, further identifies Emperor Ôjin as high spirit bearer of fruition. In the origin legend, Hachiman appears after three years of petition, as a three-year-old child, and at the triple conjunction of flourishing life energy: the rabbit. In Hakozaki's Rite of Three Origins, the offering of sea cucumber mochi echoes this same triad: male and female as embodied in the paired mirror-mochi, and the child Ôjin as represented in the sea cucumber mochi itself. More generally in Ommyôdô parlance, these same three are ciphers for yin, yang, and their offspring, all of creation. Yoshino Akiko relates this triad to heaven, earth, and humanity (1993: 213), which are simply particular names given to the former Ommyôdô categories. The Hakozaki Shrine's crest is the image of three swirling commas (*mitsudomoe*) which also echoes this same triad emphasis. Nevertheless, the Three are an emblem of fruition, of the ceaseless pairing of yin and yang which result in the emergence of new life—this process of creation made viable by the intervention of high spirits. The Spirit Tree at Hakozaki, as the divine pillar that links heaven (Ôjin-centered ritual concerns) together with earth (Tamayorihime-centered ritual), the Tree itself being indicative of the continual flourishing of life in all of its forms, brings together both ritual traditions into a single system focused on the mighty offspring of the hero: the high spirit, Emperor Ôjin. This Tree is an emblem of endless emergent life, in the form of crops, offspring, and other forms of generative life energy.

Fourth, and finally, titles used in the vision of the young Emperor Ôjin further emphasize his triumphant aspect as champion of new life. First, the term *sume* (as in his name Honda Sumera-mikoto) is an ancient title of respect applied to the emperor or to kami (*sumera*), to members of the imperial line (*sumemima*), or in China, to ancestors (Matsumura 1987: 657; Ogawa 1986: 687–88). As dealt with in Chapter Five, the ambiguities surrounding ancestors and life-granting nature spirits, from the earliest times in China, influenced similar thought in Japan. Use of this term (sume), signifying "brilliant and grand" (Ogawa 1986: 687–88), further emphasizes the ancestral character of both the emperor and high spirits (kami). The figure Ôjin exemplifies all three roles of emperor, high spirit, and ancestor at once as Hakozaki's consummate bearer of fruition. Furthermore, Hachiman calls himself the "great, transcendent king." This appellation proclaims his untrammeled ability to traverse the bounds of the seen and Unseen Realms, unencumbered by the limitations of either. His last title, bodhisattva, or "being of light," is a Mahayana Buddhist term denoting a compassionate savior figure committed to extending the benefit of his own abilities to the needs of other less fortunate beings. With this last term, Ôjin experiences a transformation and begins to take leave of characteristics of a tutelary spirit limited to only the parochial needs of a local parish. Here, he begins to take on a grander role, one as provider of life and protection for all who call upon him; this change must be in part responsible for the wide distribution of Hachiman shrines the length and breadth of Japan.

The savior aspect of Ôjin is further amplified by his birth name Honda (or Homuda) signifying "Praise Field" (Philippi 1968: 572–73) which, in terms of the Feminine archetype, adds the additional semiotic content of a life-producing field, worthy of praise. As such, Hachiman is cast in the light of conqueror over the devouring tendencies of the Terrible Mother, as evidenced by the figure of Tamayorihime at Hakozaki.

The First Rabbit Rite taking place nearest the spring equinox emphasizes the balance of yin and yang, the meeting of the Unseen and seen realms, and the congress of female and male. At this juncture, Ôjin, as the potent yang, male force equated with the Spirit Tree, meets with the Feminine earth, making her fertile with the genial seed. Similar to the gallant kami of Sumiyoshi (see Tyler 1992: 279–80), Emperor Ôjin is cast in the role of virile male force that brings offspring to the earth, thereby transforming Her (earth and womb) into the Good Mother. This role of Ôjin is signified at this rite by the offering of cooked rice pillars (*jukusen*) that represent the Ancestor/high spirit/phallus/seed, the triumphant yang bringing fruition (see Photo 6.18). Cooked rice pillars, emblematic of virile Ôjin, also are presented at the Demon Gate juncture of year end and New Year's (at the Divine Placenta Rite on S 12/31, and the following morning at the Rite of Three Origins on S 1/1). These pillar offerings represent a ritual effort to dramatically counteract the threat of this most potent yin extremity (predation of low spirits and the Terrible Mother) by cognitively invoking the male principle that renders this menace harmless through seed invigoration.

The spring equinox is also the juncture when spirits from the Unseen Realm arrive at Hakozaki's beach, bringing new life energy to its birth-soil, making it effective in warding off personal misfortune at spatial boundaries, and when sprinkled on fields, to make plants grow quickly. Such ideas obtain precisely because of the meeting of heavenly-descended, gallant Emperor Ôjin—the Spirit Tree, secondarily represented by the sakaki tree planted in the beach sand, and by the earth-bound Female spirit (Tamayorihime), cognitively linked with ocean depths. The Female earth is invigorated, and transformed into birth-soil, by the arrival of Hachiman's presence at the beach. His yang, life-giving energy, coinciding with springtime's increasing sunlight, curtails the threat of the devouring Feminine by making her fertile

Photo 6.18.   Cooked rice pillar offering

and life-giving. Therefore, Her essence, the beach sand, by extension also becomes a life-generating medium.

The Winter Solstice Observance of the First Rabbit Rite

The First Rabbit Rite at the winter solstice celebrates the ascendancy of the androgynous Empress Jingû; she is the cognitive pairing of the Great Mother's dual character, both conquering warrior and mother of Emperor Ôjin, combined with Ommyôdô cosmological considerations identified with the winter solstice and the trigram of the Threatening. The circumstances surrounding the mythic account of Empress Jingû as it appears in the *Kojiki* appears to be extremely influenced by Ommyôdô cosmology. This trigram corresponds to north, midnight, the second son, melancholy, the winter solstice, and water (Baynes 1967: 274, 277–78; Okada 1993: 137). In terms of yin and yang, *north* is indicative of cold, and *midnight* corresponds to darkness. The *winter solstice* is the shortest period of daylight in the annual solar cycle. *Water*, the most receptive and yielding of matter's five phases is the most yin. Associated with cold, darkness, water, and the shortest days and longest nights of the winter solstice, this strong yin nature indicates a female entity, Empress Jingû.

The Threatening (Empress Jingû) is also related to the *second son* and *melancholy* (Baynes 1967: 274, 277; Philippi 1968: 253, 606). Prior to his un-

timely demise, Empress Jingû was married to Emperor Chûai, whose historical particulars are sketchy at best. Emperor Chûai's name literally means
"second son" (*chû, naka*), and "sadness, melancholy" (*ai, aware*); the choice
of this particular name appears to be based on an awareness of "the Threatening" trigram in *The Book of Changes* and this emperor's relationship to
Empress Jingû.

Legends surrounding Empress Jingû bear out her unusual affinity with and
power over water, which originates in her initial identification with "the
Threatening" (Yoshino 1994: 22). Following her husband's death, Empress
Jingû levied troops, crossed the ocean, and subjugated the Korean state of
Silla thanks to the intervention of kindly sea spirits (Philippi 1968: 262–63).
Legend at Hakozaki relates that the Empress' unusual power over the waves
was due to her having been granted the "ebb and flow jewels" by Ryûjin,
dragon king of the sea (Hakozaki-gû 1928: 44, 46). While legend at Hakozaki
obviously represents a much later addition to this myth cycle, regardless of
time period, Empress Jingû's power over the waves originates in the fact that
her initial cognitive identification with "the Threatening," in turn, grants her
power over the sea. Equated with water and north she is also equated with the
shrine beach and ocean front, located to the north of Hakozaki's shrine complex.

According to the Five Phase Growth Cycle, water nourishes and produces
the phase wood. This relationship indicates that Empress Jingû (water) nourished her son Emperor Ôjin (wood). "The Threatening" trigram, of which
Empress Jingû is emblematic, also signifies pregnancy (Ota 1993: 412), and
the "propagation of life" (Yoshino 1994: 26). Before departing Kyûshû for
her military conquest in Korea, the Empress discovered by divine oracle that
she was with a male child who legend relates she kept from being born on her
expedition by tying stones around her abdomen (Philippi 1968: 260, 264).
The Growth Cycle directs that Empress Jingû, indicative of "the Threatening"
and water, will have a son, Emperor Ôjin, identified with the trigram called
"the Initiating" and wood. Winter solstice, indicative of the Mother Empress
Jingû, is the annual juncture where yang/ sunlight, relating to the embryo that
will become Emperor Ôjin, is at its weakest.[19] Ôjin as the divine offspring is
represented in the sea cucumber mochi.

The winter solstice, which I assert is related to Empress Jingû, corresponds
to the trigram "the Threatening" in *The Book of Changes*. The winter solstice
is the third most potent yin interstice in the Ommyôdô calendar, following the
primary Demon Gate, and the secondary Human Gate. "The Threatening"
corresponds to the middle of lunar calendar winter, when daytime light (yang)
has reached its shortest, most weak point in the annual cycle (Ota 1993: 412).
In terms of the Feminine archetype, "the Threatening" represents a point

where the unruly, life-threatening aspects of the Terrible Mother are in the ascendant. But in terms of the Empress Jingû myth cycle, this life-taking manifestation is outwardly directed toward the Korean state of Silla. Kami beings each possess both a rough spirit (*aramitama*) and a placid spirit (*nigimitama*). The placid manifestation seeks to maintain group cohesion and "harmony," while the rough incarnation is invoked in a more individual fashion to accomplish great tasks of "action," ones requiring great physical and mental strength and determination (Herbert 1967: 61–62). The "rough spirit" is "wild, raging, raw," and "destructive" (Herbert 1967: 61), and at some kami shrines, such as the Grand Shrine of Ise or the Great Kasuga Shrine, this unruly spirit of the kami is enshrined and petitioned separately from the placid spirit housed in the Main Hall. In her manifestation as conquering warrior, Empress Jingû exhibits her turbulent rough spirit, which corresponds to two additional aspects of "the Threatening" which The Book of Changes identifies as being "dangerous" and characterized by the physical exertion of "toil" (Baynes 1967: 268, 270, 273).

Furthermore, "the Threatening" is a trigram corresponding to the New Year's juncture in the solar cycle, Former Heaven Sequence; as such it is a boundary where yin passes into yang, this juncture represents the Great Ultimate. As such, "the Threatening" (winter solstice) is a cognitive interstice at which male meets female, life combines with death, and creation blends together with destruction. Empress Jingû manifests androgynous characteristics in her girding on armor and advancing to the battlefield to fight in a fearsome, male fashion, while simultaneously, she is a pregnant female. Her expedition to Silla, manifesting her turbulent spirit, carries in it the threat of death and destruction in the manner of the Terrible Mother, but at the same time she carries within her and nourishes her unborn son in a cognitively Good Mother fashion. As such a figure, the Empress personifies the dualities of both the Great Ultimate and the Great Mother. Her rough spirit aspect is prominent, however, and as such she is enshrined in the central, north bay of Hakozaki's Main Hall. This rough, conquering spirit, combined together with her miraculous victory, must have further endeared her to warriors who in premodern Japan were drawn to make petitions at Hachiman shrines.

Tamayorihime and the Life-Freeing Rite

Hakozaki's most elaborate, annual ritual is the Life-Freeing Rite (*hôjôya*). The Life-Freeing Rite is a week-long festival during which time the three spirits of the Main Hall are paraded through the shrine parish on their way to the beach shrine. After "taking a holiday" at the Beach Shrine, the spirits are then escorted back to the Main Hall. The parade's race back into the main shrine grounds at night is a highlight of this festival. This ritual (at Hakozaki) celebrates the ascendancy of Tamayorihime, who is: 1) a cognitive pairing of threatening spirit of the depths (predating the Ôjin ritual focus) together with the role of consort to Emperor Ôjin who yields the bounty of both womb and field, 2) a personification of pertinent Ommyôdô lore surrounding the autumn equinox and the sixth trigram "the Renewing."

This trigram corresponds to west, dusk, the third daughter, concubine, autumn equinox, and both metal and water (Baynes 1967: 274, 276; Okada 1993: 137). *West*, the direction of the setting sun, *dusk* and *water* are indicative of yin: the female, Tamayorihime. Tamayorihime seems related to the designation *third, or youngest daughter* as a younger daughter of the sea deity, Watatsumi, in the *Kojiki* and *Nihon Shoki* myth cycles (her elder sister in the *Kojiki* is Toyotamahime). The *autumn equinox* is a time of waning light and warmth (as is dusk), but it is also at this equinox that Hakozaki's most elaborate, annual ritual, the Life-Freeing Rite (hôjôya), is celebrated. This ritual occasion is a celebration of the harvest, in the emergence of new life kindled by the seed of the virile Emperor Ôjin. In terms of Ommyôdô cosmology, Tamayorihime is the consort of Ôjin and as a personification of "the Renewing," she yields the bounty of womb and field. While Emperor Ôjin fertilizes the Female with seed at the spring equinox, at the autumn equinox the seed re-emerges, as *crops* (and secondarily as offspring) from the female Tamayorihime in "the Renewing" event of harvest. This interpretation is substantiated by the fact that "the Renewing" also corresponds to "food," "harvest," "fullness," and "riches" (Ota 1993: 412)

"The Renewing" indicates the *joint* phases of *both* water *and* metal. In terms of water, Tamayorihime shares this phase in common with Empress Jingû; in Ommyôdô cosmology, water produces wood. So in terms of water, both Tamayorihime and Empress Jingû further and give rise to wood, Emperor Ôjin. Metal on the other hand, produces water and controls wood, so, Tamayorihime furthers the cause of Empress Jingû (water) while limiting the action of Emperor Ôjin (wood). In terms of the seasons, this same train of thought is validated: autumn (metal—Tamayorihime) yields to winter (water—Empress Jingû) which in turn gives rise to spring (wood—Emperor Ôjin). In terms of the conjunction of water and metal in the figure of Tamayorihime, she simultaneously nourishes (as water) Emperor Ôjin (wood), and at the same time, she limits his action (as metal). The combined roles of Tamayorihime as supporter and controller of Emperor Ôjin is the first evidence that she is his consort.

The second piece of evidence arises in the fact that "the Renewing," according to the Later Heaven Sequence, is the most yang interstice among the eight trigrams. This extremity of yang beckons a yin counter-development, but on a whole this indicates that Tamayorihime is extremely life-giving in character. The Life-Freeing Rite in premodern times was observed according to the lunar calendar, from the twelfth to the eighteenth of the eighth lunar month; it is now observed on these same days during the month of September (Hakozaki-gû 1928: 50).[20] The Hakozaki Life-Freeing Rite, as presently celebrated in September, occurs within six days of the autumn equinox and within one week of the arrival of the kami at Hakozaki's beach with its attendant gathering of birth-soil. Similar to the spring equinox, the autumn equinox, according to Ommyôdô principles, denotes the meeting of yin and yang, and signals the arrival of spirits from the Unseen Realm arriving in the realm of the seen. But while at the spring equinox the seed of Emperor Ôjin cognitively fertilizes the Female, at the strongly yang autumn equinox the seed re-emerges, as *crops* (and secondarily offspring) from Tamayorihime in "the Renewing" event of the harvest. This interpretation is substantiated by the fact that "the Renewing" also corresponds to "food," "harvest," "fullness," and "riches" (Ota 1993: 412), all indicating the bounty emerging from this Good Mother in the harvest. Tamayorihime is further identified as the consort of Emperor Ôjin by another image of "the Renewing," the "concubine" (Baynes 1967: 279). The Life-Freeing Rite is a celebration of the harvest, a male priest directed ritual presenting and offering thanks to Tamayorihime as the life-granting Mother through whom the high spirits have re-emerged from the topocosm in the fruits of the harvest. This male-managed image is gentle and reflects the placid spirit of Tamayorihime enshrined in Hakozaki's Main Hall, emphasis being placed on her as the harmonizing Good Mother.

The image of the life-generating, wife figure for Emperor Ôjin is carefully chosen to emphasize this reassuring set of ideas. As covered previously in this chapter, Tamayorihime also preserves a more fearsome, "rough spirit" manifestation linked with the lurking spirit of the depths in a more Yayoi period fashion, a more sinister Feminine spirit that seems to have predated the establishment of the Ôjin ritual complex at Hakozaki. "The Renewing" trigram also corresponds to: "west," "the setting sun," "death," "the mouth," "the cave," "insufficiency," and both "smashing and breaking apart" (Baynes 1967: 279, Kiba 1997: 159, Ota 1993: 412). In these images re-emerges the character of Nira, the insatiable Terrible Mother. Tamayorihime is here identified with the west, the region that on a daily basis devours the sun into its dark regions. The west snatches the vitality of yang, and She is further characterized as a hungry mouth that pulverizes its victims. Finally, as cave, the Terrible Mother is the tomb, the resting place of corpses. Tamayorihime's second aspect is menacing, and as such she is portrayed as the agitated, easily offended Terrible Mother, who attacks from the depths of the sea, dragging life forms into a vortex of destruction and death.

Like the Nira spirit of the Ryûkyû islands, clearly a cognitive representation of the Great Mother, Tamayorihime, as an expression of "the Renewing," displays both a life-generating and a life-destroying aspect. But at Hakozaki, the person and ravages of the threatening Tamayorihime are not addressed at the Life-Freeing Rite in September; rather, these concerns are the object of ritual the Great Exorcism, conducted at the annual Demon Gate and Human Gate interstices, junctures cognitively equated with the phase of earth. Officiating at a high spirit shrine, Hakozaki's male priests who operate from an Ommyôdô cosmological standpoint have no use for the devouring, Female spirit of the depths. At the Great Exorcism, they gravely sever all ties with her destructive influence, and by following this Ommyôdô ritual script, they exorcise and deemphasize the female powers associated with menstruation and ovulation. In this light, the Great Exorcism serves as a cognitive prevention of dissolution associated with the female cycle.

At the Life-Freeing Rite, the harvest of the seed's produce, along with the role of high spirits and the Good Mother in that process, is celebrated. At this rite, the cognitive offspring of Emperor Ôjin and his consort Tamayorihime as bearer of abundance are recognized in the year's new harvest. Tamayorihime is honored at this juncture as the Good Mother and the divine means by which the high spirits have been reincarnated, in a cyclical process that has again revived the topocosm. Nonetheless, Emperor Ôjin, as the agent that made the Feminine realm of womb/ field fruitful, is especially venerated by the male priesthood at Hakozaki. His yang energy, his seed, has quickened Tamayorihime and allowed her to bring forth her yang, life-giving energy in the form of harvest (and offspring). The Life-Freeing Rite near the autumn equinox celebrates the ascendancy of water, of the placid Tamayorihime giving birth to offspring, this offspring primarily being the harvest of earth—the multiplication and reemergence of (yang) seed.

NOTES

1. The term *itsuse* in the first son's name, Itsuse-no-mikoto, has been interpreted as "benevolent rice" (*itsushine*) (Abe 1992: 186). *Inahi*, in the second son's name, Inahi-no-mikoto, denotes "cooked rice" (Philippi 1968: 473). Mikenu-no-mikoto signifies "august food lord" (Philippi 1968: 514). Waka-mikenu-no-mikoto, later to become Emperor Jimmu, signifies "young august food lord" (Philippi 1968: 626).

2. Abe Masamichi (1992) records petitions most commonly made to particular kami in Japan; according to his work, petitions to kami in the East Shrine, in

descending order of frequency, are for: 1) agricultural prosperity (21%), 2) family and reproductive success (19%), and 3) safe passage (16%). Six of the seven kami in the East Shrine are specifically identified by Abe as presiding over safe sea travel (the three female kami of Munakata, and the three male kami of Sumiyoshi). Kami in the West Shrine most commonly receive entreaties for: 1) safe passage (22% of total requests), 2) agricultural bounty (17%), and 3) family and reproductive success (11%). The petitions made to kami in the peripheral shrines all cluster around the two main Yayoi period ritual concerns: 1) fruition and 2) protection from harm. The East Shrine represents petitions of which 60% relate to fruition and 40% to protection; the West Shrine is a collection of powers of which 52% have to do with protection concerns and 48% correspond to fruition.

3. Most Shintô ritual involves the presentation of food and drink offerings. Written petitions offered at these occasions are known as generation-invoking words (norito). Recitations that are not accompanied by food or drink offerings I translate as words of respect (haishi) (see Nishitakatsuji 1986: 132–33). The non-offering recitation at the Great Exorcism denotes a distinct severing of relations, rather than the more common establishment of relations signified with the offering of food.

4. This sacred sand is routinely called *oshioi* by practitioners at Hakozaki. One priest interviewed at Ise in 2003 was aware of the ritual use of birth-soil in shrine contexts, but he said that such earth ritual was some of that "Korean influence that exists in Kyûshû" and was not part of ritual life at Ise.

5. Feast days for the three Taoist worthies of heaven, earth, and water (*sangen*) occur on the fifteenth day of the first, seventh, and tenth lunar months (Noguchi 1994: 206–7; Okada 1993: 100–101).

6. The lunar calendar was used exclusively in Japan prior to the first of January 1873, when the Meiji government adopted the Western, solar calendar (Okada 1993: 11). Prior to 1873, the rhythm of Japanese ritual life was in harmony with the agricultural cycle, and both of these cycles were regulated according to the waxing and waning of the moon. Fewer and fewer people are now engaged in agriculture, and now that the solar calendar is used to reckon most events in modern Japan, including the majority of rites at the Hakozaki Shrine (except for the ritual of Gathering Sacred Beach Sand and the Rite of the First Rabbit), the Japanese seem to have lost touch with the cycles of the moon which were once much more of a shaping and defining influence in their lives.

7. Even though the earth is indicated by the Chinese calendar to be in its yang phase on these particular days of the year, it is noteworthy that both the birth-soil *and* the practitioners who receive it are exorcised by the shrine priests. The Feminine archetype is never an either/ or proposition; the Great Mother's threatening phases must always be purged, even when her life-bestowing powers are in the ascendant.

8. The rituals on the first and fifteenth are exactly the same with the exception that the national anthem (*kimigayo*) is sung by the group, accompanied by a reed flute and a mouth organ, following the exorcism on the first of the month.

9. Korean "red disaster" mentioned in Chapter Three as negative energy that adheres in interstitial spaces including roads, bridges, and sites of illness and death, also

appears to be an Ommyôdô influenced form of Demon Gate, and therefore female, apprehension. In Korea, this type of Demon Gate affliction is dispelled by tossing millet; at Hakozaki, the pillars of cooked rice serve a similar exorcising function at the annual Demon Gate Juncture (New Year's). The yang seed is ritually employed to dispel dangerous concentrations of yin force.

10. Korean folklore directs that azuki beans are capable of averting evil spirits of darkness (yin) ("Society & the Arts," 2002: 1). This is folklore based on azuki being a yang food item in accordance with Chinese, Ommyôdô-influenced medicine/dietary principles.

11. After every major ritual at the Hakozaki Shrine, the head priest leads the assembled group to the Box Pine, where they bow and clap in unison before proceeding to the peripheral shrines behind the Main Hall. The ritual surrounding Hakozaki's Box Pine is cognitively central and significant; if nothing else, attention paid to this location by priests and parishioners make this fact abundantly clear.

12. According to shrine legend, Ôjin's mother, Empress Jingû was given two tide-controlling jewels by the Dragon King of the sea as she set out on a sea voyage to conquer Korea. She used these jewels to control the deep (Hakozaki-gû 1928: 44–45); in this tradition, there is an emphasis on pacification of the ocean depths.

13. Such human sacrifice may function as an offering to calm the unruly local water spirit, but may also represent the cognitive creation of a new, high ancestral spirit (kami) of the locality sent to the Unseen Realm as a new tutelary being to vouchsafe the water related project.

14. The entrance into the ocean is called in the *Kojiki* the "sea border" (*unasaka*); this is the interstitial place at which Tamayorihime and her sister passed from sea to land and vice versa (see Philippi 1968: 157).

15. The Rite of Three Origins was originally conducted at midnight on the thirty-first, but due to the great influx of crowds who throng into the inner shrine area at midnight to make their first pilgrimage of the New Year, this ritual in recent years has been performed at dawn on the first.

16. Informants regularly warn that amulets must be returned to persons with credentials (i.e. shrine priests) so that these items will be disposed of properly, with no harm. Priests at Hakozaki routinely explain that their incineration of old amulets at the end of the year releases the spirits to return to the sky. Obviously, high spirits are being indicated.

17. A senior priest at Kashii Shrine in Fukuoka provides further explanation for the use of paper in kami ritual: "White paper makes evergreen-offering-branches [and other ritual items] clean (*kiyoraka*), undefiled (*kegare no nai*), and pure (*seijô*). Not just any paper either, certainly not paper made from wood pulp. We use thick, Japanese paper; the raw material that is used to make it is hemp (*asa*). From ancient times, hemp has been considered to have the power to purify pollution, impurity, and defilement. This paper made from hemp [fibers] is used to effect purification because the kami hate impure things (*fu-jô na mono*)."

18. The *Nihon Shoki* identifies the thirty-second year of Emperor Kimmei to be the year 571, which is indeed, the year of the rabbit (Aston 1990: 88).

19. The Chinese adage, "The beginning of yang (as one stroke) arrives in the Return [of winter solstice]" (*ichiyô raifuku*) is equated with the winter solstice. It is used in a figurative sense meaning that winter is ending and spring arrives, or that misfortune ends and blessing ensues at the winter solstice (Ogawa 1986: 4).

20. The fifteenth day of the eighth lunar month corresponds to the Chinese Mid-Autumn Moon Festival (*chungchiuchieh*; *chûshûnomeigetsu*), a full moon festival celebrating the harvest.

Chapter Seven

Fruit of the Spirits

The content and emphases of Shintô ritual practice, at Hakozaki and on the Japanese mainland, have undoubtedly changed with the passage of centuries. This tendency has sharply accelerated during the twentieth century, and continues at this writing. Nonetheless, as some aspects of Shintô ritual have changed, a foundation of cognitive continuity has persisted. During the Yayoi period and even as late as the Asuka period, female mediums maintained significant cognitive, and even political, clout. With the advent of the Nara period and the reorganization of political structures in accordance with Chinese models, the political role of female mediums became marginalized as the structures of power became increasingly male-centered.

Concomitantly, a Chinese set of lens in the form of Ommyôdô cosmology came to pervasively structure the social perception of time, space, and spirit relations. This change served to more firmly place the coordination of Shintô ritual into the hands of males who possessed literacy levels required to employ texts like *The Book of Changes*, and who began to conduct formal Ommyôdô rites. Notions of topocosm spirits in mainland Japan's Yayoi period came to be increasingly colored by Chinese spirit concepts influenced by Yin-Yang Five Phase thought, though not to the complete eradication of the former set of ideas. This blended system of ritual practice, in the public sphere wielded by males and in popular contexts employed by females, functioned to invoke the powers of generation, fruition, and high spirit bounty upon the communities involved. This largely continues to be the case at the present, the pattern of Shintô ritual practice has been impaired to an increasing degree since 1945, given sweeping economic, scientific, social, and technological changes seen on the Japanese mainland. The weakening of the Spirit Tree, as this ritual tradition was labeled in Chapter One, originates in Japan's growing separation from agricultural life and the weakening of the traditional family system. These two environments have historically served as essential venues for the perpetuation of Shintô ritual.

The cognitive foundation of Shintô ritual practice is the Feminine archetype. The Feminine archetype is a projection, in a Jungian sense, of two realities: earth and woman. The earth cycle is most clearly evidenced in three cycles: the cycle of the seasons, the agricultural cycle, and the lunar cycle. These aspects of experience are combined together, in social cognition, with the female cycle of fertility. As a single cognitive unit, earth and woman are the medium that receives the seed. Beginning in the Yayoi period, together with the introduction of agriculture into mainland Japan, the Feminine archetype as a social reality emerged.

The Feminine archetype has produced countless varieties of Great Mother goddesses in many human societies. In mainland Japan, this Mother goddess does not presently dominate Shintô ritual forms; rather, she is an implicit reality that is most commonly expressed in terms of her projections in the form of high spirits and low spirits. While this Mother figure was a more prominent aspect of cognition in Yayoi period Japan, de-emphasis of her presence seems to be a product of further stages of cultural development, and adoption of Chinese forms, that privileged male figures as aspects of life-giving yang realities. As a result, menacing yin and female aspects of cognition, including the Mother goddess, were suppressed and sublimated.

The Great Mother, a projection of the Feminine archetype, is an ambiguous entity simultaneously possessing both life-taking and life-giving aspects. The lunar, agricultural, and feminine fertility cycles have both waning and waxing aspects. These processes of degeneration and growth each give rise to one segment of her dual character. And as devourer of the seed, the Terrible Mother is ravenous, she takes life. As bearer of offspring and harvest, the Good Mother is beneficent; from her, life forms emerge. The Great Mother represents the entire cycle, the cognitive total of both the terrible and good aspects of earth and woman. Projections of the ambivalent Mother figure in the Ommyôdô tradition include: the ancient Chinese undifferentiated dark spirit A concept (kuei), the diagram of the Great Ultimate (yin and yang), and earth active (doyô) periods in the lunar calendar. In the Yayoi period tradition evidenced in the Ryûkyûs, the Nira spirit seems to be her primary projection. At Hakozaki, the figure of Tamayorihime seems to prominently fulfill this function, as also does Empress Jingû.

Covered in Chapter Five, sublimation of the ancient Great Mother figure gave rise to new projections: spirits. In China, with the passage of time, an ambiguous Mother concept evolved into projections of threatening dark spirits (kuei; kuei-shen), and kindly bright spirits (shen, shen-ming). In Japan, similar projections were called low spirits (mi, mono) and high spirits (kami, myôjin). Ommyôdô thought and Chinese orthography particularly influenced and certainly hastened the development of spirits in Japan that were related to their Chinese counterparts. Projections of the Good Mother in Japan include: anthropomorphic, contented, ancestral spirits who receive regular veneration (kami, tama), including the virgin field spirit (tanokami) who descends from the mountains bearing fertility in the spring; and island priestesses in the Ryûkyûs who preside over fruition rites and who traditionally serve as emblems of social cohesion and harmony. In terms of Ommyôdô-influenced cosmology, projections of the Good Mother are: the calendrical Wind Gate and Heaven Gate interstices, Ôjin equated with Hakozaki's Spirit Tree at the spring equinox, and the general tendency to equate high spirits with yang characteristics including male gender, the solar cycle, and heaven.

Earth and woman, the Feminine archetype, collectively receive the seed. This seed is analogous to the corpse that decays, that fertilizes the Great Mother, and is reincarnated as the Ancestor (high spirit; kami) as offspring, vegetation, and food. In other words, fruition. Projections of the Ancestor include the primordial sprout (kabi, me) emerging from the earth, the negotiation of an interstice, and birth from the female. All of these images are interpretations of the term "celebratory" (medetai) which functions to structure the Shintô cosmology of fruition (hare; medetasa) as opposed to decay and degeneration (kegare). In addition to the image of sprout, the Ancestor is also projected in Shintô ritual practice as the pillar, a salient example being Ise's central spirit pillar (shinnomihashira), and Hakozaki's Spirit Tree. The Ancestor is also quite often projected as the Old Man figure (okina) or the snake. The Old Man is the corporate, contented Ancestor acclaimed by Yanagita as the personification of tutelary ancestral spirits. The emperor, by means of ritual transformation, occupies the cognitive position of the "manifest ancestor" (akitsukami), also known as the "ancestor appearing in human form" (arahitogami) who is descended from the sun, a projection of dominant yang.

Projections of the menacing Feminine, the Terrible Mother that devours the seed, are several. In ancient China, fierce dark spirit B (kuei) entities that suffered an unhappy demise and preyed on the living were equated with yin forces. In addition, the Demon Gate and Human Gate calendrical interstices, points of marked Feminine power, and the predatory Nien monster at New Year's are equally projections of the Terrible Mother. In Japanese folklore and ritual practice, low spirits (chi, mi, mono) are deformed and strange entities in the landscape that lack regular ritual attention from the human community, and are hungry and predatory as a result. Water spirits (kappa) and the tired mountain spirit in winter (yamamba), given their predatory aspects, also seem to be projections of the menacing Feminine. These spirits' unusual forms denote an otherness that stands in contrast to the contented, anthropomorphic Old Man figure. Low spirits are emblematic of existence on the margins, or beyond the pale of social order. In the Ryûkyûs female shamans are socially marginal, represent anomalies to the social order, and perform ritual exorcisms and ransoms to free clients from the effects of low spirit predation. These female shamans, like the weird spirits they serve, are personifications of social non-belonging. In terms of Ommyôdô cosmology, there is a tendency to emphasize the link between yin, strangeness, lunar cycle, and earth phenomena with low spirits.

The dual aspect of the Great Mother (Good and Terrible) and the subsequent division of spirits (high and low spirits) are two poles around which Shintô ritual practice revolves: fruition and decay (exorcism). Fruition ritual is focused on generation, growth, and development; examples of these phenomena include birth and abundant harvest. Common foci in these rites include the: Ancestor, seed, and pillar. Exorcism rites are calculated to eradicate degeneration, dissolution, disintegration, and destruction. Examples of these cognitive realities include weakness, disease, injury, and death; salt and birth-soil are employed in such rites. As examined in Chapter Three, these two classes of rituals, fruition and decay, must be kept separate. Hakozaki follows this pattern; no food offerings that establish ties with spirits are offered at the Great Exorcism, and no birth-soil ritual occurs in the fruition rites performed before the Main Hall.

Three levels of cognition must be made distinct to structure this separation and begin to resolve this quagmire.[1] The Feminine archetype begins as a projection of earth and feminine cycles and projections emerge of the ambiguous Great Mother, such as the Nira spirit. At a later point the Great Mother is divided into Good and Terrible aspects, with projections such as high spirit, Old Man, or low water spirit. Next, two systems of separate ritual emerge, focused on the spirit projections of the two aspects of the Feminine archetype. Once institutionalized and defined as distinct, without dealing with the underlying cognitive foundation of the Feminine archetype, how can the two systems of ritual be explicated (exorcism and invocation of blessing), other than in terms of the ritual systems, or the two classes of spirits? In terms of the Spirit Tree analogy used in Chapter One, such explanations only focus on limb and branch strata realities. By returning to the root and soil levels, the female medium tradition and the Feminine archetype, it becomes clear that the cycles of earth, moon, and female are simultaneously life-giving and life-taking realities. Together, fruition and decay comprise the entire cycle expressed by the Feminine archetype. This cognitive unity serves to order an otherwise fragmented set of ritual practice. At Hakozaki, ritual practice confirms this interpretation. All fruition rites performed before the Main Hall begin with exorcism. This is an acknowledgment that even the high spirits equated with fruition are not separate from low spirit realities. Exorcism, as explained by shrine priests, is observed to rid the rite of low spirit interference. This exorcism ritual indicates that on an implicit level, there is an awareness within ritual form that the Great Mother, and hence the Feminine archetype, are a cognitive whole of life-bearing and life-threatening aspects.

RITUAL AT HAKOZAKI

Addressed in Chapter Six, two ritual traditions coexist in northern Kyûshû generally, and at Hakozaki particularly. Ritual coordinated by male priests at Hakozaki is most prominently structured in terms of Ommyôdô cosmology and is accorded legitimate social recognition by the prefectural and national governments. The main focus of male priest ritual are the heavenly-descended, high spirits Empress Jingû and her son, Emperor Ôjin, progenitors of the imperial line. This emphasis on heaven represents an Ommyôdô emphasis on yang, male-centered, life-giving realities. With two exceptions in the year (the Great Exorcisms), ritual performed by priests takes place at a central location, before the shrine's Main Hall. Male priests exclusively manage ritual performed at this area.

Chief among Hakozaki's male-coordinated rites are Rites of Celebration. Three of these five rites are prominent points in the annual solar cycle. At the spring equinox, ritual acknowledges the rise of the gallant Emperor Ôjin, associated with the phase of wood and the trigram of "the Initiating," in the object of the shrine's Spirit Tree. The autumn equinox celebrates the emergence of the harvest in the figure of Tamayorihime, associated with the phases of metal and water and the trigram of "the Renewing," and the pre-Ôjin sea spirit of Hakozaki that came to be cast in the role of Emperor Ôjin's consort. The winter solstice marks a ritual for the martial Empress Jingû, corresponding to the phase of water and the trigram of "the Threatening," who will give birth to Emperor Ôjin at the commencement of the New Year. Finally, in an effort to claim this point of Female power by Hakozaki's male priesthood, New Year's marks the birth of the infant Ôjin, in the sea cucumber mochi offering, and the burial of his placenta as a calming offering to seal the devouring aspect of the Feminine. These five yang (*hare*) rituals mark junctures at which the power of the seed and male are the life-conferring power that fertilizes the ambiguous Female, transforming her into the life-bearing Good Mother of fruition. The standard offering that distinguishes all five of these rites are cooked rice pillars (jukusen) that denote the male principle and the triumph of the Ancestor.

The biannual Great Exorcism rituals performed by male priests are junctures that, according to Ommyôdô cosmology, are points of Female power: the annual Demon Gate (New Year transition) and Human Gate (mid-year transition). According to Ommyôdô thought, these points in time are indicative of menstruation and ovulation respectively in the female. These two rites are the only ones in which Hakozaki's male priests use birth-soil in exorcism. These rites take place outside of the Main Hall ritual arena and serve to exorcise the concentration of yin forces (kegare) associated with the Feminine archetype.

On the other hand, ritual observed by females at Hakozaki, while being partially structured by Ommyôdô cosmological principles, seems to be based on an older, more vague set of principles. This set of unofficial, popular practices is more Female-centered, focused on the local earth and sea spirit, Tamayorihime. While women who observe these rituals also acknowledge the male priesthood and the rites it leads before the Main Hall, their popular rituals are focused on more peripheral shrine areas and yin, female concerns. Their ritual revolves around the peripheral shrine complexes, the other dimension shrine near the beach, and the shrine beach itself.

The most salient Female-centered rituals for women at Hakozaki are Yang Earth Rites that are cognitively oriented in terms of lunar cycles. Women, many now elderly, gather birth-soil on the first and fifteenth of the month at the shrine beach to use for exorcism at the entryway of their homes. These two dates recall the new and full moon junctures of the old lunar calendar. According to Ommyôdô cosmology, the new moon corresponds to the monthly Demon Gate juncture while the full moon is indicative of the Human Gate. These two times, in turn, relate to the female fertility cycle events of menstruation and ovulation and are not times at which male priests advertise the gathering of birth-soil. Women at Hakozaki gather soil at these two monthly junctures as a means of obtaining the Great Mother, Tamayorihime's power for themselves. These same two days each month, male priests conduct a special exorcism near the Main Hall at the northeast, Demon Gate, corner as an expression of apprehensions regarding Feminine power associated with this most potently yin juncture in Ommyôdô cosmology. Women also gather birth-soil at the spring and autumn equinoxes, times when ancestral spirits from the Unseen Realm bring power to the sand. The Yayoi period cosmology based on the Feminine archetype seems to structure three classes of popular, female conducted ritual in northern Kyûshû: soil-release rituals involving birth-soil, Feminine interstice shrine rites (focused on the well, hearth, and soil), and red rice ritual.

CONCLUDING THOUGHTS

A great deal more research has yet to be done on Ommyôdô influences in Japan, including a more thorough examination of is its role in ritual life. The majority of Japanese citizens, perhaps owing to a growing unfamiliarity, do not recognize aspects of Yin-Yang Five Phase cosmology as such. For many persons, these phenomena are simply traditionally "Japanese" ideas. Strained relations experienced by Japan with neighboring countries during and following the Second World War have been an impetus for some Japanese scholars to skirt the issue of Ommyôdô thought as an organizing force in traditional Japanese cultural forms. For Western scholars, too, it is perhaps more convenient to consider Japan in a vacuum apart from its neighbors. An insularity of research scope for Japanese studies in general has perhaps unwittingly colluded with the former tendencies, rendering dormant a broader acknowledgment of Japan's explicit relatedness to the larger sphere of Chinese cultural influences. Studies that examine Ommyôdô influences in Japanese cultural contexts will begin to remedy this situation and establish Japan as an extension of East Asia rather than a "special case."

In particular, more work should be done to account for shared history and relatedness of pattern between mainland Japan and its neighbors, Korea and the Ryûkyûs. Relatedness of language, ritual practice, and history need to be explicated in a more concerted and dedicated fashion. If as scholars we fail to account for such vast similarities, then we do not deserve to inherit a clearer picture of Japan's genetic, cultural, and historical identity.

In a country that is constantly competing with itself to become evermore rational and modern, largely along Western lines, comparatively few bother to maintain what many, even some sheepish practitioners, now call superstitions (*meishin*) from the past. Needless to say, it is often the elderly, their immediate offspring, and others whom these repositories of the past happen to admonish that concern themselves with kami ritual. One priest at Hakozaki explained that the mobility of families in modern Japan has been the main cause for breaking with all sorts of tradition, particularly kami ritual. "The lack of contact between the elderly and the younger generations, many of whom used to help raise the children of the neighborhood, and the increasingly lower incidence of elderly relatives living in homes with their extended family, has seriously impaired this intergenerational flow of tradition," he said.[2]

In the contemporary age, the Tamura family of the Hakozaki Shrine is persevering to keep public support constant. Shrine personnel pursue ever more extensive advertising campaigns to draw the public into its seasonal festivals.

The Chief Priest's son is presently being groomed to become the fifty-third chief priest as he assumes increasing levels of responsibility at Hakozaki. In 2003, a grand refurbishing of the Main Hall was completed, which included the major renovation of cedar bark roof shingles, massive amounts of red lacquer and guilt work, and new furnishings for the interior. In addition to a small amount of money provided by the national government for this, the priests worked hard to raise millions of dollars to fund the project in its entirety. It is a heavy burden to be the inheritors and custodians of items designated by the government as National Treasures.

Hakozaki lays claim to a glorious architectural legacy; it also maintains a priceless treasure of mankind's cognitive inheritance preserved in its ritual practice. Located at the top of Kyûshû and facing the mainland of Asia, Hakozaki preserves in its legitimate male and popular female coordinated rituals a living cross section of cognitive history. The Spirit Tree standing before the Main Hall flourishes in the local soil while the Spirit Tree of the Shintô worldview struggles to do likewise, at Hakozaki and in other venues throughout Japan.

NOTES

1. Some practitioners explain the spirits addressed in each set of ritual are mutually incompatible, and are prone to actively dispute if combined. Furthermore, their natures are incompatible: high spirits are pure (seijô; hare) while low spirits are defiled (kegare). These basic differences make a meeting undesirable. Another explanation is that a combination of these two separated realms is unlucky (*engi ga yokunai*). In other words, fruition ritual (for example a noshi-bearing envelope) at a decay ritual occasion (a funeral) will encourage the growth and development of more death and decay to the recipient family and is therefore taboo. These explanations are circular; they provide no clear means of resolving the issues involved.

2. Robert Smith, citing a study conducted by Morioka Kiyoshi in the mid 1960s, indicates that among the ten-year-old children that were interviewed, grandparents seemed to have been an important factor in teaching children to venerate ancestors, but mothers were mentioned by children with even greater frequency as the familial influence who had trained them to venerate (*ogamu*) ancestors (Smith 1974: 120–23). While grandparents do seem to be a significant source of training for younger Japanese with regard to ancestor and kami veneration, based on the previous children's responses, they do not seem to be the *only* or the most prominent source of that training. Intriguingly, however, it is predominantly elderly parishioners who attend the only *public* rite at the Hakozaki Shrine that is still reckoned according to the lunar calendar, the Gathering of Sacred Beach Sand.

Appendix A

Chronology of Japanese History

Jômon period	10,000 BC–250 BC
Yayoi period	200 BC–250 AD
Kofun period	250–552
Asuka period	552–645
Nara period	645–794
Heian period	794–1185
Kamakura period	1185–1338
Muromachi period	1338–1568
Momoyama period	1568–1615
Edo period	1615–1867
Meiji period	1868–1912
Taishô era	1912–1926
Shôwa era	1926–1989
Heisei era	1989–present

Roster of Peripheral Shrine Spirits

East Shrine

Bay 1: Inari-sha
    a. Inari-sha
      1. Ugamitama-no-kami
    b. Ta-no-kami-sha
      1. Haniyasu-himegami
Bay 2: Sumiyoshi-dono
    a. Sumiyoshi-san-shin
    b. Suwa-ôkami
      1. Hiko-gami
      2. Hiko-gami
    c. Ameno-minakanushi-no-mikoto
Bay 3: Otoko-dono
    a. Uji-no-waka-no-mikoto
    b. Wakino-irazuko
    c. Ujinowaki-iratsuko
Bay 4: Take-no-uchi-sha
    a. Take-no-uchi-no-sukune

West Shrine

Bay 1: Minjun-sha
    a. Minjun-sha
      1. Haniyasu-no-kami
    b. Aragorô-jinja
      1. Ukemochi-no-kami
    c. Take-no-uchi-sha
      1. Hayato-no-kami
    d. Suga-sha
      1. Takehaya Susanoô no kami
Bay 2: Itsukushima-dono
    a. Ichikishima-no-mikoto
    b. Izanagi-no-mikoto
    c. Izanami-no-mikoto
    d. Keigo-san-bashira-ôkami
    e. Atago-ôkami
    f. Amano-nibu-no-kami

Bay 5: Ikeshima-dono
  a. Munakata-mi-megami
  b. Kôjin-sha
    1. Kaguzuchi-no-mikoto
    2. Okutsuhiko-no-mikoto
    3. Okutsuhime-no-mikoto
  c. Shuzô-jinja
    1. Sukunabiko-no-mikoto
    2. Ôyama-kui-no-mikoto
    3. Uganomitama-no-
       mikoto

Bay 3: Chûai-dono
  a. Emperor Chûai
  b. Amaterasu-ômikami
  c. Shika-san-bashira-ôkami
  d. Ameno-koyaneno-mikoto
  e. Takara-tamatare-no-
     mikoto
Bay 4: Wakamiya-dono
  a. Emperor Nintoku
  b. Waka-hime
  c. Ura-hime
  d. Kure-hime
Bay 5: Ryûô-sha
  a. Watatsumi-no-kami

Glossary

aitai suru	相対する	to face one another
akafujō	赤不浄	red impurity
akitsukami	明津神 現つ神	manifest ancestor, the Emperor
amatsukami	天津神	high, heavenly spirits
arahitogami	荒人神 現人神	ancestor in human form, the Emperor
aramitama	荒魂	rough spirit
asa	麻	hemp
bakemono	化物	transformed-object apparition
bōchibō-uchi	穂打棒打ち	striking the grain head staff rite
bosatsu	菩薩	bodhisattva
bunai (Ryu.)	ブナイ	sister priestess on Dunang
bunke	分家	branch family
butsudan	仏壇（佛壇）	family Buddhist altar
chakai	茶会（茶會）	tea gatherings
chapkwi (Kor.)	잡귀 (雜鬼)	sundry low spirits, ghosts
chesa (Kor.)	제사 (祭祀)	Confucian ancestor ritual
c'hi (Man.)	氣 （気）	Primordial Breath, vital energy
chifijing (Ryu.)	貴婦人	Ryūkyū kingdom chief priestess
chihayaburu	千早振る	"impetuous," said of kami

chijin	地神	earth spirit, in Seto region
chilsŏng (Kor.)	칠성 (七星)	the Seven Stars
chinokamisama	地の神さま	kami of the earth/place
chisin tongbŏp (Kor.)	地神動法	unruly earth spirits
chito	地戸	Earth Door (Wind Gate)
chōju	長寿 （長壽）	longevity
chosang (Kor.)	조상 (祖上)	ancestor spirits
chosang malmyŏng (Kor.)	祖上말명	restless ancestor spirits
chū	丑	earthly branch equated with the cow
Chunchiu-tsoshih-chuan (Man.)	春秋左氏傳	*Tsuo Commentary*, 535 BC
chungchiuchieh (Man.)	中秋節	Mid-Autumn Moon Festival
chūshūnomeigetsu	中秋の名月	Mid-Autumn Moon Festival
daidai	橙／代々	bitter orange / many generations
dango	団子 （團子）	round rice dumplings
dokujin	土公神	tutelary earth spirit in Ommyōdō
doyō	土用	earth active period
ekibyōgami	疫病神	epidemic spirits
emaden	絵馬殿	hall of votive tablets
engawa	縁側	veranda-under-the-eaves
engi ga ii	縁起がいい	auspicious
engi ga yokunai	縁起がよくない	inauspicious
enmusubi no kami	縁結びの神	spirit of male-female relations

feng shui (Man.)	風水	geomancy
fūfu	夫婦	husband and wife
fūfu emman	夫婦円満 (圓滿)	conjugal harmony
fūfu ga mutsumajiku	夫婦が睦まじく	conjugal harmony
fūfuwagō	夫婦和合	conjugal harmony
fu-jō na mono	不浄なもの	impure things
fūmon	風門	Wind Gate
fushi sōzoku	父子相続 (相續)	continuation of generations
Fusō-ryakki	扶桑略記	*Abbreviated Record of Japan*, late 11th century
futasu-futatsu	二つ二つ	two and two
genkansaki	玄関先 (玄關先)	at the entryway
Gishiwajinden (Man. *Wei chih*)	魏誌倭人傳	*Chronicles of Wei*, 297 A.D.
gogyō	五行	the Five Phases of matter
gohei	御幣	zigzag paper offering wands
gosenzosama	御先祖様	contented ancestors, high spirits
goshintai	御神体	object of veneration (literally: "kami body")
gozutennō	牛頭天王	Cowhead Heavenly King (Gion)
gūji	宮司	Chief Priest of a shrine
haiden	拝殿 (拜殿)	veneration hall of a shrine
haishi	拝詞 (拜詞)	words of respect, without offerings

hakama	袴	divided skirt
hakomatsu	筥松	the Box Pine
hakozaki	筥崎	Box Cape
Hakozaki Hachiman-gū	筥崎八幡宮	Hakozaki Hachiman Shrine
hamaya	破魔矢	demon-crushing-arrow, talisman
hanei	繁栄（繁榮）	prosperity
haraigushi	祓い串	exorcism wand
harame-uchi	孕打ち	dealing a filling blow rite
haramu	孕む	to fill, impregnate
harau	祓う／払う	to exorcise / to clear, sweep away
hare	晴れ	concentrations of yang force
hashi-me-no-tokoro	端目の所	source places
hashira	柱	pillar, counter word for kami
hatsuusai	初卯祭	the First Rabbit Rite
heiwa	平和	peace, harmony
henge	変化（變化）	changling
higashi	干菓子	dry rice flour sweets
hito-bashira	人柱	human pillar sacrifice
hitotsume kozō	一つ目小僧	one-eyed apparitions
hōjōya	放生会（放生會）	the Life-Freeing Rite
honden	本殿	Main Hall of shrine
hongaek (Kor.)	홍액 (紅厄)	red disaster

honke	本家	main house
hoshigaki	干し柿	dried persimmons
hotoke-sama	仏様（佛様）	Buddha, ancestor spirits
hou tien pa kua t'u (Man.)	後天八卦圖（図）	Later Heaven Sequence
houtugung (Man.)	后土公	Chinese earth spirit
hsien tien pa kua t'u (Man.)	先天八卦圖（図）	Former Heaven Sequence
Hsi-wang-mu (Man.)	西王母	Queen Mother of the West
hun (Man.)	魂	yang soul, during life
hun-ch'i (Man.)	魂氣（魂気）	yang soul breath
hyakki yagyō	百鬼夜行	nighttime demon procession
ibi (Ryu.)	イビ	inner enclosure shrine
ichimabui (Ryu.)	生きマブイ	living life-soul
ichiyō raifuku	一陽来復／福	"Yang begins at winter solstice."
ido	井戸	well
ie no kamisama	家の神さま	household kami
ii kamisama	いい神さま	good kami, high spirits
ikazuchi	雷	thunder spirit (*Kojiki*)
inkamuro (Ryu.)	インカムロ	water spirit of ocean
inokami	亥の神	harvest (boar) spirit, Kansai region
inyōgogyōsetsu (see *Ommyōdō*)	陰陽五行説	Yin-Yang Five Phase cosmology
itako	イタコ	female medium, Tōhoku area
iwai	祝い	celebratory

iwakura	磐座	stone vessel altar (ritual area)
iwasaka	磐境	rock boundary (ritual area)
izumi	泉／出水	spring (of water)
izuminoshita	泉の下	underworld
Izumo taisha	出雲大社	Great Shrine of Izumo
jangdokte (Kor.)	장독대 （醬독臺）	storage platform
jiaguwen (Man.)	甲古文	oracle bone texts
jichinsai	地鎮祭	soil pacification rites
jikkan	十干	the ten heavenly branches
jinja	神社	kami shrine
jinja honchō	神社本庁 （本廳）	Central Bureau of Shrines
jimmon	人門	Human Gate, or Rear Demon Gate
jū (Ryu.)	ジュー (穣)	fruition
jujutsu	呪術	magical incantation
jukusen	熟饌	cooked rice pillars
jūnishi	十二支	the twelve earthly branches
k'a (Ryu.)	力	island priestess on Dunang
kabi	牙／穎	sprout, bud
kadomatsu	門松	gate-pines
kagutsuchi	火の迦具土	fire spirit (*Kojiki*)
kākaro (Ryu.)	カーカロ	water spirit of springs and wells
kamado	竈	the traditional hearth structure

kamekan	甕棺	Yayoi period ceramic urn coffins
kami	神	spirits, ancestral spirits
kamidana	神棚	kami altar
kamikatarai	神語らい	spirit intercourse
kan (Ryu.)	カン (神)	spirit, ancestral spirit, priestess
kandin (Ryu.)	神瓶	sacred vase
kanbunaga (Ryu.)	カンブナガ	major, high spirit ritual occasions
kanji	漢字	Chinese characters
kan-nu-michi (Ryu.)	神の道	Spirit Trails (on Dunang Island)
kansai	関西 (關西)	West of the Barrier (western Japan)
kantō	関東 (關東)	East of the Barrier (eastern Japan)
kappa	河童／河伯	water spirit
karahitsu	唐櫃	wooden chest for ritual use
kegare	汚れ (穢れ)	concentrations of yin force
kegare no nai	汚れのない	undefiled
kidō	鬼道	sorcery
kiyoraka	清らか	clean, pure
Kimigayo	君が代	Japanese national anthem
kimo	肝／胆	liver, gall bladder, vitality
kimon	鬼門	Demon Gate
kiyomeru	清める	to purify, to make yang

Glossary

kodama	木霊／谺	echo (literally, tree spirit)
Kojiki	古事記	mythology/history, 712 A.D.
kōkotsumoji	甲骨文字	oracle bone texts
kokugaku	国学（國學）	National Learning scholarship
kosa (Kor.)	고사 (告祀)	offering to household spirits
kōshin-no-gi	降神の儀	rite of kami descent
kotodama	言霊信仰（言靈）	word-spirit belief
koyomi	暦	lunar calendar almanac
kudii (Ryu.)	クディー	sister priestess on Okinawa
kuei (Man.)	鬼	dark spirit A: all deceased spirits dark spirit B: threatening spirits
kuei-shen (Man.) (Jpn. *kijin*)	鬼神	dark spirits; dark-bright spirits; dark *and* bright spirits
kukunochi	茎の靈	tree spirit (*Kojiki*)
kunitsukami	国津神	low, earth spirits (*Kojiki*)
kut (Kor.)	굿	female medium's ritual
Li-chi (Man.)	禮記（礼記）	*Ritual Records*, third century B.C.
mabui (Ryu.)	マブイ	life-soul
magatsuhi	禍津日	misfortune-working spirit
magatsukami	枉津神	twisted, malevolent spirit
mamono	魔物	low spirit, demon, evil spirit
mayoke	魔除け	to avert evil, to dispell yin
mansin (Kor.)	만신 (萬神)	female medium, shaman

Manyōshū	万葉集（萬葉集）	eighth century poetry anthology	
massha	末社	peripheral shrine	
medetai	芽出たい	celebratory	sprout emerging
	目出たい	celebratory	interstice emerging
	雌出たい	celebratory	Feminine emerging
medetakunai	目出たくない	non-celebratory	
medetasa	目出たさ	fruition, life-giving production	
me ga deta	芽が出た	the bud, sprout has emerged	
meishin	迷信	superstition	
me-no-hashi-me	女の端目	source of womanhood	
miao (Man.)	廟	familial ancestral hall	
miko	巫女	female medium, shrine maiden	
mitsudomoe	三つ巴	three swirling commas crest	
mizuchi	水霊（水霊）	water spirit (*Kojiki*)	
mizuhiki	水引き	water-applying knots	
mochi	餅	glutinous rice cake	
moe-agaru	萌騰がる	to bud or sprout	
moksin tongbōp (Kor.)	木神動法	unruly tree spirit	
mon	門	gate	
mono	モノ	low spirit, demon	
mononoke	物の怪	low spirit, demon, evil spirit	
moromuki	諸向	two facing together, fern name	

muenbotoke	無縁佛	relationless deceased spirit
munaci (Ryu.)	ムナチ	female shaman on Dunang
mutsu	睦	friendly, intimate, harmonious
musuhi / musubi	産巣日	generative force (*Kojiki*)
myōjin	明神	high spirits
namakomochi	なまこ餅	sea cucumber mochi
nanten	南天	*nandina domestica*
nan wo tenzuru	難を転ずる	diverting misfortune
naohi / naobi	直毘	healing spirit (*Kojiki*)
naorai	直会（直會）	meal of rapport
nigimitama	和魂	placid spirit
Nihon Shoki	日本書記	mythology / history, 720 A.D.
nikoniko	ニコニコ	two and two / all smiles
nōgami	農神	farming spirit, in Tōhoku region
norito	祝詞	generation-invoking words
noshi	熨斗	lengthened-abalone ornament
nozuchi	野槌	field spirit (*Kojiki*)
nunka (Ryu.) (see *sunka*)	ヌンカ	Other World (of death)
nuru (Ryu.)	ヌル	island priestess on Okinawa
ōamu (Ryu.)	大母	Great Mother priestess
o-enasai	御胞衣祭	the August Planceta Rite

ofuda	お札	amulet-tablet
ogamu	拝む　(拜む)	to venerate
ōga-no-morime	大神杜女	Usa's great female priest, 749 A.D.
ōharai	大祓い	biannual Great Exorcism rite
oharaijo	お祓い所	place of exorcism
ōharai no kotoba	大祓詞	Words of Great Exorcism
ohigan	お彼岸	the far shore period, Unseen Realm
o-kagami	お鏡	mirror-mochi
okina	翁	Old Man, high spirit, Ancestor
okumiya	奥宮	removed, interior shrine
Ōkuninushi	大国主	Great Earth (Topocosm) Lord
o-mamori	お守り	protective-talisman
omiki	お神酒	rice wine offering
Ommyōdō	陰陽道	Yin-Yang Five Phase cosmology
ommyōji	陰陽師	Ommyōdō practitioner
ommyōnotsukasa	陰陽寮	Bureau of Ommyōdō at court
Ōmononushi	大物主	Great Lord of Earthly Spirits
omote	表	frontside realities
ōna	媼	Old Woman, high spirit, Ancestor
oni	鬼	low spirit, demon
o-no-hashi-me	男の端目	source of masculinity

Glossary

onryō	怨靈 （怨霊）	menacing low spirit
ōpu (Kor.)	어푸	tutelary serpent spirit
Ōsaka	逢坂	Meeting Slope, a Ōtsu
osameru	納める／治める	to garner / to manage, subdue
oshahi	お社日	birth-soil day
oshioi	お潮井	birth-soil
oshioi-tori	お潮井取り	gathering sacred beach sand
otabisho	お旅所	other dimension shrine
otsukai	お使い	spirit familiar, messenger
paksu (Kor.)	딱수	male medium
Pa kua (Man.)	八卦	the Eight Trigrams
Pei-tou-hsing-chun (Man.)	北斗星君	Lord of the Northern Dipper
p'o (Man.)	魄	yin soul, during life
p'o-hsing (Man.)	魄形	yin soul [physical] matter
sakaki	榊	evergreen, *Cleyera ochnaces*
sainan	災難	calamity, misfortune
saisei	再生	extension of life, rebirth
sakaeru	栄える	to flourish, thrive
saku	裂く／割く	to tear, rip / to sever, separate
sambō	三方	wooden ritual offering stand
sangen	三元	worthies of heaven, earth, & water

sangensai	三元祭	the Rite of Three Origins
sanokami	サの神	field-spirit
sansin (Kor.)	산신 (山神)	mountain spirit
saotome	早乙女	field-spirit maidens
sarashi	晒し	bleached white cloth
sasa	笹	bamboo grass, *Sasa kozassa*
satoimo	里芋	taro, *Colocasia antiquorum*
satokotoba	里ことば	village language
segakie	施餓鬼会	ritual to feed the wandering dead
seijō	清浄	pure
sekihan	赤飯	red rice
senjutsu	占術	divination
shanichi	社日	birth-soil day
shen (Man.)	神	bright spirits
shen ch'i (Man)	神氣 (神気)	bright energy
shen ming (Man.)	神明	bright spirits
shide	紙垂	zigzag streamers of cut paper
shigan	此岸	this shore, the seen realm
Shih-chi (Man.)	史記	*Annals of History*, ca. 91 B.C.
shikaku	資格	qualifications
shikigami	式神	familiar spirit sent on errands
shimboku	神木	Spirit Tree, divine tree

shimekazari	しめ飾	entry-decoration
shimenawa	注連縄	rice straw festoon
shinnomihashira	眞御柱	central spirit pillar
shinsei-dokoro	神聖處	sacred place
Shintō	神道	cycle of high spirits
shison han'ei	子孫繁栄	abundance of offspring
shizen	自然	nature, natural order
shizume-mono	鎮めもの	calming offering
shōshin-no-gi	昇神の儀	rite of kami ascent
sillyong (Kor.)	신령 (神靈)	spirit, god
sumera	皇ら	title for kami or Japanese emperor
sumemima	皇御孫	imperial line descendants
sunka (Ryu.) (see *nunka*)	スンカ	this world (of fruition)
T'ai chi (Man.)	太極	the Great Ultimate
taiin	太陰	moon, the Great Yin
taiyō	太陽	sun, the Great Yang
tama	玉／魂	life-soul on Japanese mainland high spirit
tamagaeshi	魂返し	returning the soul rite
tamagushi	玉串	evergreen offering branches
Tamayorihime	玉依姫	Hakozaki's Female spirit of the west

tamuke	手向け	safe travel offerings
tanokami	田の神	field spirit
tanuki	狸	badger-dog
tanzaku	短冊	fancy poem tablets
Tao (Man.)	道	the Way
Tao-te-ching (Man.)	道德經（道徳経）	*Classic of The Way and Its Power*
tao-t'ieh (Man.)	饕餮	monster on Shang bronzes
tatari	祟り	curse, retribution
tenmon	天門	Heaven Gate
tōju (Kor.)	터주 (基主)	house site spirit
tokiwagi	常磐木	eternally celebratory tree
tokkaebi (Kor.)	도깨비	low spirit, demon
tokonoma	床の間	ritual alcove
tori-tsuku	取付く	to possess
toshi no hajime	年の始め	beginning of the year
Tou-mu-yuan-chun (Man.)	斗母元君	Mother of the Northern Dipper
tsao hua (Man.)	造化	Mother Nature, creative change
tsuchi-no-e	戊／土の兄	yang earth, heavenly stem
tsukinamisai	月並祭	the monthly ritual (1st & 15th)
tsukurigami	作り神	growing spirit, in Kinki region
tudigung (Man.)	土地公	old man earth spirit

tudima (Man.)	土地媽	earth mother spirit
Tung-wang-kung (Man.)	東王公	King Sire of the East
ubaishi	姥石	Old Woman Rock
ubazuki	姥月	Old Woman Moon
ubusuna	産砂	birth-soil; tutelary spirit of local earth
ujigami	氏神	ancestral tutelary beings
umaku chōwa	巧く調和	smooth interplay (of yin and yang)
uminokami	海の神	sea spirit
uminosachi	海の幸	bounty of the sea
unasaka	海坂	sea border entrance (*Kojiki*)
ura	裏	backside realities
urajiro	裏白	fern, *Gleichenia glauca*
urakimon (see *jimmon*)	裏鬼門	Rear Demon Gate
urami	恨み	ill will, grudge
ushirogami	うしろ神	shiver-from-behind spirits
utaki (Ryu.)	お嶽	High Peak shrine
utsubo	空	sealed vessel
warui kamisama	悪い神さま	bad kami, low spirits
washi	和紙	thick Japanese paper
watatsumi	綿津見	sea spirit (*Kojiki*)

yaku-yoke	厄除け	protection from evil, yin dispelling
yamakotoba	山ことば	mountain language
yamamba	山姥	mountain hag
yamanokami	山の神	mountain spirit
yamanosachi	山の幸	bounty of the mountains
yamatsumi	山津見	mountain spirit (*Kojiki*)
yang-chieh	陽界	seen realm, corporeal existence
yaso-magatsuhi	八十枉津日	twisted, malevolent spirit
Yi-ching (Man.)	易經 (易経)	*Book of Changes*, ninth century B.C.
yin-chieh (Man.)	陰界	the Unseen Realm of spirits
yin-yang-chia (Man.)	陰陽家	geomancer, sorcerer, astrologer
yōkai	妖怪	changling spectre
yōngsan (Kor.)	영산 (靈山)	ghost
yorishiro	依代	materializing-medium for kami
Yuan chi (Man.)	元氣 (元気)	Primordial Breath
yukionna	雪女	Snow Woman
yuta (Ryu.)	ユタ	female shaman (on Okinawa)
yuzuriha	交讓葉	*Daphiphyllum macropodum*

Select Bibliography

Abe Hajime. *Nihon kûkan no tanjô: kosumorojii, fûkei, takaikan*. Tôkyô: Serika shobô, 1995.

Abe Masamichi. *Nihon no kamisama wo shiru jiten*. Tôkyô: Nihon bungeisha, 1992.

Akiba Takashi. "A Study on Korean Folkways." *Folklore Studies* 14 (1957): 1-106.

Amamoto Takashi. "Minzoku no naka no kappa densetsu." In *Kyûshû kappa kikô*, edited by Kyûshû kappa no kai. Fukuoka: Asahi shobô, 1993.

Arai Ken. "New Religions." In *Religion in Japanese Culture: Where Living Traditions Meet a Changing World*, edited by Tamaru Noriyoshi and David Reid. Tôkyô: Kôdansha International, 1996.

Ashkenazi, Michael. *Matsuri: Festivals of a Japanese Town*. Honolulu: University of Hawaii Press, 1993.

Aston, W. G. *Shintô: The Way of the Gods*. New York & Bombay: Longmans, Green, and Company, 1905.

_____. *Nihongi: Chronicles of Japan from the Earliest Times to A.D. 697*. Tôkyô: Charles E. Tuttle Company, 1990.

Bargen, Doris G. *A Woman's Weapon: Spirit Possession in the Tale of Genji*. Honolulu: University of Hawaii Press, 1997.

Basic Terms of Shintô. Tôkyô: Kokugakuin University Institute for Japanese Culture and Classics, 1985.

Baynes, Cary F., trans. *The I Ching*. Bollingen Series XIX. Princeton University Press, 1967.

Berger, Peter L. & Thomas Luckmann. *The Social Construction of Reality*. New York: Doubleday, 1966.

Birrell, Anne, trans. *The Classic of Mountains and Seas*. London: Penguin Books, 1999.

Blacker, Carmen. *The Catalpa Bow: A Study of Shamanistic Practices in Japan*. London: Allen and Unwin, 1975.

Blunden, Caroline and Mark Elvin. *Cultural Atlas of China*. New York: Checkmark Books, 1998.

Brandon, Reiko Mochinaga & Barbara B. Stephan (editors). *Spirit and Symbol: The Japanese New Year*. Honolulu: Honolulu Academy of Arts and University of Hawaii Press, 1994.

Brown, Delmer M., ed. *Ancient Japan*. Vol. 1, The Cambridge History of Japan. Cambridge, England: Cambridge University Press, 1993.

Buckley, Thomas and Alma Gottlieb. *Blood Magic: The Anthropology of Menstruation*. Berkeley, California: University of California Press, 1998.

Campbell, Joseph. *The Mythic Image*. Bollingen Series C, Number 100. Princeton, New Jersey: Princeton University Press, 1974.

_____. *The Inner Reaches of Outer Space: Metaphor as Myth and as Religion*. New York: Harper Perennial, 1995.

Chamberlain, Basil Hall, trans. *The Kojiki: Records of Ancient Matters*. Tôkyô: Charles E. Tuttle Company, 1982.

Chang Chu-kun. "An Introduction to Korean Shamanism." In *Shamanism: The Spirit World of Korea,* edited by Yu Chai-shin and R. Guisso. Berkeley, California: Asian Humanities Press, 1988.

Cheng Chen-hsiang. "A Study of the Bronzes with the Ssu T'u Mu Inscriptions Excavated from the Fu Hao Tomb." In *Studies of Shang Archaeology*, edited by K. C. Chang. New Haven: Yale University Press, 1986.

Clayton, Anita H. et al. 1999. "Assessment of Sexual Functioning During the Menstrual Cycle." *Journal of Sex and Marital Therapy* 25:281-291.

Covell, Jon C. & Alan Covell. *Japan's Hidden History: Korean Impact on Japanese Culture*.Elizabeth, New Jersey: Hollym International, 1984.

Covell, Alan C. *Folk Art and Magic: Shamanism in Korea*. Elizabeth, New Jersey: Hollym Corporation Publishers, 1986.

Crump, Thomas. *The Death of an Emperor: Japan at the Crossroads*. Oxford: Oxford University Press, 1991.

Czaja, Michael. *Gods of Myth and Stone: Phallicism in Japanese Folk Religion*. New York: Weatherhill, 1974.

Dinnerstein, Dorothy. *The Mermaid and the Minotaur: Sexual Arrangements and Human Malaise*. New York: Harper and Row, 1976.

Douglas, Mary. *Purity and Danger: An Analysis of the Concepts of Pollution and Taboo*. London and New York: Routledge and Kegan Paul, 1966.

Ebersole, Gary L. *Ritual Poetry and the Politics of Death in Early Japan*. Princeton, New Jersey: Princeton University Press, 1989.

Egami, Namio. *Kiba minzoku kokka*. Tôkyô: Chûô Kôronsha, 1968.

Egashira Kô. *Shatô shunshû*. Fukuoka: Nishinippon shimbun, 1988.

_____. *Hakata e-nikki*. Fukuoka: Puraningu Shukôsha, 1995.

Eliade, Mircea. *Patterns in Comparative Religion*. Translated by Rosemary Sheed. London and New York: Sheed and Ward, Inc, 1958.

Evslin, Bernard. *Gods, Demigods, and Demons: An Encyclopedia of Greek Mythology*. New York: Scholastic Book Services. 1975.

Feng Gia-fu and Jane English, trans. *Tao Te Ching*. New York: Random House, Inc, 1972.

Fong Wen C. & James C. Y. Watt, eds. *Possessing the Past: Treasures from the National Palace Museum, Taipei*. New York & Taipei: The Metropolitan Museum of Art & National Palace Museum, Taipei, 1996.

Fuji Tatsuhiko. *Chôfuku daihôten: meishin zokushin daihyakka*. Tôkyô: Gakushû kenkyûsha, 1996.

Fukuoka-ken jinja-chô. *Heisei hachi-nen jinja-chô koyomi*. Fukuoka, Japan: 1995.

Fukuyama Toshio, ed. *Kodai izumo taisha no fukugen*. Tôkyô: Gakuseisha, 1989.

Gale, Simon J. "Orientation," in Process: Architecture. *Japan: Climate, Space, and Concept*. 25 (1981): 36-50.

Gaster, Theodore H. *Thespis: Ritual, Myth, and Drama in the Ancient Near East*. New York: Shuman, 1961.

Geertz, Clifford. *The Interpretation of Cultures: Selected Essays*. New York: Basic Books, 1973.

"Gishi wajin-den." <http://www.inetmie.or. jp/~jin/ GWAJIN. html> (15 May 2002).

Grapard, Allan. *The Protocol of the Gods: A Study of the Kasuga Cult in Japanese History*. Berkeley and Los Angeles: University of California Press, 1992.

Gutherie, Stewart. *A Japanese "New Religion:" Risshô Kôsei-kai in a Mountain Hamlet*. Ann Arbor, Michigan: Center for Japanese Studies, 1988.

Hafuri Miyashizu, ed. *Nihon minzoku bunkazai jiten*. Tôkyô: Daiichi hôki shuppan, 1969.

Hagiwara Shûsaburô. *Me de miru minzokugami*. Vol. 1, *Yama to mori no kami*. Tôkyô: Tôkyô bijutsu, 1988.

_____. *Me de miru minzokugami*. Vol. 2, *Hôjô no kami to ie no kami*. Tôkyô: Tôkyô bijutsu, 1988.

_____. *Me de miru minzokugami*. Vol. 3, *Sakai to tsuji no kami*. Tôkyô: Tôkyô bijutsu, 1988.

_____. "Ine ga tsutaeta taiko no uchûkan." *Ise jingû to nihon no kamigami*. Tôkyô: Asahi shimbunsha, 1993.

Hakozaki-gû. *Hakozaki-gû-shi*. Fukuoka: Hakozaki-gû, 1928.

_____. *Hakozaki-gû shiryô*. Tôkyô: Hakozaki-gû, 1970.

_____. *Gochinza sennanajû-nen: Hakozaki-gû daihômotsu-ten*. Fukuoka: Hakozaki-gû, 1993.

Hanihara, Kazurô. "Estimation of the Number of Early Migrants to Japan: A Simulative Study." *Journal of the Anthropological Specify of Nippon* 95 (1987): (3) 391-403.

Hardacre, Helen. *Kurozumikyô and the New Religions of Japan*. Princeton: Princeton University Press, 1986.

_____. *Shintô and the State, 1880-1980*. Princeton: Princeton University Press, 1989.

Hattori Shirô. "Nihongo no keitô." *Zusetsu nihon bunkashi taikei* 1 (1956): 117-130.

Hattori Yukio. *Sakasama no yûrei*. Tôkyô: Heibonsha, 1989.

_____. *Ôinaru koya: Edo kabuki no shukusai kûkan*. Heibonsha Library Number 21. Tôkyô: Heibonsha, 1994.

Herbert, Jean. *Shintô at the Fountainhead of Japan*. London: George Allen and Unwin, Ltd, 1967.

Hill, Gareth S. *Masculine and Feminine: The Natural Flow of Opposites in the Psyche*. Boston and London: Shambhala, 1992.

"Hinode-chô kyôdoshi aikô-kai." <http://www/3/coara.or.jp/~primrose/kensyu2.html>(10 June 2002)

Hirata Atsutane zenshû kankô-kai. *Hirata Atsutane zenshû*. Tôkyô: Meichô shuppan, 1977.

Hirowata Masatoshi, ed. *Hakozaki-gûshi*. Tôkyô: Bunken shuppan, 1999.

Honda Sôichirô. *Nihon shintô nyûmon*. Tôkyô: Nihon bungeisha, 1991.

Horai Satoshi et al. "mtDNA Polymorphism in East Asian Populations, with Special Reference to the Peopling of Japan." *American Journal of Human Genetics* 59 (1996): (2) 579-590.

Hori Ichiro. "Manyôshû ni arawareta sôsei to takaikan reikonkan ni tsuite." In *Shûkyô shûzoku no seikatsu kisei*. Tôkyô, 1963.

Hori, G. Victor Sôgen. "Teaching and Learning in the Rinzai Zen Monastery." *Journal of Japanese Studies* 20 (1994): 1:5-35.

Hucker, Charles O. *China's Imperial Past: An Introduction to Chinese History and Culture*. Stanford, California: Stanford University Press, 1994

Hudson, Mark and Gina L. Barnes. "Yoshinogari: A Yayoi Settlement in Northern Kyûshû." *Monumenta Nipponica* 46 (1991): (2) 211-235.

Iijima Yoshiharu. "Hitobashira densetsu." In *Nihon shinwa densetsu sôran*. Tôkyô: Shinjimbutsu ôraisha, 1992.

Imoto Eiichi. *Kyôkai: saishi kûkan*. Tôkyô: Hirakawa shuppansha, 1994.

Inoue Nobutaka, ed. *Shintô jiten*. Tôkyô: Kobundô, 1994.

Ishii Kenji. "Urbanization, Depopulation, and Religion." In *Religion in Japanese Culture: Where Living Traditions Meet a Changing World*, edited by Tamaru Noriyoshi and David Reid. Tôkyô: Kodansha International, 1996.

Ishii Masami. *Zusetsu nihon no mukashibanashi*. Tôkyô: Kawade shobô shinsha, 2003.

Itô Tsugio, et al, eds. *Chôsen wo shiru jiten*. Tôkyô: Heibonsha, 2000.

Japan Times Online. "Ties to China unearthed from Yoshinogari ruins." <http://www.japantimes.com>(17 May 2002).

Jinja Honchô. *Nature, It is Divine*. (Pamphlet.) Tôkyô, 1998.

Jones, George Heber. "The Spirit Worship of the Koreans." *Transactions of the Korea Branch of the Royal Asiatic Society* 2 (1902): 37-58.

Jordan, David K. *Gods, Ghosts, and Ancestors: The Folk Religion of a Taiwanese Village*. Berkeley, California: University of California Press, 1972.

Jung, Carl Gustav. *The collected works of C. G. Jung*. Volume 12. New York: Pantheon Books, 1953.

Kakuda Iwao. *Musubi: mono to ningen no bunka-shi*. Tôkyô: Hôsei daigaku shuppankyoku, 1972.

Kanda Hideo. *Kojiki no kôzô*. Tôkyô: Meiji shoin, 1959.

Kamata Tôji. "Kami to wa nanika." In *Ise jingû to nihon no kamigami*. Tôkyô: Asahi shimbun-sha, 1993.

Kato Kei. *Shimokita: shinbutsu to no deai no sato*. Tôkyô: Hirakawa shuppansha, 1992.

Kawai Hayao. *The Japanese Psyche: Major Motifs in the Fairy Tales of Japan*. Dallas, Texas: Spring Publications, Inc, 1988.

Kawara Yoshio, ed. *Butsuzô no mikata miwakekata hyakka*. Tôkyô: Shufutoseikatsuha, 1995.

Kawazoe Shôji. *Fukuoka-ken no rekishi*. Tôkyô: Yamakawa shuppansha, 1997.

Kendall, Laurel. *Shamans, Housewives, and Other Restless Spirits: Women in Korean Ritual Life*. Honolulu: University of Hawaii Press, 1985.

Kiba Akeshi, ed. *Inyô gogyô*. Tôkyô: Tankôsha, 1997.

Kim In-hoe. "Korean Shamanism: A Bibliographical Introduction." In *Shamanism: The Spirit World of Korea*, edited by Yu Chai-shin and R. Guisso. Berkeley, California: Asian Humanities Press, 1988.

Kim Yung-sik. *The Natural Philosophy of Chu Hsi 1130-1200*. Vol. 235, *Memoirs of the American Philosophical Society*. Philadelphia: American Philosophical Society, 2000.

Kinsley, David. *Hindu Goddesses: Visions of the Divine Feminine in the Hindu Religious Tradition*. Berkeley, Los Angeles, and London: University of California Press, 1986.

Kishi Yûji. *Te ni toru yô ni minzokugaku ga wakaru hon*. Tôkyô: Kanki shuppan, 2002.

Kitazawa Masakuni. *Nihon shinwa no kosumorojii*. Tôkyô: Heibonsha, 1991.

_____. *Saijiki no kosumorojii*. Tôkyô: Heibonsha, 1995.

Kôdansha Encyclopedia of Japan. Volume 8. Tôkyô: Kôdansha, 1983.

Komatsu Kazuhiko. *Yôkaigaku shinkô: yôkai kara miru nihonjin no kokoro*. Tôkyô: Shôgakkan, 1994.

_____. *Kami-naki jidai no minzokugaku*. Tôkyô: Serika shobô, 2002.

Krupp, E. C. "Queen of the May." *Sky & Telescope* (May 1994): 64-65.

Kuroda Toshio. "Shintô in the History of Japanese Religion." In *Religion & Society in Modern Japan*, edited by Mark R. Mullins, Shimazono Susumu, and Paul L. Swanson. Berkeley: California: Asian Humanities Press, 1993.

Kuroita Katsumi. *Nihon shoki*. Vol. 1, *Kokushi Taikei*. Tôkyô: Yoshikawa Kôbunkan, 1966.

LaFleur, William R. *Liquid Life: Abortion and Buddhism in Japan*. Princeton: Princeton University Press, 1992.

Lagerway, John. *Taoist Ritual in Chinese Society and History*. New York: Macmillan Publishing Company, 1987.

Leach, Maria, ed. *Standard Dictionary of Folklore, Mythology, and Legend*. New York: Harper and Row Publishers, 1984.

Lebra, William P. *Okinawan Religion: Belief, Ritual, and Social Structure*. Honolulu: University of Hawaii Press, 1966.

Lewis, I. M. *Ecstatic Religion : A Study of Shamanism and Spirit Possession*. Baltimore: Penguin Books, 1971.

Liang Shih-chiu. *A New Practical Chinese-English Dictionary*. Taipei: Far East Book Company, Ltd, 1972.

Liu Ying-fu. *Chungkuo lidai dashih nienpiao*. (Timeline.) Taipei: Yichun hsutien, 1986.

Manyôshû (Part 2). Vol. 5, *Nihon koten bungaku taikei*. Tôkyô: Iwanami shoten, 1959.

Marcus, George E. and Michael M.J. Fischer. *Anthropology as Cultural Critique.* Chicago: University of Chicago Press, 1986.

Mason, J. W. T. *The Meaning of Shintô.* Port Washington, New York: Kennikat Press, 1967.

Masuda Hidemitsu. *Fûsui no hon.* Vol. 23, *Books Esoterica.* Tôkyô: Gakken, 2001.

Matisoff, Susan. *The Legend of Semimaru, Blind Musician of Japan.* New York: Columbia University Press, 1978.

Matsumura Akira, ed. *Ôbunsha kogo jiten.* Tôkyô: Ôbunsha, 1987.

McCullough, Helen C., trans. *Genji & Heike: Selections from the Tale of Genji and the Tale of the Heike.* Stanford: Stanford University Press, 1994.

Miles, Margaret R. *Carnal Knowing: Female Nakedness and Religious Meaning in the Christian West.* Boston: Beacon Press, 1989.

Miyata Noboru. *Hime no minzokugaku.* Tôkyô: Seidosha, 1987.

Mizoguchi Yûzô, et al., eds. *Chûgoku shiso bunka jiten.* Tôkyô: Tôkyô daigaku shuppankai, 2001.

Mizuhara Shukiko, ed. *Shinnen.* Vol. 1, *Nippon dai-saijiki.* Tôkyô: Kôdansha, 1981.

Mizuki Shigeru. *Yôkai 100 monogatari.* Vol. 88, *Shôgakkan nyûmon hyakka.* Tôkyô: Shôgakkan, 1989.

_____. *Nippon yôkai taizen.* Tôkyô: Kôdansha, 1991.

Mori Kôichi. "Yoshinogari iseki ga katarikakeru mono." In *Yoshinogari: Yamataikoku ga miete kita* (pp. 142-144). Tôkyô: Asahi Shimbunsha, 1989.

Morris, Ivan. *The World of the Shining Prince: Court Life in Ancient Japan.* New York: Kôdansha International, 1994.

Nakano Hatayoshi. *Hachiman shinkô jiten.* Tôkyô: Ebisu Kôshô Shuppan, 2002.

Nelson, John K. *A Year in the Life of a Shintô Shrine.* Seattle and London: University of Washington Press, 1996.

_____. *"Enduring Identities: The Guise of Shintô in Contemporary Japan".* Ph.D. diss., University of California at Berkeley, 1993.

_____. *Enduring Identities: The Guise of Shintô in Contemporary Japan.* Honolulu: University of Hawaii Press, 2000.

Neumann, Erich. *The Great Mother: An Analysis of the Archetype.* No. 47, Bollingen Series. Translated by Ralph Manheim. Princeton, New Jersey: Princeton University Press, 1963.

Ng Wai-ming. *The I Ching in Tokugawa Thought and Culture.* Honolulu: University of Hawaii Press, 2000.

Nihon kokugo dai-jiten, Vol. 1, 2nd Edition. Tôkyô: Shôgakkan, 2000.

Nihon no kamigami. No. 3, *Geijutsu Shinchô.* Tôkyô: Shinchôsha, 1996.

Nishitakatsuji Nobuyoshi. *Ima shitte okitai: kamisama, jinja, saigi.* Tôkyô: Shufutomosha, 1986.

Nitschke, Gunter. *From Shintô to Andô: Studies in Architectural Anthropology in Japan.* London: Academy Group, Ltd, 1993.

Noguchi Tetsurô, ed. *Dôkyô jiten.* Tôkyô: Hirakawa shuppansha, 1994.

Nomoto Kan'ichi. *Kamigami no fûkei: shinkô kankyô-ron no kokoromi.* Tôkyô: Hakusuisha, 1990.

Nomura Jun'ichi, ed. *Yanagita Kunio jiten*. Tôkyô: Bunsei shuppan, 1998.

Oba Iwao. *Saishi iseki: shintô kôkogaku no kisoteki kenkyû*. Tôkyô: Kadogawa shoten, 1970.

Ogawa Shin'ichi. *Usa jingû to ôga-shi*. Tôkyô: Bungeisha, 2003.

Ogawa Tamaki, ed. *Kadogawa shin-jigen*. Tôkyô: Kadogawa shoten, 1986.

Ôhazama Reizô. *Nippon no shikitari*. Tôkyô: Gakuyô shobô, 1985.

"Ohigan wa naze nihon dake no gyôji?" Television program in NHK series: *Nazo-toki saijiki*,1999.

Ohnuki-Tierney, Emiko. *Illness and Culture in Contemporary Japan*. Cambridge: Cambridge University Press, 1984.

_____. *The Monkey as Mirror: Symbolic Transformations in Japanese History and Religion*. Princeton, New Jersey: Princeton University Press, 1987.

Okada Yoshirô. *Gendai koyomi yomi-toki jiten*. Tôkyô: Kashiwa shobô, 1993.

Ômori Takashi. *Ommyôdô no hon*. Vol. 6, *Books Esoterica*. Tôkyô: Gakken, 1993.

Ômoto Keiichi and Saitô Naruya. "Genetic Origins of the Japanese: A partial Support for the Dual Structure Hypothesis." In *American Journal of Physical Anthropology*. 102 (1997): 437-446.

Ono Sôkyô. *Shintô: The Kami Way*. Rutland, Vermont and Tôkyô: Charles E. Tuttle Company, 1962.

Ôshima Akio. *Minzoku tanbô jiten*. Tôkyô: Yamakawa shuppansha, 1983.

Ôshima Tatehiko. *Dôsojin to jizô*. Tôkyô: Sanmii shoten, 1992.

Papinot, E. *Historical and Geographical Dictionary of Japan*. Tôkyô: Charles E. Tuttle Company, 1988.

Pepper, Stephen C. *World Hypothesis: A Study in Evidence*. Berkeley: University of California Press, 1972.

Peris, Anna, ed. "Female Body: Reproductive Organs and How They Work." <http://www.fertilitext.org/p1-101/femal_repro_systm.html# typicalMenstrual Cycle>(23 June 2002).

Perry, Susan and Jim Dawson. *Secrets Our Body Clocks Reveal*. New York: Ballentine Books, 1988.

Philippi, Donald L., trans. *Norito: A New Translation of the Ancient Japanese Ritual Prayers*. Tôkyô: The Institute for Japanese Culture and Classics, Kokugakuin University, 1959.

_____, trans. *Kojiki*. Tôkyô: University of Tôkyô Press, 1968.

Picken, Stuart. *Shintô: Japan's Spiritual Roots*. Tôkyô, New York, and San Francisco: Kôdansha International, Ltd, 1980.

_____. *Essentials of Shintô*. Westport, Connecticut and London: Greenwood Press, 1994.

Piggot, Juliet. *Japanese Mythology*. Yugoslavia: Newnes Books, 1984.

Platania, Jon. *Jung for Beginners*. London: Writers and Readers, Ltd., 1997

Plutschow, Herbert. *Matsuri: The Festivals of Japan*. Richmond, England: Curzon Press, 1996.

Reader, Ian. *Religion in Contemporary Japan*. Honolulu: University of Hawaii Press, 1991.

Røkkum, Arne. *Goddesses, Priestesses, and Sisters: Mind, Gender, and Power in the Monarchic Tradition of the Ryûkyûs*. Oslo: Scandinavian University Press, 1998.

_____. Email exchange with author, 19 July 2002.

Samples, Robert. *The Metaphoric Mind*. 2nd ed. Torrance, California: Jalmar Press, 1993.

Sanari Kentarô, ed. *Yôkyoku taikan*. Volume 3. Tôkyô: Meiji shoin, 1982.

"Sashima-chôshi, seikatsu shôgai gyôji, shi to sôshiki no junbi." <http://www.town.sashima.ibaraki.jp/jiten/shogai/maiso/shi.htm> (29 May 2002).

Saso, Michael R. *Blue Dragon, White Tiger: Taoist Rites of Passage*. Washington D.C.: The Taoist Center, 1990a.

_____. *Taoism and the Rite of Cosmic Renewal*. Pullman, Washington: Washington State University Press, 1990b.

"Sekihan no yurai." <www.narumi-nochu.jp/yurai.html> (17 September 2003).

Senge Yoshihiko. Personal communication at Izumo Taisha, Shimane prefecture, Japan. April 28, 1996.

Service, Elman R. *Primitive Social Organization: An Evolutionary Perspective*. New York: Random House, 1962.

Shinmura Izuru, ed. *Kôjien*. Tôkyô: Iwanami shoten, 1969.

Shintani Takanori, ed. *Minzokugaku ga wakaru jiten*. Tôkyô: Nippon jitsugyô shuppansha, 1999.

Skinner, Stephen. *The Living Earth Manual of Feng-Shui*. Singapore: Graham Brash, Ltd., 1982

Smith, Robert J. *Ancestor Worship in Contemporary Japan*. Stanford: Stanford University Press, 1974.

Smith, Huston. *The World's Religions*. New York: Harper Collins Publishers, 1991.

Smyers, Karen. *The Fox and the Jewel: Shared and Private Meanings in Contemporary Japanese Inari Worship*. Honolulu: University of Hawaii Press, 1999.

"Society & the Arts: Plays Based on Popular Fairy Tales." <http://kn.koreaherald.co.kr/SITE/data/html_dir/ 2002/02 /27/200202270009.asp> (1 July 2003)

Swanson, Guy. *The Birth of the Gods: The Origin of Primitive Beliefs*. Ann Arbor, Michigan: University of Michigan Press, 1960.

Takahashi Yôji, ed. *Kyô no hyakusai*. No. 82 *Bessatsu taiyô, Nihon no kokoro* . Tôkyô: Heibonsha, 1993.

_____,ed. *Nihon no kami*. No. 68 *Bessatsu taiyô, Nihon no kokoro*. Tôkyô: Heibonsha, 1989.

Takatori Masao. *Shintô no seiritsu*. Tôkyô: Heibonsha Library, 1993.

Tamaru Noriyoshi. "Buddhism." In *Religion in Japanese Culture*, edited by Tamaru Noriyoshi and David Reid. Tôkyô and New York: Kodansha International, 1996.

Tanikawa Ken'ichi, ed. *Taiyô to tsuki: kodaijin no uchû-kan to shisei-kan*. Vol. 2, *Nihon minzoku bunka taikei*. Tôkyô: Shogakkan, 1983.

_____, ed. *Nihon no kamigami: jinja to seichi*. Vol. 1, *Kyûshû*. Tôkyô: Hakusuisha, 2000.

Tatematsu Wahei. "Gendai ni yobi-modosareru kodai no chie." In *Ise jingû to nihon no kamigami*. Tôkyô: Asahi shimbunsha, 1993.

Teeuwen, Mark. *Watarai Shintô: An Intellectual History of the Outer Shrine in Ise*. Leiden, Netherlands: Research School CNWS, 1996.

Toita Michizô. *Nô: Kami to kojiki no geijutsu*. Tôkyô: Serika Shobô, 1972.

Turner, Victor. *The Ritual Process: Structure and Anti-Structure*. New York: Aldine de Gruyter, 1995.

_____. *Dramas, Fields, and Metaphors*. Ithaca, New York: Cornell University Press, 1974.

Tyler, Royall. *Japanese Tales*. New York: Random House, Inc, 1987.

_____. *Japanese Nô Dramas*. New York: Penguin Books, 1992.

Ueda Atsuo, ed. *Japan 1997 An International Comparison*. Japan Institute for Social and Economic Affairs, Keizai Kôhô Center, 1997.

Ueda Kenji. "Shintô." In *Religion in Japanese Culture: Where Living Traditions Meet a Changing World*, edited by Tamaru Noriyoshi and David Reid. Tôkyô: Kodansha International, 1996.

Ueda Masaaki, ed. *Kasuga taisha: ikiteiru shôsôin*. Tôkyô: Kadogawa shoten, 1995.

Umehara Takeshi. *Mori no shisô ga jinrui wo sukû*. No. 71, *Shôgakkan Library*. Tôkyô: Shôgakkan, 1995.

Uryû Naka and Shibuya Nobuhiro, eds. *Senjutsu to uranai no subete*. Tôkyô: Nihon bungeisha, 1997.

Van Gennep, Arnold. *The Rites of Passage*. Chicago: University of Chicago Press, 1960.

Vindenes, Haakon. Conversation with author, 30 June 1992.

Warashina Tetsuo and Higashimura Takenobu. "Sekki Genzai no Sanchi Bunseki." In *Nihon Bankazai Kagakukai Dai-7 Kai Taikai*. April 1990: 66-67.

Webster's Ninth New Collegiate Dictionary. Springfield, Massachusetts: Merriam-Webster, Inc., 1983.

Werkhoven, Jennifer. Conversation with author, 23 May 2003.

Williams, Eldred Leslie. *"Earth, Boundaries, and the Foundations of Folk Shintô"*. Ph.D. diss., University of Pittsburgh, 1997.

_____. "A Unity of Pattern in the Kami Tradition: Orienting Shintô Within a Context of Pre-Modern and Contemporary Ritual Practice." In *Journal of Ritual Studies*. 14 (2): 34-47.

_____. "Will the Real Ancestor Please Stand Up? The Social Construction of Ancestors, Kami, and Obake in Contemporary Japan." Forthcoming manuscript.

Yamaori Tetsuo. "Shinwa no kami." *Nihon no kami*. Volume 68 in series *Bessatsu taiyô*. Tôkyô: Heibonsha, 1989.

Yanagita Kunio. *About Our Ancestors: The Japanese Family System*. Translated by Fanny Hagin Mayer and Ishiwara Yasuyo. Tôkyô: Japan Society for the Promotion of Science, 1970.

_____. *Imôto no chikara*. Tôkyô: Kadogawa Bunko, 1971.

_____. *Saiji shûzoku go-i*. Tôkyô: Kokusho kankôkai, 1987.

Yokoi Kiyoshi. *Moto to ena*. Tôkyô: Heibonsha, 1988.

Yoshino Hiroko. *Inyô gogyô to nihon no minzoku*. Kyôto: Jinbun shoin, 1983.

_____. *Eki to nippon no saishi*. Kyôto: Jinbun shoin, 1993.

_____. *Jûnishi: Eki gogyô to nihon no minzoku*. Kyôto: Jinbun shoin, 1994.

_____. *Inyô gogyô shisô kara mita nihon no matsuri*. Kyôto: Jinbun shoin, 2000.

Index

relationship to "the Initiating", 113, 115–16

Empress Jingû: and fire element relationship to Emperor Ôjin, 169 ; and winter solstice First Rabbit Rite, 166–68; enshrined at Hakozaki, 112; relationship to "the Threatening", 116; sea cucumber mochi offered before, 150; tide-controlling jewels, 173n12

entry to the home: exorcism with sacred beach sand, 47; gate pines (*kadomatsu*) placed at, 156–57; Heaven Gate unfavorable direction for, 85; New Year's entry-decoration (*shimekazari*) placed at, 157; ritual locus at New Year's, 160–61; spiritual beings recognized, 25; Wind Gate most auspicious direction for, 79

equinox(es), 76; ancestor ritual, 37; arrival of ancestor spirits, 103, 180; cooked rice pillars, 106; cross quarter days, 91; First Rabbit Rites, 161–165; gathering sacred beach sand, 129–36, 139, 180; Rites of Celebration, 146; Yang Earth Rites, 120, 129, 139, 180; yin/ yang balance, 74, 103; *See also* autumn equinox; spring equinox

evergreen: in New Year's decorations, 152, 157; ritual use of branches, 42, 123–26, 129, 134, 173n17; trees as home to spiritual beings, 25

exorcism: at equinoxes (Hakozaki), 134; at sealing of well, 142; at spatial and temporal boundaries, 160; in *Tale of Genji*, 47; low spirit focus of, 6, 159; of Demon Gate quadrant (Hakozaki), 138; of earth and tree spirits (Korea), 46; of ghost by wife (Ryûkyûs), 49, 56; of house boundaries (Korea), 50; of "red disaster" with millet (Korea), 50, 173n9; of sacred beach sand pilgrims (Hakozaki), 131, 172n7;

temporary place of (*oharaijo*), 134; using birth-soil (Hakozaki), 138; using hemp, 161; using nandina, 161; using salt, 144, 145–47, 160–61; wand (*haraigushi*), 134; water closet, 158, 161. *See also* Great Exorcism

female cycle of fertility: central to logic of Later Heaven Sequence, 74, 86; Demon Gate analogous to end/beginning of cycle, 78, 86–88; Heaven Gate relates to last quarter of cycle, 89–90; Human Gate analogous to middle of cycle, 88–89; Wind Gate relates to first quarter of cycle, 89

Feminine archetype: and mountain taboos, 35–36, 38; capitalization of Feminine, 15n1; conceptual linking of woman and earth, 5; grounded in natural cycles, 6; implicit reality for practitioners, 3, 6, 30; kami ritual informed by, 30; life-giving aspect: equated with mountains, 32, 35; high spirits as expression of, 7; offerings indicative of, 33; life-taking aspect; low spirits as expression of, 7; possesses positive and negative aspects 31, 38; seed metaphor linked to, 17; Spirit Tree analogy, 1

field spirit, 37–38, 54, 158, 177; and Five Phase cosmology, 79, 89–90, 91n7, 93n14; named in *Kojiki*, 51; resemblance to spring spirits of Dunang, 40; rituals, 79, 89–90

fifteenth of the month: and Yang Earth Rites, 120, 127–29; mid-autumn moon festival, 174n20; popular rites at the shrine, 138–41, 180; popular rituals in the home 141–46, 158–59; shrine-sponsored rites, 133–38; Taoist feast days, 172n5

fire spirit, 45, 51. *See also* hearth spirit

first of the month: and Yang Earth Rites, 120, 127–29; Japanese national